THE IRISH MERCHANT OF ALICANTE

MOORE HALL

AND

FOUR GENERATIONS OF IRELAND'S
ARISTOCRATIC MOORE FAMILY

MICHAEL GERARD

Copyright © 2023 Michael Gerard

All rights reserved. No part of this publication may be reproduced, stored in a retrieval system, or transmitted in any form or by any means, mechanical, photocopying, recording or otherwise, without prior permission in writing of the author.

ISBN: 9798394731280

HEARTFELT THANKS

To – Mary and Todd for taking me to visit the Moore Hall ruins

Paddy K for tireless efforts on my behalf in Ireland

Eoin and Adam for all your computer help

Diane for your patient support

My proofreaders – Mike S and Tom S

For sweet Harlow and fearless Finn – my future fans

Killala – coastal town where French expedition landed in 1798
Castlebar – site of French-Irish victory over large British forces

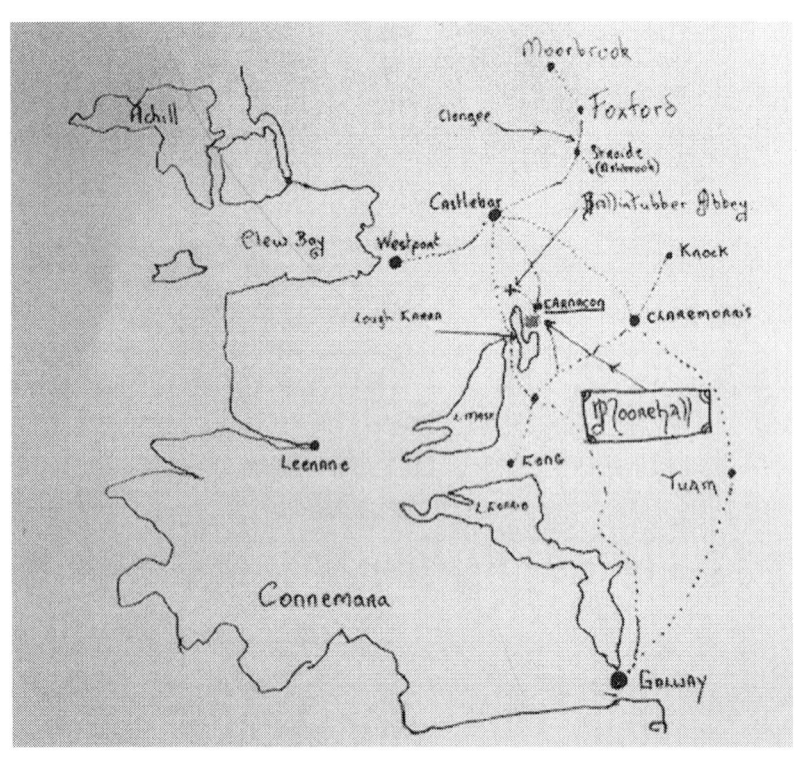

Note locations of Moore Hall, Castlebar, Westport and Straide

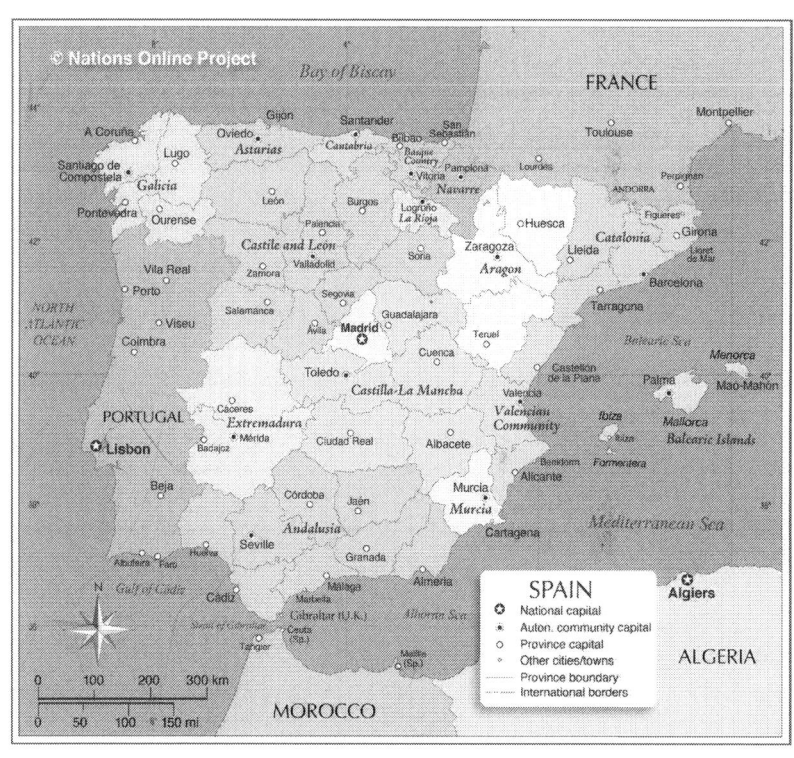

Note Alicante on Southeast Coast, Bilbao on North Coast, Cadiz and Seville on Southwest Coast

Won the Chester Cup for George Henry Moore in 1846 and 17,000 pounds. This enabled George Henry to charter a ship load of American cornmeal into Westport to feed the starving Mayo people

The Moore Family Burial Vault beside Moore Hall, County Mayo

TABLE OF CONTENTS

Prologue	xiii
Chapter One	1
Chapter Two	23
Chapter Three	34
Chapter Four	50
Chapter Five	68
Chapter Six	84
Chapter Seven	99
Chapter Eight	115
Chapter Nine	135
Chapter Ten	150
Chapter Eleven	169
Chapter Twelve	190
Chapter Thirteen	214
Chapter Fourteen	232
Chapter Fifteen	246
Chapter Sixteen	259

Chapter Seventeen	281
Chapter Eighteen	306
Chapter Nineteen	319
Chapter Twenty	338
Chapter Twenty-One	356
Chapter Twenty-Two	374
Chapter Twenty-Three	391
Chapter Twenty-Four	413
Chapter Twenty-Five	437
Epilogue	449
Notes / Research Acknowledgements / Inspiration for This Book	453
Meet the Author	455

PROLOGUE

When most people think about Irish history, they focus on the long struggle endured by the persecuted Catholic peasants to gain control of their farmland and their country. That struggle was real, particularly for those of us who were directly affected. My own father fought in the Irish War of Independence (1919-1921), and as a youngster I met many of these old IRA rebels who came to gatherings at our tailor shop in County Mayo – usually on the occasion of funerals because these heroes were aging and dying.

The other constant during my formative years in Mayo in the 1960's was hearing everyone repeating how poor and backward that County Mayo was. 'Mayo, God Help Us' was a statement I heard over and over again. I was not ashamed of Mayo, but I didn't feel that I had anything to brag about as I made my way through school, college and into the workforce. Putting distance between myself and Mayo, between myself and Ireland, allowed me to view both places through a different lens – to see the bigger picture. The America that I found myself living in later was one of diversity – in religion, in history, in ethnicity, in ancestry. Gradually I began to see a new richness in Irish history and the important place that County Mayo played in that history – my perspective expanded further as I read and researched for my recent book 'Ireland's Final Rebellion and an American Dream'.

Yes, the struggle of the poor Catholic peasants was a vital component of our history, but the landed gentry/aristocracy, both Catholic and Protestant, also played an important part in the achievement of Irish Independence and the making of Modern Ireland. Characters in that narrative moved back and forth across the religious divide, be it for reasons of intimate love or to take advantage of privileges on offer by the choice of sides. I felt the need to tell the story of these settlers who were 'planted' in Ireland centuries ago, after the old Gaelic Chieftains were defeated by the new ruthless Model Armies of England – settlers who were part of the master plan to subdue Ireland and integrate it into the Anglican Protestant British Empire.

History tells us that over time, a great number of these settlers 'became more Irish than the Irish themselves'. Settlers were planted extensively in County Mayo, and being a Mayoman myself, I wanted to tell the history of their transformation as a distinctive Mayo story. A few years ago, while on a home visit to Mayo I went on a day trip with my sister and brother-in-law to visit the ruined Moore Hall, near Carnacon, a few miles south of Castlebar – a 'Big House' that was burned in 1923 during the Irish Civil War. I was enchanted by its location on the shore of Lough Carra, but even more so by the history of the Moore family who built it and held it through four generations of turbulent Irish history. Many details of the Moore family history have been lost but their story immediately struck a chord in me – they were a personification of another side of Irish history that had been simmering in my brain.

Starting with the sparse details of George Moore's emigration to Spain I have reconstructed his life there, his triumphant return to Ireland, his building of Moore Hall and piecing together a large, landed estate which became a family dynasty. His vision was pivotal and laid the groundwork for the extraordinary influence the Moore family have had – not only on County Mayo but also on the founding of the Irish Free State, and the revival of Irish literature and theatre.

CHAPTER ONE

Galway Bay, Ireland – summer of 1754 –

George Martin climbed aboard the anchored merchant ship from a local fishing boat tied alongside it – no problem to this lean and agile gentleman. As he stepped over the rail, a tall muscular swarthy middle-aged man identified himself as Pierre Lacombe, the ship's captain and greeted him with a friendly 'Bonjour Monsieur Martin' to which George answered in fluent French.

"Thank you for waiting on our boat, we had a rowing issue and strong currents. I am happy to be here and look forward to a pleasant voyage to Bilbao."

Pierre was surprised by his passenger's response and delighted to have a French speaker on board.

He replied in French – "Sir, my crew is a mix of illiterate Portuguese and Irish, so I am very pleased to welcome you on board. Where did you learn to speak such excellent French?"

"Thank you for the compliment, I was educated at 'College

des Grandes Anglaise' in Douai, Flanders. I fear that my French is a little rusty after several years back in Ireland where I have had little opportunity to converse in French."

"No please, your French is music to my ears. If you would be so kind as to join me for dinner at 8 o'clock in my cabin, whence we can continue our conversation, in French of course. For now, I must oversee our departure – is eight good for you?"

"C'est bon, Merci."

Such was the beginning of a new chapter in the life of George Moore, twenty-five-year-old second son of John Moore of Ashbrook Estate in County Mayo – travelling under the assumed name of George Martin, posing as a wine merchant going to inspect wine cargos prior to importing the product to Galway. George was a member of the Irish landed gentry, the aristocracy comprising mostly Protestants but some Catholics who between them owned the huge, landed estates into which Ireland was divided. He understood and reluctantly accepted the system of inheritance amongst his aristocracy class where the first-born son was heir to the entire estate – his older brother Robert would inherit the house and the five-thousand-acre estate, and he was already being groomed for that position. He and other siblings would get a minimal inheritance and they would have to make their own way in life. Most of the estate was leased in very small parcels to poor tenant farmers who struggled to pay their rents. This was the Irish system, a nasty but profitable business that had been going on since the seventeenth century when the British Crown confiscated the land of the defeated Gaelic Chieftains. Britain wanted to create a land-owning class of British Protestants in Ireland to rule over the Irish Catholic tenants, believing that over time the few remaining Catholic estate owners would convert to Protestantism and the peasant masses would follow their example. These tenants lived in poverty while the ruling gentry lived in luxury – either in Big Houses on their Irish estates or were absentee landlords living in England while their agents ran the estate and collected the rents on their behalf. Tenant farmers grew grain and other crops in order to pay their rents and in the process made Ireland the breadbasket for the expanding British Empire.

His own storied family history as passed down to George was a bit different than most. After the bloody subjugation of the Irish Chieftains, the Cromwellian Plantation followed, where English and Scottish Protestants were 'planted' on the confiscated Irish land. The Crown devised a system where the Irish peasant masses were forced to work the land in small parcels for the greater good of their masters and in turn the greater good of the British Crown. The lands at Ashbrook were gifted to a Protestant ancestor named William Moore, for services rendered in Oliver Cromwell's New Model Army campaign, and the land was then left untouched for many years. Later, a descendent, Captain George Moore served in King William's Army at the Battle of the Boyne in 1690 and after William's victory, the captain took possession of the family's Mayo estate and built Ashbrook House a short time later. It was a rather simple functional farmhouse, a detached three-story building constructed in a T-shaped plan which served the dual purpose of a comfortable home while having solid stone walls that conferred aspects of a fort to the structure and made it easier to defend in this Mayo wilderness. The West of Ireland is a hauntingly beautiful landscape and over time the family became thoroughly intrenched in the place and became 'as Irish as the Irish themselves'.

By the early years of the eighteenth-century John Moore became Master of Ashbrook. He took stock of his situation and saw that his future could be much improved by an alliance with the local power base which happened to be in Catholic hands. Thereafter, he married Jane Lynch-Athy of Galway, whose family was a staunchly Catholic member of the 'Tribes of Galway' – a group of a dozen or so Catholic merchant families who had controlled all aspects of business life in the city of Galway for as long as anyone could remember. For this marriage to happen Jane persuaded John to convert to Catholicism. The change in church affiliation had little impact on the way the Moore family was treated in the West of Ireland. Most of the landed gentry in Ireland at the time were Protestants – members of the established Church of Ireland which was part of the Anglican Church of England created by King Henry VIII when he severed England from the Roman Catholic Church. Protestants had relocated to Ireland to take possession of land granted to them in line with the policy of Britain to make

Ireland a Protestant country. Many of the old Catholic landed families had converted to Protestantism in order to hold onto their lands – such as the Browne family of Westport who were acquaintances of the Moore's. The bond between the upper classes was one of power and money, more than it was one of co-religion – and changing religion did not exclude either party from socializing together. With John Moore's marriage the family benefitted from their Galway connections – increased wealth and influence seemed to trump religious affiliation. Meanwhile, life for the poor Catholic tenant farmers of the estates continued as before – they toiled in misery to keep the aristocracy in luxury. John Moore, like most landlords of his time had little contact with his tenants, preferring to employ managers to collect the rents and do the dirty work of evictions. He and Jane raised three boys and two girls as Catholics, and Jane instilled in them the rebellious nationalism of her ancestors. Those ancestors from the 'Tribes' had been officers in King James' Jacobite army defeated by King William at the Boyne in 1690. After defeat at the Battle of the Boyne and the surrender of Galway, the signing of the Treaty of Limerick forced these defeated Jacobite soldiers to leave Ireland – a departure so profound that it became known in history as the 'Flight of the Wild Geese'. So many of them joined the armies of France and Spain that they formed their own Irish Brigades.

The passage of the Penal Laws which came into existence beginning in 1695 changed life for Irish Catholics. They were forbidden from being elected to Parliament, denied voting rights, excluded from holding any offices of trust and severely restricted from owning property – laws that were of no consequence to the poverty-stricken tenant Irish illiterate masses whose lives were already totally consumed with day-to-day survival. These laws were aimed at pushing the Catholic gentry towards Protestantism, but the reality on the ground was that well-connected Catholic families like the Moore's were able to circumvent most of these restrictions, and Ashbrook continued to prosper. By the time George returned from his schooling in France his prospects were severely limited by these Penal Laws, and his station in life as second son meant that his older brother Robert would be the sole inheritor of the estate. He and Robert were reasonably close but very different personalities. Robert was a bookworm studying to become a medical doctor, had little interest in outdoor pursuits or the landed estate – he planned to be a doctor in Galway. George had an engaging personality – he was an outdoors type, loved riding and hunting and was out on the estate so much that he learned to converse in the Irish language – a rare attribute among the gentry. He studied law but as a Catholic he was not allowed to obtain a degree. There were opportunities for him in the merchant business in Galway, but his mother Jane wanted more for him and so did George himself.

A significant number of Jane Lynch's Wild Geese ancestors had laid down their swords and set about rebuilding their family fortunes in their new adopted homelands of Spain and

France. They had generations of experience as merchants in Galway, and had strong trading links with France, Spain and Portugal by the time of the 'Wild Geese' exodus. Trading was a natural route for the exiles to follow and in a few short years they had set up successful commercial operations in the ports of Bordeaux, Bilbao, Lisbon, Seville, Cadiz and Alicante – some even broke into the trade in Bruges and Rotterdam. Jane wrote letters to several trusted family connections in these exotic locations and as replies filtered back, she began to develop a plan with George and convinced him to participate in a management level apprenticeship with a respected Galway merchant family, so that the young man could learn the basics of the merchant trade. Surprisingly, he enjoyed the experience and became eager to move to the next level of her plan. He possessed a competitive spirit, was desperate to prove that he could achieve more than his older brother and saw no reason why he could not emulate the success that the exiled Irish merchants had achieved in Spain. Together, he and Jane formulated their 'George Plan' which culminated with George boarding that ship for Bilbao. Before his departure for his new life, they sat down for a rehearsal of the plan.

"George, are you sure you want to take on this risky adventure? Your challenges begin with the sea voyage itself – sickness, storms, pirates, the British fleet, loneliness and the risk of failure."

"Dear Mother, I am looking forward to the challenge – I relish it. The Irish before me have been successful and I am confident I can do the same. There is no opportunity for me here, so I have nothing to lose. No offense to Robert but I think I am smarter than him. I intend to make my fortune in short order and come back home to invest that money here once the Penal Laws subside. Maybe I can create a large estate to compliment Ashbrook and make you and Father proud."

"Promise me that you will always honor your Catholic faith, your Irish heritage, and you will write to me frequently – I will be eagerly waiting for those letters."

"I promise, Mother."

Young George had good sea legs and spent most of that first afternoon on the deck as the ship's crew ran sails up and down the mast, searching for favorable winds that would carry them south around the coast of Kerry and set them on a direct course for Spain. The Galway coastline soon disappeared from his view over the horizon, bringing a tear to George's eye amid the sadness of not knowing when he might see his homeland again. He pulled himself out of that despair and took time to study his notes before going to his cabin to check that his luggage was in order, and to freshen up for dinner. At precisely 8 o'clock he presented himself at Captain Pierre's cabin and was ushered inside. It was quite a compact area, as to be expected on such a ship – two or possibly three small rooms, the largest being the room with a decent sized table that no doubt served as a map and conference room when not in use for dining.

Their conversation was entirely in French.

"Thank you for joining me Mr. Martin, I trust you have settled into your cabin. Is everything to your liking – if it is not so, then tell me and I will have it corrected immediately."

"Everything is very comfortable, thank you. Please call me George."

"Very well, Mr. George. Would you like to join me in a glass of sherry before dinner, or do you prefer wine or rum?"

"Sherry is perfect, thank you."

"Let's drink a toast to a safe and smooth voyage."

They chatted about the ship, in answer to George's questions and compliments. Pierre told him they were sailing under the Portuguese flag, which meant less likelihood of aggressive behavior from the British fleet which they were likely to encounter at some stage of the journey. He was expecting good weather and helpful winds. The cook produced a chicken dish with rice and a very French sauce seasoned with garlic, washed down with a bottle of claret.

"Mr. George, I have you listed as a wine merchant – what do you think of this claret?"

George swirled the wine around in the glass, held it to his nose and after another swirl he tasted it.

"It is a rather young wine but has lots of flavor and great potential if aged – I like it. I am rather new to the wine industry I must confess – this is my first wine trip; part of my training is to meet the wine producers and see their operations. What do you think of the wine Pierre?"

"It goes down easily, something I picked up very cheap the last time I was in Bordeaux. I have made this voyage many times and have carried passengers before. Every one of them had a story to tell – what is your story Mr. George?"

George shifted nervously in his seat, wondering how much Pierre knew about him and how much he should tell him.

"I don't understand, what do you mean?"

"I am an old seadog and have carried many types of passengers – people escaping persecution, highwaymen running from the law, rebel leaders after one of your frequent Irish rebellions – and so on. Do you fall into any of those categories? I ask mainly so that I can best handle the situation when we are confronted by a British warship."

"Thank you for your frankness, Pierre. I fall into none of these categories, but I do indeed have a story – does your cook understand French?"

Pierre smiled and topped up their glasses. "He is Portuguese and speaks no other language other than a few words of Spanish. I have enough Portuguese to instruct him – you can speak French without worrying about him."

"The real story is that I am an Irish Catholic whose family have a landed estate in County Mayo, which is some forty miles northeast of the port of Galway. You may or may not know this, but the British have enacted some very harsh laws against Catholics in Ireland which makes it very difficult for a man of my age and education to rise to my proper place in society. I have an older brother who will inherit the family estate, which means that I must create my own future, and a suitable career in the army is not available to me at this time because of those laws. Ireland is not a good place for me to stay at present, so I am moving to Spain to find better prospects. Does that answer your question?"

"Thank you for being so candid about your situation. Yes, I am aware of these Penal Laws, and I understand your predicament – I myself am Catholic and must hide it most of the time. Do you have people ready to help you in Bilbao?"

"My mother is from a merchant family who have regular business dealings with several ports in Spain and France – she has been able to provide me with contacts who are expecting me and will help me to get established."

"Where is your final destination?"

"I will be spending a few weeks in Bilbao, then I will be travelling on to Alicante in a ship that is owned by my contact family."

"Alicante is a beautiful place, warm and lush, with wonderful, aged wines – you have made a good choice. Now let us drink to your future in Spain."

George was somewhat uneasy that he had told Pierre so much, and the older man sensed it – he reassured George that he was in safe hands. The owners of Pierre's ship were paid handsomely for carrying passengers like George, and he was in the care of their best Captain. They moved on to other topics – Pierre was from near the port of Brest on the northwest coast of France and had a wife and four children there which he seldom saw. He had been to several of the Irish ports but had never travelled inland in the country. George described the layout of the estate farmland amid the well-stocked rivers and lakes, told him about the Irish language spoken by the peasants and a little about Ireland's troubled history. He spoke several sentences in Irish to demonstrate the language to Pierre, who said he had heard it spoken while in port and that his Irish crew members spoke it between themselves.

"Pierre, do you expect to have contact from British navy ships, and if so, when?"

"They have a constant presence in the waters that our route takes us and will monitor us as we cross the approaches to the Channel between England and France. It will depend on what other activities are consuming their time at present, but this ship is quite familiar to patrolling British warships and they may not bother us at all. I keep a good supply of wine on board, plus quart bottles of whiskey, rum and gin that their inspectors can slip into their pockets – it helps keep them on our side. There is no need to worry, I have been dealing with them for many years – just make sure you are not carrying a pistol on your person, and do not have any incriminating documents with you."

"I am clear on both of those points."

Their conversation moved on to more relaxed subjects. Pierre was able to tell George more details about the history and layout of Bilbao which made it sound like a very nice place with a good climate and a strong merchant class. While

Spanish was the predominant language there, the merchants were also able to converse in English and French, so George need not worry on that front, but he suggested that he should plan on learning Spanish as soon as possible.

"I totally agree," George replied. "To prosper as a merchant in Spain I need to speak Spanish, and maybe Portuguese also to add to my French. I have a very good feeling about my future business prospects in Spain. Please provide me with contact details for your ship owners and your good self, so I can put some business your way and help you also, my friend."

Pierre told him that his home port of Brest was another place worthy of adding to any merchant trade list, as were several ports east of that, stretching along the Dutch coast.

George agreed to join Pierre for dinner each evening of the voyage, which would be three to five days depending on the winds and weather. The second and third days brought good sailing conditions and the two men had lively discussions – ranging from trade to rural pastimes and even the politics of the major countries of this region – Ireland was no longer the main subject, which was fine with George. He needed to know as much as possible about his soon-to-be-adopted new homeland, so he absorbed as much information as he could from Pierre's ramblings. On the morning of day four they encountered three British warships, one of which sent a boat to inspect their ship. It was a routine visit which Pierre handled very well, and he soon sent the boarding party on their way with flat pint bottles of liquor in their britches. By the morning of day five they were in the Nervion River estuary approaching Bilbao. George quickly got up on deck to view the port and the city. Pierre motioned for him to join him on the bridge and as they proceeded into the port, he gave George a descriptive layout of the city.

"The old city occupies the western bank. The main center is the Siete Calles or Seven Streets that run parallel to the riverbank. That steeple you see is the Cathedral of Santiago which has been here since the fourteenth century. Where are you meeting your contacts?"

"As soon as we land, I am to send a messenger to an address in the city and they will send a carriage to collect me and my luggage."

"That seems like a good plan."

Once at anchor Pierre sent a few crew members to the quay to find a messenger who ran off to find George's hosts at a nearby merchant business. George said goodbye to Pierre after noting down his ship owner's details, promising to send them a letter praising Captain Pierre's abilities and assuring them of more shipping business as soon as he got settled in Spain. A carriage appeared at the same time as George landed ashore and the crew placed his luggage trunk on the back. He thanked them and looked one last time toward Pierre's ship, waved goodbye and was on his way.

A few minutes ride had the carriage at a comfortable looking house at the edge of the city. George was ushered to an inside room where a gentleman and lady greeted him. Raul

Torres and his wife Maria managed the merchant house in Bilbao for the Lynch-Bagen wine family of Bordeaux. They spoke enough French for George to understand their plans for him. He was to remain in Bilbao for approximately ten days until a ship coming from Bordeaux would arrive with cargo. Once it was reloaded it would be sailing for Alicante and would take George aboard. After a welcome toast of sparkling wine, he was shown to his guest room where he freshened up and relaxed on his porch. It had a view of the city and the port, so he retrieved his long sight-glass from his trunk and spent a few hours watching daily life in Bilbao unfold in front of him. It was far different than Ireland, warm and sunny, a prosperous looking city by the activity and dress of the local working population. Later at dinner with his hosts Raul and Maria, they told him a more detailed story of Lynch-Baden history.

Joseph Lynch had emigrated to Bordeaux from the Galway, Ireland many years before, as part of the 'Wild Geese' exodus of the defeated Jacobite army. He set up as a wine merchant, found success, married well and bought land on which he planted vines and he set up a winery. His son inherited the business and continued to expand to other regions in France and then into Spain. Bilbao had good shipping connections via Seville to the Spanish colonies of the New World of the Americas, so it was a good trans-shipping point for their wine, brandy and other commodities. It also had long established shipping connections to several ports in England and Ireland, including Galway

– hence the opportunity for George to find passage on board Pierre's ship.

During the following days George was able to visit their warehouses at the port where he studied their operations and was impressed at how efficiently this business functioned. Their warehouse managers were a mix of French and Spanish, some with Irish ancestors – overseeing the import and export business and managing their local Spanish work force. He was allowed full access to their operations and was made to feel very welcome. Later he did some exploring of the city by himself and visited the Cathedral of Santiago to give thanks and to marvel at its architecture. While there he was engaged in conversation by a young man who turned out to be one of the assistant priests, Father Ernesto Perez. Ernesto was also a past pupil of Douai, and it turned out that they had several mutual acquaintances, and of course he spoke fluent French. They became immediate friends and after hearing that George was moving on to Alicante in a matter of days, Ernesto arranged to meet him the following day at the church, promising to have information and contacts for him for Alicante. He was as good as his word and gave George two pamphlets devoted to Alicante's long history and some letters of introduction to the Catholic hierarchy of the city, plus information on influential Irish-Spanish families at the important Atlantic ports of Seville and Cadiz. They met again two days later at Sunday Mass, which George attended in the company of Raul, Maria and their three children in their family-reserved front pew.

Father Ernesto served Holy Communion to them all and chatted with them for quite some time after the service.

A few days later the Lynch-Bagen ship arrived into port from Bordeaux early in the morning and George watched as the workers unloaded the mixed cargo of dry goods plus lots of French wine, and then loaded new cargo bound for Alicante and two other ports along the route.

By late afternoon George said his good-byes to Raul and Maria and boarded his new ship for his next sailing adventure. It was quite a small ship of some 250 tons, said to be fast but with modest accommodations. George had pride of place as a special guest of the ship owners and was welcomed aboard by the French captain. He apologized that the guest living quarters would have to be shared with another travelling gentleman, who came aboard a little later. George was pleased to see that he was a young man of similar age to himself. The captain introduced him as Jorge O'Reilly, Spanish born but with a likely Irish family connection based on his name. To George's delight Jorge spoke French and they immediately struck up a friendly conversation.

"George, you may not know it but Jorge – while sounding very different than your name – is Spanish for George. Our grandfather emigrated here from Ireland and established a wine merchant business in Seville – I was born here, as was my older brother Gerardo and two sisters."

"I did not know the name Jorge – what an amazing coincidence and that your family came from Ireland. I myself am from County Mayo and am on my way to Alicante. Where is your family from in Ireland?"

"County Meath. My brother Gerardo is an officer in the Spanish army serving with the Hibernia regiment. I work in our family merchant business and was visiting with our trading partners in Bilbao."

The two young men were of very similar disposition and hit off an immediate friendship. During their voyage south they talked extensively about Ireland and the wine merchant business. George admitted that he was a newcomer to the wine industry, on his way to start a career with the Lynch-Baden operations in Alicante and openly asked Jorge for guidance. Jorge recounted the history and importance of Seville and explained why his family's business was based there.

"Seville is a large and ancient city on the Guadalquivir River located some sixty miles from the sea. After the discovery of The Americas, it became the economic nerve center of the Spanish Empire. The sailing route to the Americas is defined by the constant currents and winds in the Atlantic Ocean. That route commences in the Canary Islands and extends on to the Lesser Antilles which means that the departure port must be on the Atlantic coast of Andalusia. Only Seville was large enough to absorb and lodge the massive population of mariners, merchants and passengers who were embarking on the fleets of ships heading to the Americas – so the Spanish Crown chose it as the main hub. It was already an established port and transit point between East and West, and between

Europe and North Africa. It is an economic center producing an abundance of grain, wine, oil and salted fish capable of feeding the crews of dozens of ships which sail in fleets at the same time. Seville is also the home of the very influential Casa de Contratacion (House of Trade) who governs all aspects of the shipping fleet operations – and it has a long-established base of Genoese bankers who provide the loans, insurance and letters of exchange that also are needed. When my father settled in Spain, he opened a merchant business in Cadiz and later expanded to Seville in order to participate in supplying the fleets of merchant ships and military Galleons bound for the Americas with all the provisions they needed for those long voyages of discovery. We ourselves have a fleet of supply ships, but I could not wait for one as I needed to get to Seville to take care of urgent business – hence I found passage on board this ship."

"I'm glad you are here to educate this ignorant Irishman on these matters. Thank you for that history lesson – I had no idea that Seville was such a large city and so central to the Spanish Empire."

"Tell me more about the Americas – sounds fascinating."

"I have not been there, so I only have secondhand information. Spain has been sending out expeditions into the western oceans for well over one hundred years and have made great discoveries of what they call Inca gold and silver in the Americas which is vitally important to the expansion of the empire, provided they can get the precious metals home safely to Spain. They have a fortified place called Havanna at an island just south of the great land mass named America and another one called St. Augustine on the east coast of La Florida which is part of the land mass. The Galleons carrying the gold gather at Havanna and sail north along the eastern coast of La Florida to a very large bay they call Santa Elena where they regroup again before catching the winds and currents to sail home across the Atlantic in fleets for added safety. These fleets need lots of supplies to sustain themselves in both directions and that is where we come in."

"I look forward to seeing Seville and I would dearly love to see this great land called the America someday."

"I hope to sail to America during the next year. Unfortunately, you will not see Seville on this trip, George. I know that the ship we are on now will berth at Sanlucar de Barramada, at the mouth of the river which is a long way from Seville. Cargo will be transferred there to smaller boats and probably new cargo added for your ongoing voyage. Bigger ships do not venture upriver past Las Horcadas because of the shifting sandbars and water depth limitations – smaller faster boats are used to ferry cargo and people to and from Seville to this transloading point. I myself will also transfer to a member of our fleet of smaller supply boats for the journey up the river."

"Hopefully I can visit Seville some other time."

"You should indeed, and Cadiz also. Before I disembark, I will give you the address of our business in both ports – send me a letter advising when you are planning to visit, and I will be happy to have you as my guest."

"That is very kind of you, Sir. Once I get settled in Alicante I will indeed come and visit."

The following day they arrived at Sanlucar at noon. It was an absolute hive of activity with lots of large ships in port. There was a flotilla of small ships and boats plying the waters and huge numbers of men laboring to transfer supplies. George's ship made its way to a reserved dock where Jorge's supply boat awaited him. He wasted no time transferring and they said goodbye with a promise to meet again in Seville. George was advised to stay on board as the crew busied themselves with unloading and reloading – he found his highest vantage point to observe his surroundings and made good use of his eyeglass. Within hours they were underway again, this time bound for Cadiz.

During this part of the journey George made it his business to get friendly with the ship's captain, Francois, who told him about the history of Cadiz.

"It is an ancient city with a lot of architecture from its Muslim past. Crusaders in route to the Holy Land in the thirteenth century attacked it and shortly after that the Muslims were ousted by Alphonso of Castile. A few of Christopher Columbus's voyages originated from the port and it later became the home of the Spanish treasure fleet, which made it a target of the enemies of Spain. It was raided by pirates, then by the English under Drake to delay the Spanish Armada, then captured by an Anglo-Dutch fleet who burned much of it before leaving. About fifty years ago it was attacked again by the English who laid siege for a long time before being repelled. All is quiet at present, and the city and port continue to prosper because of its excellent access to the Atlantic Ocean – it has many rich merchants including some Irish families like that of Senor O'Reilly whom you met already. There are rumors that Cadiz will soon become the center for our trade with the Americas, taking over from Seville – as the growing sand bars choke the Guadalquivir and the city port."

CHAPTER TWO

George began to sense that the Irish in Spain had acquired a powerful place in the merchant and military fields. He had a gut feeling that great opportunities awaited, and he was eager to get started. He busied himself on the trip studying maps of coastal Spain while also keeping detailed records of the ships they passed and all local navigation terminology he gathered from Francois and remembered from his first captain Pierre. The ship arrived in Cadiz at night, got unloaded and reloaded, and it was back on its way before first light. George could see it was a busy place and kept out of the way as cargo was unloaded and replaced with more.

A day later they sailed through the narrow straits of Gibraltar as they left the Atlantic Ocean for the Mediterranean Sea, passing close to the rocky shore. George saw many odd-looking boats plying the waters that Francois told him were of North African origin, traditional sailing vessels that had been used for trade between North Africa and Spain for centuries.

Once back in the open sea George pulled out all his accumulated information on Alicante and began studying his soon-to-be home.

Alicante also had its own long and storied history, first inhabited by native tribes of hunter gatherers as early as 4,000 BC. By 1,000 BC the Phoenician and Greek traders began to visit, established small trading posts and introduced iron and pottery wheels to the natives. The Carthaginians later conquered most of the area and established the fortified settlement that became the new city – before being themselves conquered by the Romans who remained in control for hundreds of years. When the Roman empire declined in the fifth century the Iberian Peninsula fell to the Goths. They in turn were conquered by the Arabs in the eighth century, in the personage of the Moors. It was they who named the place Alicante, which is Arabic for city of lights. George was astounded by the coincidence of this – the Moors had named this place and here he was, another Moore coming to conquer the city for himself. He interpreted this history as a sign of great optimism and luck – how could he NOT succeed.

There were passages in his readings referring to when King Felipe had expelled thousands of Moor descendants from the area in the early years of the seventeenth century, which unfortunately removed the backbone of skilled artisans from Alicante. The chapter on the recent War of Spanish Succession recounted further heartache for the area when the Valencia region which includes Alicante, backed Charles in the war – he lost to Felipe who punished the entire region for their bad choice. George ignored these signs of possible decline in the area, preferring to see the situation as an opportunity for someone like himself. By the time he arrived in Alicante he had convinced himself that he was in the right place at the right time and that he was going to succeed.

Francois berthed the ship at their company wharf about mid-morning. There seemed to be a distinct lack of activity which puzzled both George and Francois. A lower-level clerk called Carlos came on board to greet them and told them the sad news. Diego Garcia, the manager of merchant operations had been killed the previous day in a freak accident. They were relocating barrels of wine using a hoist when a rope broke, dropping two full barrels on top of him. Carlos had taken control as best he could while awaiting the arrival of their new leader whom he had been told to expect any day – that being George. After suitable expressions of condolence George had to take immediate control of the port facility. Thankfully Francois was able to interpret from Spanish to French, as Carlos tried to explain the status of stored products, shipments needing to get sent out and details of expected incoming cargo. It took several hours to get a good appraisal of the operations and to formulate a plan to go forward with. By the late afternoon the workers were loading out a ship that had been waiting all day. George, with rolled up sleeves watched the sweating laborers with a sense of satisfaction. In the space of a few hours, necessity had propelled him from being a newly arrived guest to taking charge of the situation. Francois was impressed and told him he had never seen the facility run more efficiently during many visits there. Next order of business was to find a replacement interpreter for Francois so that he could get loaded and leave in the following few days – they put out inquiries for someone who could preferably handle English and Spanish, but French and Spanish would do. That first night George worked until midnight and decided to sleep on the ship where he was also fed.

The next day he was able to venture out locally after getting his labor force lined up for the day's tasks. Diego's wife and family had a little company-owned cottage nearby – where he and Carlos visited with his widow. It was a very sad situation, and all George could offer her was that she could continue to stay there for the moment. Next, he went to see the company's Genoese banker Luigi, to make sure there was sufficient funds to pay the workers and have the necessary papers readily available for all the moving cargo coming in and going out, as well as the products like wine that they purchased locally. Luigi spoke French so George asked him for help finding an interpreter, and to find some good accommodations nearby for himself.

"All of this is no problem. I have a niece who speaks French, Spanish, Italian, some Portuguese and some English – she would be ideal as an interpreter for you. I will ask my brother Ricardo tonight to escort her to your offices tomorrow to meet you. As regards accommodation I will write down the address of a client who has what I think you need in a good part of the old city and is not too distant from your facilities. Bellissimo! Welcome to our humble city of Alicante, Monsieur George."

After a quick check on his workers George made his way to the address Luigi gave him. The proprietor Giuseppe turned out to be a cousin, but a delightful man with a hearty laugh who happily showed him a second-floor suite of furnished rooms that George thought would be suitable for his needs. It was difficult for George to figure out what was a suitable rental fee, so he offered half of the amount asked.

"Did Luigi tell you to offer half of whatever price I asked?" he said with a loud chuckle. "However, I accept your offer because you seem like such a nice young man, and we love the Irish."

"Very good then. I will have my people bring over my belongings tomorrow afternoon. One other thing, I need a good horse and a nearby stable arrangement."

"No problem. I have a stable with four good horses just up the street. For you, I will let you borrow any of my horses anytime you wish. Come by once you settle in and take your pick. When you are ready to buy your own horse, I will sell you one of mine or help find you to find another horse of your choosing – and you can stable it with me."

"Thank you so much, I will come visit the stables in a few days."

Back at the wharf he found that Carlos's laborers had almost completed the loading of his second ship, under the watchful eye of Francois. When George and Francois ate dinner on board the ship that night George told him they would start unloading and reloading Francois's ship the next day. He also shared his plans for an interpreter and that he would be moving his belongings to new accommodation in the city on the following afternoon.

• • •

So began George Moore's merchant career in Alicante. According to people who knew the previous difficulties with the Alicante operations, George had them running better than ever before – all within three months. He received letters of praise from Bordeaux and relatively generous bonus payments, but George wanted to rise above the status of employee. He floated the idea of getting some equity share in the business but that was quietly ignored – so he started planning for the setting up of his own commercial merchant enterprise. By the end of his first year on the job George had excellent relationships with the producers of the classical Alicante wine, Fondillon – a robust sweet wine made from Monastrell grapes that is fortified to sixteen percent alcohol. This product was a favorite among the British and Irish aristocracy and George longed to tap into that market directly. White wines from the region had good potential also – especially from the Merseguera grapes, while Garnacha grapes yielded rose wines. He had access to the excellent sherries and ports from nearby regions, and local brandy that he could repackage and export. The region had plenty of oranges, almonds and other agricultural products, rich fisheries and even a shoe making tradition. George also cultivated good relationships with the local Catholic hierarchy using Father Perez' list of contacts, as well as with bankers, ship builders, farmers, wineries and fishermen.

He had made sure he kept up a regular schedule of written correspondence with his mother, who in turn kept him abreast of happenings in Ireland – the family were doing their best under the ongoing harsh laws and conditions. Mother thought that his best prospects lay with the Lynch-Baden merchants – he was moving in a different direction but didn't want to worry her or to have information out in the open before he was ready to go his own way. He told her that he dutifully attended Mass every Sunday and politely sidestepped questions about his personal life by saying that he had been introduced to several very nice young ladies but had not yet met anyone with whom he wished to pursue. The real story was rather different. Luigi's brother Ricardo had escorted his daughter to meet with George and to be considered for the job of interpreter. Francesca spoke good French and of course Spanish and Italian, some Portuguese but he could not assess its level, and her English was just a smattering of words and phrases. Her husband had developed some health issues that prevented him from doing any heavy work, but he could care for their two young children and do some artisan work at home, which freed her to find employment to help the family make ends meet financially. She was a pretty girl with a friendly disposition, had some understanding of business and promised to help him to learn Spanish, so he agreed to employ her daily from mid-morning to mid-afternoon six days a week. They started the following day on a good business footing, and she did indeed begin to tutor George in Spanish as she helped him negotiate with workers, suppliers and shippers. Within a month their relationship changed after she told him that her husband's condition meant that he could no longer satisfy her – and she offered herself to George. They became lovers – it was a situation that satisfied the personal needs of both while providing a perfect cover story, and they agreed that they would not show any mutual affection in public or in front of other employees. She interpreted for him, cooked lunch for him, took siestas with him and then went on home happily. George was free to concentrate on his work while living the life of a carefree bachelor.

• • •

Meanwhile, Spain itself was going through much upheaval and strife. The Bourbon King Felipe V had taken control of the monarchy in the early years of the eighteenth century at a time when Spain was weakened by wars. It continued to be the world's greatest imperial power and his priority was to hold onto its remaining European possessions, and its American Empire. He began a series of reforms aimed at reducing the power of the old provincial councils and to subject the Church to the absolute monarch. Britain's great sea power was a huge threat to Spain in the Atlantic, while its main continental enemy was the Austrian empire. Austria refused to recognize Felipe and that led to the War of Spanish Succession. The British and Austrian armies became allies and invaded Spain in order to replace Felipe with the Austrian preferred candidate named Charles. Felipe survived some severe defeats and he eventually triumphed over Charles at the battle of Almansa in 1707, then integrated Catalonia into Spain and began to impose what they called 'full Regalism' over everyone, which was a big win for the reformers. He took an Italian lady called Isabella Farnese as his new wife in 1714 and that began a less rigid administration which made compromises with the Church.

An unexpected benefit of the war was that it had created a unitary Spanish state except for the Basque provinces, but Spain had lost many possessions outside Iberia – notably Belgium, Luxemburg, Milan, Sardinia, Sicily, Naples and had lost Gibraltar and Minorca to Britain. It also had to give Britain the right to send one ship per year to trade with Spanish America. Continued Atlantic rivalry over British trade privileges in Spanish America led to another war in 1739 which lasted through 1743. King Ferdinand VI succeeded to the Spanish throne in 1746 and concentrated on domestic recovery of their lost possessions like Gibraltar. His minister Ricardo Wall tried a policy of neutrality to shield Spain from the hostility of Austria, France and Britain. The practice of sending convoys of ships to America was abandoned in favor of individual sailings. That, and the creation of privileged trading companies greatly increased American trade. Spain's big weakness was the inability of its economy to supply America with enough consumer products in return for its exports to Spain. These needs were met by 'legitimate' trade from Cadiz by independent merchants and by the increase in contraband trade. After 1749 Spain used crown officers called intendants to rule the provinces, which strengthened royal control over local government, especially over financial aspects like upgrading the tax structure – and royal receipts increased greatly. The net effect of the reforms was that the old social structure based on the nobility and the peasantry began to show cracks. Due to the gradual development of commerce and industry, a middle class began to grow alongside the growing bureaucracy of the Bourbon Rule.

By the time George Moore arrived in Alicante in 1754 the Spanish postal system had been reorganized and new provincial public works projects had taken place, which resulted in a huge improvement in the amount and quality of roads. A cotton-based textile industry and a tobacco industry began to flourish in the region, and a brandy industry was growing in Catalonia – all of which brought prosperity to the entire eastern region of Spain. Charles III succeeded Ferdinand in 1759 and began to implement even more dramatic reforms – appointing reforming ministers who adhered to a philosophy of government derived from the ideals of European Enlightenment. The prejudices of the nobility and the old system of traditional privileges were not allowed to stand in the way of the government's ideals of greater prosperity and greater tax revenue for the state. A decree was issued in 1783 ennobling the mechanical trades and it served the administration as another route to establish government factories. Charles and his ministers failed in their attempts to get Britain to respect Spain's American possessions and that eventually led to the Seven Years War (1756 – 1763) between Britain and a French-Spanish alliance. The war broke the Spanish monopoly on trade with the colonists in Spanish America, including Cuba and the Caribbean – and it seriously disrupted France's prospects as an American power. Spain lost territory between Florida and Mississippi but got Louisiana from France. The revolt against Britain by its North American Colonies was timely for Spain and enabled it to recover some of its lost possessions, notably the Florida territories.

CHAPTER THREE

Now that he had a good feel for this merchant business George set himself a deadline of one to two years to gain an equity foothold with Lynch-Baden but by the autumn of 1755 he concluded that his overtures were falling on deaf ears. He had sent a letter some months earlier to his new friend Jorge O'Reilly and received a renewed invitation to visit him in Cadiz. He took up this offer in October that year and spent a few weeks there as a special guest of Jorge. By this time George had a decent grasp of Spanish and used it to impress all those he met, including many of Irish descent – Guillermo White, Lorenzo Plunket and Ricardo Fitzgerald being among them. He found that these people were sympathetic to the plight of Ireland's desire to free herself from the British Empire and he surprised himself with his own nationalist fervor and how well it was received. In a morning meeting at the sprawling O'Reilly compound George decided the time was right to pitch his plans for his own merchant operation and see what help he might be able to get from his friend.

"I have increased Lynch-Baden's business in Alicante tenfold but other than a slap on the back and some extra bonus money there is little future for me with them. They are a tight family business and have no desire to allow an outsider like me into the fold."

"My friend, here in Spain the only way to gain entry into a family business like that is to marry into the family. Are there any ladies in the family that might offer you a path forward?"

"Seems to be only one, and oddly enough that same Marie came to Alicante in November from France with a delegation of auditors, and she was not there only to look at the books. I was expected to entertain her while also keeping operations going and spending time with the auditors. Of course, I did my duty and showed her around. She complained constantly about my city and showed me no endearing qualities that would convince me to look past her plain and plump features. I quickly decided that I was not cut out to cater to her, regardless of what company opportunities may come with her."

"Having firmly closed that door what is your next move, George?"

"I am going to resign from Lynch-Baden and set up my own merchant business in Alicante – and very soon, I hope."

"Tell me more."

"I now have very good working relationships with a wide range of suppliers of goods that I know are in demand in

Spanish America where your biggest market is. I can supply your company with these goods that you can then export to the colonies."

"We do indeed have a bigger need for more kinds of commodities to export to America than we are able to supply. How do you plan to get them to us, do you have ships coming to Cadiz?"

"This is where you can help me and help yourselves. I need someone to help me acquire a few small ships to run the Barcelona-Alicante-Cadiz route. Can you help me on that front?"

"We have a substantial fleet of ships as you know, and we are constantly replacing older ships with new ones. At present we are planning to replace as many as ten in the next few years and could sell you some older but good ships."

"That would be great but let me be totally honest with you – while I do have excellent relationships with local Genoese Bankers, I do not have the finances to purchase your ships outright. Do you think your family would consider selling me ships in some structured deal whereby I can gradually pay for them – especially when your business will be receiving the goods and will make a profit from your exports to America."

"I like the sound of that. Prepare a list of the quantities of products you can provide and an outline plan of what moneys you project that you can use to pay off the ships. I will take this to our next family meeting in a few days."

"In anticipation of this I already have the information

prepared and here with me – I can give it to you within the next few hours."

"I like the way you think, George, and I assure you that I will do everything I can to find a way to make this happen."

Later that day George provided the documents promised. At the same time Jorge introduced him to his brother Gerardo, a high-ranking officer in the army who was home for a few days. It was fortuitous indeed to have the opportunity to meet such a powerful figure and they had quite a long discussion about Ireland, covering the plight of Catholics under the Penal Laws and Spain's own difficulties in combatting Britain in European waters and in the American colonies. The man was very amiable, and George felt that he had gained another friend among the O'Reilly clan. That evening George attended a soiree with Jorge and Gerardo at the house of Fitzgerald's where he met several pleasant and influential new contacts, including a few eligible young ladies from Cadiz's best families. They were all enamored with his Irish accent and his progress with Spanish – he walked away with invitations to visit them on his next visit.

Jorge was as good as his word. He did a sales job on behalf of George and by the following week there was an outline agreement in place for him to acquire a retiring 200-ton ship from the O'Reilly fleet, with options on several more. George was delighted with the outcome and decided to return to Alicante as soon as possible to set in motion his plan for 'Alicante Merchant Line' and his resignation from Lynch-Baden. The first thing he had to do was to lock in his tentative hold on wharf and warehouse space. Lucky for him he was the only person with direct contact to Bordeaux and it was too far away for surprise visits, so he was free to plan without interference. Francesca picked up on the new activity by several of their workers at the new location and was happy enough with his vague explanation and she did not press him with more questions. Next part of his plan was to meet with suppliers and ensure that he personally would have control over their future business dealings regardless of what name he had over the door. Once he got the local suppliers locked in, he set off for Catalonia to visit the brandy distillery owned by the Cruz-O'Donnell family, who had Wild Geese connections to Ireland. It was on that visit that he met Maria, a young and vivacious woman whose grandfather had emigrated from Limerick after the defeat of the Jacobite army – she was the business manager and daughter of the owner, Bruno. She was fiery and passionate about their brandy, and surprisingly knowledgeable about Irish history. Over several days they had long discussions about their planned business dealings and even longer ones about the situation in Ireland that he had largely pushed out of his head while he worked to rebuild his life in Spain. Their discussions rekindled more of the sparks of rebellion in him that his mother had ingrained into his head as a child and he again surprised himself with his nationalism, to the point of feeling homesick. Maria longed to visit Ireland and see for herself the places her ancestors came from. She was betrothed to an army officer, an acquaintance of Gerardo, so George treaded very carefully. They became close friends from their first meeting, and she helped George to convince her very conservative father to put his faith in this young Irishman. He locked up an exclusive agreement to ship their brandy from Barcelona to Alicante with the understanding that he was to repackage it and ship it further afield through his Cadiz associates, and he promised that he would open a market for it in Ireland.

George returned to Alicante and began to put his long-term plans into motion with renewed vigor. Within four months he had his premises ready, had resigned from Lynch-Baden and enticed Carlos and several other good employees to come and work for his Merchant Line. The first ship was named Queen Maeve in honor of the legendary warrior queen of Connaught. He convinced Jorge to supply a captain and crew for several months while he built up the business and was able to hire his own people. George was a workaholic by anybody's standards. During the first year he slept at the warehouse as often as he slept in his own bed. His business with O'Reilly Shipping grew at a record pace and ship number two and three were soon added. After feeble attempts to compete against him, Lynch-Baden ceased operations in Alicante and George promptly took control of their docks and warehouses allowing him to grow even more. By year two he had full mastery of Spanish and was picking up Italian and Portuguese, which helped him hire better captains for his ships and they brought better crew members along with them. His success brought him into contact with people of influence and wealth which in turn put more pressure on his personal schedule. He no longer had need or time for Francesca's company or her interpreting skills but felt a loyalty to her and her family while he continued leasing rooms that he seldom used. The dilemma was solved when she told him she needed to stay home and take care of her ailing husband and children. He gave her some money to help the family when she departed and soon afterwards terminated his lease of rooms from Giuseppe – instead he purchased a free-standing house on several acres.

His next major move was to expand his sailings further west – picking up cargo from Lisbon and beyond, in order to establish a profitable sailing schedule to Irish ports. In this regard George had another stroke of luck. Word got back to him that a French ship captain was in port in Alicante and was inquiring of him. It turned out to be Pierre, who had carried him from Galway to Bilbao. George made his way to Pierre's ship with haste and was greeted warmly by the Frenchman.

"I hear that Mr. George is already a major player in shipping from here to Seville. Congratulations my young friend."

"Thank you, Pierre. How have you been doing since our voyage together and how are your family doing? What brings you to Alicante?"

"Family all well, thank you. I am returning from Sardinia

to Bilbao and was told to find a cargo of Fondillon wine to carry back."

"I can certainly help you in that regard. What else is news in your life?"

"The owner of my shipping company based in Bilbao recently died, and his widow Madame Lafond is attempting to operate it – not very successfully I might add. She needs help and money. I suggest that you consider purchasing the business from her."

"You have given me much food for thought, I think you and I need to have a drink to help us digest that food."

Pierre took leave from his ship and George's carriage ferried them both to George's villa where he showered Pierre with hospitality. A whole day went by before the subject of the widow's shipping business came up in conversation, spurred by Pierre's noting that George was a bachelor and wondering whether he should entertain marrying the widow. He quickly withdrew that idea as he described the woman to George, and they laughed about it for over an hour. There were only four good ships left in her fleet and they mainly plied routes along the coast from Lisbon to Brest, and across the channel to Liverpool and to the Irish ports of Cork and Galway. George was hesitant about approaching the woman until Pierre told him about the potential for a new cargo – that of carrying kelp from Ireland's west coast to locations on the coast of France and Spain where it was used to make iodine and other products. Being able to fill ships for the return journey would make trips to Ireland very profitable. Pierre assured him that the market for kelp was there, George only needed to get more of it and thought that with his Irish connections he could muster an army of Irish peasants to harvest the plentiful product. The next day Pierre was able to use his company letters of credit to secure a sizeable cargo of wine which George's workers moved from local warehouses to the ship. George sent a letter via Pierre addressed to Madame Lafond with an outline proposal of his interest in acquiring her shipping company over a five-year period of regular payments, and invited her to respond positively, after which he would travel to Bilbao to finalize the sale. Pierre would vouch to her on his behalf and do all he could to convince her to sell to George. The friends parted ways with a hearty embrace, the ship sailed, and George got back to work – fulfilling the supply contracts with O'Reilly.

It was at this time that George felt the need to get out and about in society. He went to Mass more frequently, not because of a new-found devotion to God, but because church was an ideal setting to see and be seen among the best families and get invited to social events. He was now in his thirty-first year and thoughts of finding a wife began to occupy his mind. He attended events frequently but found a distinct lack of desirable candidates, while he became adept at finding polite excuses to avoid suitors that he had no interest in. He had almost forgotten about Pierre's visit when he received a letter from Madame Lafond expressing a strong interest in an agreed purchase, and she invited him to come visit her as soon as possible. While he began to plan for such a trip, he received a letter from Pierre; in which he told him that Madame was ready to agree to just about any purchase plan that assured her enough funds for her to live comfortably for the rest of her life. Pierre also urged him to come to Bilbao with haste and assured him that the market for Irish kelp was stronger than ever. Six weeks later George was able to co-ordinate a profitable voyage to Lisbon aboard one of his own ships and then continued to Bilbao. He surprised himself that he remembered in detail his first visit there and found the city to be every bit as spectacular as before. He had sent word ahead and as luck had it, Pierre was there to meet him and to introduce him to Madame Lafond at her residence in the old city. She looked older than he expected from Pierre's description, short and plump, with what could only be described as crazy hair. His eyes met those of Pierre just as he completed his introduction and both men shared a wry smile. She rambled on about her visits to Ireland and how she found it a very spiritual place, with its old, ruined abbeys and holy wells, and had visited St. Patrick's holy mountain. He explained that he was raised within sight of that mountain and had climbed it all the way to the top. It was like he was visiting his aunt as she doted over him with offerings of food and drinks. Within a few hours he had an agreement whereby he did not have to pay very much money up front, could take almost immediate control of her shipping operations and take over the company debt which was substantial but manageable. She was happy with his offer, so long as she was assured of a quarterly stipend that allowed her to continue to live at the comfort level that she was accustomed to and would allow her to be able to support her beloved church.

George asked her if Father Ernesto Perez was still serving the faithful at the Cathedral of Santiago. Madame Lafond was pleased and amazed that George knew her priest and told him that Ernesto was now the parish priest. Any lingering doubts she may have had were now gone and she had her legal advisors draw up the necessary papers over the following few days. Before one week passed George was at the cusp of realizing his dream – to have his own ships carrying cargo into and out of Galway. He made Pierre the head of shipping operations and they began to formulate plans. George wrote a hurried letter to his mother, telling her the great news and that he would be coming to visit Ireland soon. He asked her for introduction letters to the bigger merchant houses of Galway, most of which were related to her through family, and told her of his plans to help the local peasant population by purchasing dried kelp for export – imploring her to find suitable middlemen that could help him to grow that business quickly. While Pierre was busy writing up business plans George went to the Cathedral to give thanks and to find Father Perez. There was a service in progress and Ernesto was the celebrant. George went to the altar to receive Holy Communion and noticed the searching look that Ernesto gave him at the time. After the Mass he lingered in the pew until the church was almost empty, then approached the sacristy door, which was open.

"Father Ernesto", he called out, "I have come back to visit with you."

"It is great to see you again my son – as soon as I heard you speak, I remembered that Irish accent. God be with you, welcome."

They embraced for several moments, and Ernesto took George's hands in his own.

"I know you have made a success for yourself because I can see it in your face. What brings you Bilbao, Mr. George?"

George briefly told him of his Alicante merchant business and that he had come to purchase Madame Lafond's shipping company.

"She and I prayed for a suitable person to relieve her of this business burden. I must confess that I did not think of you, but I am delighted that you found each other, and I give you both my blessings. Have you found a nice Spanish lady to marry or perhaps you have brought over a sweetheart from Ireland to share your life with?"

"Neither is the case, Father. In truth I have worked day and night since my arrival in Alicante and it is only now that I am finding some time to accept invitations to social gatherings and of course church related events."

"Of course."

"I am in a quandary and invite your advice. Firstly, I want to find a lady of high standing, a Catholic lady with a strong connection to Ireland, and I do not have a long-lost sweetheart in Ireland whom I plan to carry over here. I did not realize until I settled in Spain just how much of an Irish nationalist I was – until I heard myself speak of England's subversion of my homeland and was applauded for my words by the exiled Irish that I encountered in Alicante, Cadiz and Seville. The other fact I have come to understand is that I have a strong desire to return to Ireland later in life and to build a house in the land of my ancestors in Mayo, assuming I am able to accumulate enough money here to make that possible. That means that whomever I marry must know this and accept that we will in time move back to Ireland, and hopefully they will help me achieve that dream. Maybe that is too tall of an order, eh Father?"

Father Ernesto stroked his chin as he absorbed the full meaning of George's statement.

"Well said my son. That is indeed a tall order but not insurmountable. How long are you planning to stay in Bilbao during this trip?"

"About another week or so. Madame Lafond and I must complete our business and I must reorganize the new business here so that our ships and people are busy and profitable under my new manager, Pierre, who is one of her ship captains and the man who told me about this opportunity. Of course, I will be back here frequently to oversee our operations."

"I think I may have the perfect match for you. Let me explore it further before I say something out of place. Write down the address of your lodgings for me, and I will send you a message in the coming days – after I have had the opportunity to speak to this lady and her family."

They shook hands warmly again and George headed back to work. Pierre had written up a three-month and six-month plan showing what voyages they had on the books. It was obvious that they were unable to fill their ships and he brainstormed with Pierre about ways to add more cargo. There were details of the kelp business to study – current quantities were insufficient to make it profitable and it was agreed that George would go to Galway aboard their next ship heading there and drum up business for both the import side and the export side. One of the Bilbao ships needed repairs and he and Pierre visited with a recommended repair yard to put that process into motion. When George returned to his lodgings there was a letter from Father Perez waiting for him, asking him to visit the rectory that evening at seven o'clock and to plan to have dinner there.

He sent a messenger confirming the plan and his carriage deposited him at the rectory door at the stroke of seven. Ernesto greeted him warmly and guided him into the well-appointed rooms where George found a table for two laid out with all the finery. After a few pleasantries and glasses of sherry they sat down to dinner and Ernesto got straight to business.

"I can introduce you to a young lady who is eligible and very pretty, lives here in Bilbao, who is interested in meeting with you – and she fits the criteria you expressed to me the other day. Would you like to know more?"

"Yes please."

"Her name is Catherine de Kilkelly. She was born in Galway, Ireland and was brought to Spain at a very young age by her father Dominick, of Castle Lydican, Galway – I do not know the exact location there. She is very much a Spanish lady, so much so that most people have no idea that she was born in Ireland. She is several years younger than yourself, a staunch Catholic and a member of my congregation here. The family can trace their ancestry to the O'Neill's of Tyrone, Ireland and the Burkes of Galway – she is as Irish as the day is long while being very proud of her Spanish family also. Off the record I will tell you that their wealth has deserted them. Her father is old and has been in poor health for many years, while her brother is a respected officer in the army, Spanish army of course. So, she cannot bring money into the marriage but from what I see of your circumstances you have no need for that. Look at this recent pencil sketch of Catherine drawn by a local artist – I can assure you that the sketch does not flatter her, she is indeed beautiful, and slim I might add."

"Very interesting, she is indeed very pretty. I have heard of Castle Lydican but I don't know anything about it, although I think my mother would be able to educate me as she seems to know every castle, tower and big house in the region. Yes, I would like to meet her – can you arrange that?"

"She is coming to a service here tomorrow evening at six

with her father. Plan to come also and I am inviting you both to meet me here in this very room afterwards. Once I introduce you to each other I will leave you to your privacy – her father may want to be there also, at least initially – I cannot speak for him on that fact."

CHAPTER FOUR

As the time approached for the evening service – a rosary prayer meeting, George struggled with what to wear. He had noticed that Spaniards were dressing somewhat less formally than he was dressing and agreed that they were wise considering their climate. Knowing from Ernesto that Catherine was very Spanish in her dress and mannerisms he decided to be less formal. He assumed that their conversation would be in Spanish, and he was comfortable with the language now, although sometimes he had difficulty in finding the best words to express himself in delicate situations – he could only do his best and be himself, so he was not going to put stress on himself worrying about it.

He decided to be early and to sit off to the side in the church so he would have a clear view of the people as they entered. It was a large church, and it was quickly obvious that there would not be a full congregation in attendance. The people filtering in were mostly older and mostly women, their heads and faces partially obscured by veils. Just before the starting time there was a last-minute increase in attendees, amongst which was an old gentleman using a walking cane and accompanied by two ladies, an older lady who was probably a servant and a tall young lady in a colorful dress which showed off both her figure and her good looks – it had to be her. Once they settled in a pew near the alter George noticed that this young lady sneaked a look around the church and even back in his general direction. The service started soon afterwards, and Father Ernesto asked people further back to please move forward. George complied and again noticed her looking back. Now that he was closer, he clearly saw her long silky dark hair despite the covering veil, not pure black hair like so many Spanish women but a softer brown color. She was paler skinned than most locals but had an outdoors look about her – maybe she liked to ride horses. The old man had a distinct Irish look about him; he looked like any of a thousand old Irishmen George had seen. He was quite feeble, and his attendant mopped his brow several times – he stayed sitting and did not kneel at the appropriate times like the rest of the congregation. Whether he was deaf or not as familiar with Spanish, George could not decipher, but he did not join in the responses and sometimes just moved his lips. The young lady was totally engaged with the prayer sequence and George could hear her strong responses which made him try harder also.

After the final blessing George stayed in his seat while

people began to filter out, including the threesome. As they passed down the aisle, she made momentary eye contact with George – he noticed her striking facial features and especially her lips. He lingered in his seat till they had exited the door and allowed extra time for the old man to shuffle towards the rectory. Only then did he make his way out and moved slowly towards the rectory door – seeing Ernesto beckoning him to come on.

The attendant lady was seated outside the door to the main room as Ernesto opened it and showed George in. The old man was seated at the table allowing him to use his left arm for support, and beside his chair stood his daughter, looking directly at George as he entered the room.

Ernesto began, in slow clear Spanish, "Mr. George Moore of Alicante, formally of County Mayo, Ireland – I am pleased to introduce you to Mr. Dominick de Kilkelly and his daughter Catherine de Kilkelly, of Bilbao, and formally of County Galway, Ireland."

Then Ernesto left the room.

George moved forward and shook the extended hand of Dominick, and then took Catherine's extended hand briefly in his own hand while bowing gracefully. He was surprised when Dominick spoke in English, with a decided Irish brogue.

"Father Perez tells me you are part of the Moore's of Ashbrook, in Straide, County Mayo and that you are a recent immigrant to Spain. Tell us more about yourself, young man, and about your family."

"Yes sir. My father is John Moore of Ashbrook, County Mayo and my mother is Jane Lynch-Athy, of Renvyle, County Galway – her family are part of the Tribes of Galway. My older brother Robert is a doctor in the city of Galway, and I am their second son. Being Roman Catholic, the repressive Penal Laws forced me to leave Ireland and I have settled here in Spain. I am delighted to make your acquaintance sir, and that of your daughter Catherine. Do you mind if we all sit and get more comfortable?"

"I cannot stand for very long anymore – please sit near me George, that way I will be better able to hear you. I brought Catherine to Spain when she was just a little girl, many years ago. Ireland has not been a welcoming place for us Catholics for a very long time. I thank God for Spain every day – we have been very well received here in Bilbao and I am pleased to hear that you too have been made welcome in Alicante."

He then addressed George in Irish, asking him if he could converse in the language – George said that he could. The old man continued in Irish – "My daughter does not understand Irish, so I want to say a few private words to you before I leave you two to talk. She is the light of my life and has put her own life on hold as she has cared for me during my several years of sickness since my wife died. I have told her all about Irish history, so she knows the place even though she has never been there. A few years ago, she was betrothed to an officer serving alongside my son in the Spanish army – alas he was killed, and her heart was broken. I don't want her to go through any more heartache.

You seem like a nice young man and Father Perez speaks highly of you. I trust that your intentions are honorable – I beg you to be honest and truthful in your deliberations with her. May Almighty God bless the two of you. I will leave you now."

"Sir, I already feel affection for both of you. I appreciate your sincere words and I assure you that my intentions are honorable in the utmost. God Bless you Sir."

George and Catherine helped the old man to his feet as he called for his attendant. She appeared instantly and they shuffled out, causing a few moments of awkward silence, finally broken by Catherine in English, spoken deliberately slow and with a Spanish accent.

"I hate it when he speaks a language I don't understand. I apologize if he said anything to offend you."

George answered her in Spanish – "I haven't heard any spoken Irish in a very long time – he was telling me how much you meant to him. Thank you for speaking English – I suggest we use both languages – your Spanish is better than mine and I suppose my English is better than yours. So, you have been in Spain since you were a child – have you ever visited Ireland since then?"

"No. There were many planned trips, but something always got in the way. Another Irish rebellion, a war between England and Spain, my mother's death, my father's business and in recent years his failing health – we never made that return voyage, but I will someday, and I do regard myself as Irish despite all these years here."

"Catherine, I have found out during my time here that the further away from Ireland I am the more it kindles my Irish spirit. I must admit that despite my success here I miss Ireland every day. You already know who my family are and that I am a merchant based in Alicante. What else would you like to know about me?"

"What age are you, have you ever been married, are you betrothed to anyone, do you drink heavily, what do you like to do in your spare time?"

"I'm thirty-five, never been married, never betrothed to anyone, have had a few too many drinks on several occasions but I drink very little alcohol on a regular basis. I have very little spare time but when I have the chance, I love to ride a good horse and to gallop."

She blushed at his frank answer, smiled and continued – "I'm twenty-six, never been married but was betrothed once – he was an officer in the army and was killed in battle last year, one month before we were due to be married. It is still a difficult subject for me to talk about. I drink wine only sparingly and I too love to ride my horse."

This initial mutual confession seemed to melt any tension that was present. They chatted more freely about Bilbao, Alicante and other places in Spain that they were both familiar with. She told him her father was very ill with his heart and she needed to take him home very soon. They agreed to meet at her stables the following afternoon where she could provide him with a suitable horse for a ride on one of her favorite trails, and so he escorted her to her carriage where George spoke a few more words of Irish with Dominick before wishing them farewell.

Father Ernesto was waiting at the rectory door when George returned with that 'how did it go' expression on his face.

"She is an exceptionally nice lady. Our meeting had to be cut short so she could bring her father home. We are going riding together tomorrow afternoon – that is all I have to say for now. Thank you for introducing me to Catherine and her father. He spoke to me in Irish, which she doesn't understand, telling me how much she means to him and warning me to treat her with utmost attention and respect – I have not spoken any Irish since I left home."

"Recently she has had a few tough years, with his illness and other things."

"Yes, she told me about her impending marriage that was cancelled when her betrothed was killed."

"I have done my work, Mr. George. It's now up to you and Catherine and the will of God. Go in peace my friend."

"Thank you again Father Ernesto. I'll talk to you soon."

• • •

Extract from the diaries of Catherine
de Kilkelly, Bilbao, Spain

George M, a charming Irishman was introduced into my life yesterday. Father Perez has turned matchmaker! Bless him, he has been wonderful to me in so many ways since the passing of Javier. And to think that I was only going to a prayer evening – cannot help wondering if Daddy had something to do with this. He chatted happily with GM in Gaelic and God only knows what they were saying about me – I now regret never learning the Irish language. He comes from nearby to Daddy's ancestral home, from a well-known Irish landed estate family. However, he lives in Alicante which is just about as far away from here as one can go while remaining in Spain. Let's not count our chickens yet. We are to ride out together this afternoon when I hope to get to know much more about this man who speaks halting Spanish with an Irish accent – how utterly enchanting. Alas, he sails back to Alicante very soon while I must remain here.

• • •

Pierre sensed that something was going on and asked George why he was so giddy as they deployed their workers the next morning and continued with their future planning.

"Does it show that much Pierre? I thought I was doing a good job of keeping calm."

"It's a lady friend I venture to say – us old married guys can sense this kind of thing."

"Yes, it is a lady I just met – you are correct. I had limited time to talk with her yesterday, so I am going riding with her this afternoon. Be prepared to cover for me if I am indisposed over the coming days – I have only a short amount of time here before I return to Alicante. Now, what have you got for me on the sea kelp front?"

"We have two agents in Galway area who can get supplies from several peasant farmers, but the overall quantity is not enough to fill a ship. I know from sailing the route that there is lots of kelp around the Arainn Islands and plenty along the coastal counties of Clare, Kerry and Cork. Can you enlist help from your family connections to secure more supplies?"

"There is lots of kelp around the Mayo coast and its islands – within a short distance of my family's estate. I have already written to my mother asking her to seek out local suppliers and this can be a great boost to the local subsistence farming community. Have you ever sailed into Clew Bay and Westport?"

"I did put into Westport once and that should be no problem for our ships if we can get kelp loaded there. The question is when can we make that trip and what products do we carry in there?"

"Wine and brandy of course, with some other commodities to balance the bill of lading and cover our tracks."

"I don't understand Mr. George – 'cover our tracks'."

"Pierre, there are restrictions and heavy tariffs on importation of liquor into Ireland, and we all know how much the Irish like liquor. They make lots of illegal whiskey and 'poitin'- fire water made from potatoes. They love brandy but don't have the ingredients or resources to make it locally. England wants brandy imported into English home ports and then they want to re-export it to Ireland in their ships, at much higher prices after taxes and tariff fees, where they make all the profits. Our ship manifestos will show the regular boring cargo, but we will carry a secret cargo of brandy that we will put ashore quietly into the hands of trusted merchants. Everyone in the chain will benefit from my plan, right up to the person drinking it because they will pay much less for it than the brandy coming in through England."

"I love smuggling, but I don't have a source of brandy to send over there."

"I do, my friend – I secured a large and regular supply of Spanish brandy direct from the makers in Catalonia when I visited them a few months ago. We already have a substantial amount of their brandy in our warehouses in Alicante and are shipping some to our business partners in Seville for export to the Americas. It's just a matter of getting some onto our ships going to Ireland. Those same ships will then be loaded with kelp for those factories you already have lined up on the French and Spanish coast, where they will extract iodine from the kelp and make other products. I think this is going to be a very profitable business and Madame Lafond's ships are the final pieces of the puzzle to get us into the Irish ports."

"This sounds like a masterly plan. How soon can we get everything into place? We must get the brandy to our ships but I'm not keen to send them all the way to Alicante for it."

"You don't have to. Can you send your ships to Seville, or more precisely to Sanlucar de Barramada at the mouth of the Guadalquivir River, which is where cargo for Seville is transloaded into smaller boats for the sixty-mile journey to Seville. We can carry extra brandy on our regular voyages to Sanlucar and transfer that product to our Bilbao ships. We can find cargo that we can bring from Bilbao to Seville to make the voyage profitable."

"Absolutely, we have plenty of products we can send to Seville and even send some on back to Alicante with your ships after transloading."

"That's it then – we can complete the loop. Keep our men busy here and figure a plan for whatever cargo you can send to Galway and Westport in about four to six weeks. I will be on that ship, I'm overdue a visit to see my family and I will use the trip to find middlemen for our brandy and for enough kelp to fill our returning ships. That's it for now Pierre – I've got some courting to do."

"Good luck."

With that, George went home to freshen up and change into riding clothes and to get his mind focused on this important event – he was reluctant to call it a date. A handwritten note from Catherine had arrived giving him the address of the riding stables outside the city and mentioned that it would include jumps and opportunities to gallop. His carriage driver knew the area and he arrived some fifteen minutes early. George told the driver to wait for instructions while he proceeded into the stables. He asked a stable boy nearby where he should go and was told where the lady was waiting for him. As he drew near, he saw that she was talking with a man who turned out to be the owner of the stable.

Catherine saw him approaching and waved, then spoke to him in English as he came close – "Mr. Moore, welcome. I have been talking to Pablo, the stable owner about choosing a horse for you, and he has recommended a fine stallion on the assumption that you are an accomplished horseman."

She then switched to Spanish and introduced George to Pablo. George first took her hand and thanked her for the invitation, then shook hands with Pablo. He played down his horsemanship even though he was indeed an excellent horseman and complimented her on her own horse before they went to see his mount – a splendid specimen which Pablo told him was highly spirited and one of his own personal favorites. The horse seemed to take well to George, who made a point of making friends with it, to the obvious satisfaction of Pablo. Catherine looked even better than when he saw her at church, now in her all-black shapely riding skirt with her hair pinned neatly under a tight-fitting hat. Pablo made some saddle adjustments to suit George who was a bigger man than himself. A short time later they set off and George let her lead the way. They were immediately in farm country with fruit orchards, corn fields and vineyards in the distance. Catherine was a strong rider for a woman on a side saddle and after they skipped over some small jumps, she set off in a fast gallop that caught George unaware. He quickly made up the ground and pulled alongside her. She was smiling, obviously enjoying herself and she gave him a nod to compliment him on his riding. They slowed to a canter and then to a walk and she opened a conversation, mostly about the area and about her love of horses and being outdoors. He was happy to go along with this pleasant conversation – neither party asking any searching questions while they enjoyed the verdant countryside. When they arrived at an overlook with distant views of the fields below them, she told him this was one of her favorite places and suggested they should dismount for a while and allow the horses to rest. She produced a picnic of bread, cheese and fruit from her saddle bags, complete with a small carafe of wine and two silver goblets. As they shared her feast using a rock outcrop for a primitive table they talked with more intensity.

"George, tell me more about the current situation in Ireland, what is daily life like there at present. All I ever hear from my father are tales of war, destruction and famine. Surely there is some good news to be told about the place and about your area and your family."

"Ireland is constantly going through various degrees of turmoil. Recent letters from my mother indicate that it is relatively peaceful at present, but a rebellion may well have occurred since then or could break out at any time. England will never subdue the Irish people or get them to turn away from their Catholic faith, but they insist on making life very difficult for the peasant masses, and indeed for those of us in the upper classes who are Catholic. The Penal Laws that have been in force now for many years have been tough on people like me – in fact those laws are the reason I am here. Catholics cannot purchase or lease land, practice law, be a member of parliament and such. Because my older brother will inherit the family estate, I had no opportunities in Ireland unless I converted to the Protestant faith, and that was a price I was not willing to pay. Most of our estate lands are leased in very small parcels to poor Catholic tenants who grow crops for export to England to pay their rents and grow potatoes to feed their own large families. It is the system that has been put in place – we are lucky to be in the upper echelons of the system, a system I do not like but am powerless to change at this time, but I hope to be part of a future change. And so, I am in Spain and have become a merchant in Alicante, and here I am now sharing a picnic with a beautiful lady in Bilbao – life is good for me. Tell me about yourself, Catherine."

She blushed and thanked him for his compliment. "I was brought here by my father when I was a little girl, and I don't remember anything about Ireland other than what I have been told. Father and a business partner used to own most of these orchards and some of the vineyards that we see in the distance. The partner deceived father about their debts and despite his efforts to save it, most of the holdings were eventually lost to the bankers, leaving us with a few acres and our home. The strain of all this took a terrible toll on my parents – my mother died during all this stress and as you saw, my father is in poor health. My brother, Michel, is an officer in the army, who is stationed away most of the time, and I am here caring for my father. Pray tell me, George, what are your aspirations in life?"

"That is a tough question, my dear. I have worked very hard these past years since coming to Alicante and am now realizing the fruits of these labors. Ironically my first port of call in Spain was Bilbao and I met Father Ernesto Perez at that time. I have returned here to purchase the shipping interests of Madame Lafond which allows us to expand our fleet of ships and add voyages to include Ireland, something that I have always wanted to do. Pierre, my chief Captain, and I are at present figuring out suitable cargo to make that expansion profitable and I hope to be on our first ship to Galway, Ireland very soon. I am a bachelor at present but have expectations of finding a life partner soon – please do not interpret that statement as pressure. This is for your ears only, my dear – I would like to live in Ireland later in life, to return there with wealth and a brood of children, where we would find a beautiful location to build our own grand estate in Mayo. These Penal Laws will not last forever, and I firmly believe that England will see the fallacy of their treatment of the Irish Catholic majority and will eventually enact laws that will allow us all to prosper together."

"Well said. I do so want to see Ireland but for now the only home I know is Spain. When are you going back to Alicante?"

"In a matter of days, as soon as I have concluded my dealings with Madame Lafond and have our new Bilbao wharf and warehouse complex ready to roll. I will be back again in about five weeks and will then proceed to Ireland on our maiden voyage. I very much want to see you again and I hope that you will allow me to call on you during my next visit."

"I would like that. We should be heading back to the stables soon. I would be most grateful if you could find room in your carriage to bring me to my home on your way back to the city – then you will know where to find me when you return in the coming weeks."

"It is my pleasure to do so, my dear Catherine."

They had a spirited ride back to the stables where Pablo attended to them. George made a special effort to compliment him on his choice of horse for him and mentioned that he would like to engage his services to help him find suitable permanent horses and stabling in the coming months, as his business will bring him to Bilbao on a regular basis. The carriage ride to Catherine's home was short but it gave them the opportunity for easy conversation. The house was quite modest, with a mature walled-in garden full of fruit trees and flowers – they maintained a large beehive which produced the best honey in Bilbao, or so Catherine bragged. George asked her to pay his respects to her father. He promised to send her a letter once he knew the details of his next trip schedule. She took his hand as he helped her dismount from the carriage, a delicate hand with long fingers. He kissed it and released her into her garden. She watched the carriage leave and was still waving when he looked back. He leaned out and waved to her.

• • •

Extract from the diaries of Catherine de Kilkelly, Bilbao, Spain

George was a most charming companion on our first ride together. He is an excellent horseman and was kind enough to compliment me on my own riding abilities. Alas, he had to return to Alicante and will not return here until a month or more from now. Daddy advises me to be patient and he is correct as always – George will be back soon, and I know he will want to come visit me again.

I had not thought seriously about Ireland for a long time, and now I cannot think of anything else. Daddy has been kind enough to retell me the stories of Ireland that he used to tell me when I was a little girl. I know he has embellished the details in the stories, but he insists that the countryside is full of old stone castles and other forts with sweeping views of the ocean – the wild Atlantic Ocean. He has described the area George comes from as being rugged, full of mountains, rivers and lakes. He thinks their family estate is a little further inland where people are more refined, and the landscape consists of rolling hills – not unlike my riding route here, he said. Every time he tells these stories he gets emotional and before I know it, he becomes tearful, sad that he had to carry me away from Ireland as a child, sad that my mother did not survive to see me grown up and married, but happy that my brother and I have had such a nice life here in our adopted homeland. Next, he gets animated about how terrible Britain has treated Ireland since taking it in the twelfth century as part of the Norman Conquest of Ireland, and he agonizes over all the rebellions the Irish have lost, especially the one that ended with the Treaty of Limerick and forced so many great soldiers like Sarsfield into exile – dubbed 'the Flight of the Wild Geese'. It was in the aftermath of that event that he too was forced to leave, and to some degree at least, he has never forgiven himself. When I comfort him, he places his hands on my cheeks and looks deep into my eyes as he declares that the descendants of the Wild Geese will return and help to liberate Ireland – and I nod in agreement till he becomes calm.

When I ask him whether he would like to return to Ireland he always says no, but I can see it in his eyes that he still dreams of the old country, and later I hear him reciting those long Gaelic poems to himself, from memory, as he sits on the porch. He recited one out loud last evening at my request, it had a melodic sound to it even though I did not understand the words. It tells the story of a brave young boy who unwittingly tastes the salmon of knowledge while it is being cooked over an open fire and he sucks his scalded thumb; he acquires magical powers from the fish and grows up to be a great warrior who saves Ireland from all kinds of serpents and invading giants. Maybe George will take me to see Ireland for myself.

• • •

CHAPTER FIVE

The Alicante operations had suffered while George was in Bilbao, and O'Reilly Shipping was griping about delays and missing cargo. Carlos was doing his best but was out of his depth. The new Bilbao facilities and expanded fleet with new shipping routes meant that George would be away even more – he knew he needed a better qualified and experienced general manager. He decided upon a bold approach – he went after a top manager of his main competitor and lured him away within days. Pierre captained a ship to Alicante a month later as planned, and within days they set sail again for Sanlucar with a fully loaded ship, much of it being brandy and Fondillon wine. Other than the wine and half the brandy, all the rest of the cargo was transloaded onto O'Reilly's boats. They carefully hid the remaining brandy in the hull with the wine cargo over it acting as a disguise, took on other mixed cargo and set sail for Bilbao. The plan was to stop and reload there, give George time to progress with his courting of Miss

Catherine and then proceed to Galway and later to Westport. Letters from his mother in Mayo promised plenty of dried kelp would be ready to load and Pierre was confident his iodine customers would take all they could get. The wine had buyers but not the brandy – not for now. George planned to give it to his chosen contacts and middlemen to win both their loyalty and future illicit brandy business.

After arriving in Bilbao Monday morning, George sent a messenger to Catherine inquiring about when he could call on her. The return message suggested two days hence for lunch as her father had taken a bad turn, was recovering, but she wanted him to improve more so that he would be well enough to converse with George during his visit. This was good because it gave George time to inspect and improve the local operations while Pierre worked on getting cargo ready for shipment to Ireland.

On Wednesday morning George had a large bouquet of flowers brought to him, while a basket containing several bottles of Fondillon wine, plus two bottles of brandy was also made ready. At eleven o'clock his carriage was brought to his quarters, the basket and other gifts loaded aboard. He left the flowers in the cool of the house until the moment before he set off. At precisely noon he arrived at the Kilkelly residence. He personally carried the flowers to the front porch and presented them to Catherine who was totally delighted and ushered him inside, where the bouquet was placed on a polished round table in the foyer. She then formally greeted George and happily allowed him to kiss both her hands as she held them forward in a welcoming gesture. The old man was already seated at the lunch table and greeted George with an Irish blessing, and apologies that he had to remain seated for fear of falling over. His female attendant was standing nearby, and she helped the two servant women with the food when all were seated. George was seated opposite Catherine with Mr. Dominick at the head of the table. Lunch was beautiful and they had a lively and wide-ranging conversation. George's impending voyage to Ireland was very much the main topic despite his efforts to steer them away from it. Dominick told him the history of Lydican Castle, now sadly just a ruin, and the story of his family connections in that area of County Galway. For his part, George promised to make every effort to call on their relatives and convey best wishes from everyone in Spain.

Catherine excused herself to supervise the unloading of the gift baskets George had brought, a timely opportunity for the men to talk privately. George formally declared his interest in Catherine and asked the old man's permission to proceed with his courtship. Dominick rambled on in Irish about all his misfortune and lamented his ability to provide for Catherine in the manner he would have wished – clearly embarrassed by their family circumstances. He basically admitted that this match was a golden opportunity for Catherine, but he was shrewd enough to see that George was at a point in his life when he wanted a mate and to start a family, so it had the makings of a win-win situation. When Catherine returned, she brought a bottle of wine and brandy from the gift basket to show her father. He promised to try some of the brandy as soon as he was feeling better and thanked George for his kindness. Then he said that it was time for him to rest but wished to say a few words to say before he departed – this time in English.

"My dearest Catherine – Mr. George Moore has formally declared to me his affection for you, my dear, and has asked my permission to seek time with you to grow that affection. I am pleased to give you both my blessing and I will now get out of your way so you two can talk and make whatever plans you desire. George, God Speed you on your voyage to Ireland, give our kind regards to your parents and if you have time, please call on our relatives in County Galway. I hope to see you here very soon, and to be in better health for that meeting. Good day to you, Sir."

After he shuffled away George and Catherine went for a walk in the garden. He took her hand as they walked, and she smiled with joy. She brought him to her favorite spot where she bade him sit with her.

"I wish you were not heading off over the dangerous ocean, but at the same time I wish I was going to Ireland with you. Father needs me here and you need to go to visit your family. Are you going to tell them about me?"

"Yes, unless you wish me to not do so. My mother will sit me down and will want me to relate every detail of what I have been doing since I left Ireland. She will be delighted to hear about you and especially proud that your family roots are in Galway. My own father is also in poor health, and from what I have been told in recent letters he is slipping fast, so I know what you are going through with your father. My brother Robert is being groomed to inherit the Moore estate and should do a fine job in that capacity. It will be wonderful to see everybody again – so much has changed in Ireland since I left and so much has changed in my life here in Spain, that I really do not know what to expect. Our ship will deliver a mixed cargo to the ports of Galway and then proceed to Westport, which is in Mayo and is quite close to our family estate. On our return voyage we are carrying a ship full of dried seaweed from Mayo and Galway coastal areas to factories along coastal France, where they extract a medicinal product called iodine from it, plus other products before the remainder becomes crop fertilizer. Luckily, the west coast of Ireland is teaming with kelp which is left on the rocks during low tide. Locals fit baskets called cleaves onto their donkeys' backs and carry the kelp ashore, where it is laid out to dry. That dried product is what we fill the ship with on our return voyage. The key to success in shipping is to have the ships that are full in both directions, and that is what we are hoping to do. But, enough about business – let us talk about us, about what it is going to take for me to win your heart."

"Maybe that heart has already drifted in your direction. I will wait eagerly for your return. Hopefully my father's health will have improved by then so that you and I will be able to spend more time together, I might even be able to join you on one of your voyages – I would like to see Alicante."

"That would be wonderful, I would love to show you the city and the lush countryside surrounding it – which is a great place to ride also. Unfortunately, I need to go shortly my dear, I have much to do to get the ship ready for Ireland and we must sail very soon."

They held hands again as they sat, and George kissed her on her forehead. He could hear her heart beating as he did so, and it filled his own heart with joy. He longed to take her in his arms but knew that the time was not yet right. They sauntered back to the house, and he set off for the port soon afterwards. Again, they waved to each other until he rounded the bend that blocked their view.

The voyage to Ireland was uneventful, weather was fair, and they had no issue with British navy ships. Pierre knew the route well and brought along a junior shipmaster to train as a future captain. They docked at Galway in the morning and George immediately got a carriage, which was loaded with several crates, and he set off for Ashbrook, leaving Pierre to sort out the unloading and restocking of the ship and do some repairs that had become apparent during the voyage.

It felt good to be back in Ireland again and everything seemed peaceful, but he did bring along one of his tall and strong Spanish sailors as an armed guard on the trip because of the danger of brigands and highwaymen. He had forgotten how bad the roads were, compared to Spain, and the carriage had to slow its speed considerably. The bonus side of that was having more time to enjoy the countryside. When he got within a few miles of Ashbrook he sent a rider ahead with news of his arrival – and when he did pull onto their own driveway, he could see people assembling ahead in the distance. His brother Robert took center stage and gave a speech, welcoming him home – reminding everyone that George had left several years earlier and praising him for his success, and for arriving home on his very own ship. His father was the only person seated and looked very ill; his mother was beaming with joy – Robert's wife and their two children stood beside him, his younger brother John, sisters Sarah and Judith with husbands and children that George had never met – they were all assembled there, flanked by a group of servants. After the speech everybody cheered, and George spoke a few words of thanks in English, and some in Irish for the benefit of the servants. Then his mother hugged him for several moments, he greeted his father who became very emotional which was not his usual demeanor – he hugged Robert, and then it was hugs all round with all the family members. The kids had never seen anybody from Spain before and they were amazed by this tall, tanned guard in clothes that were very different from those worn by Irish people.

A feast was waiting for them inside the house, and it was quite some time before George was able to sit and talk with his parents and Robert. His father had suffered a few strokes, was paralyzed on one side of his body which affected his speech, and he was unable to walk more than a few steps. He seemed to be able to understand George if he spoke slow and looked straight at him, but he was not able to put sentences of any length together – Jane was used to it by now and helped to finish his sentences for him. It was obvious that Robert was on the verge of being the master of Ashbrook, and for all practical purposes was already in that position.

Later that evening when the house was quiet his mother captured him alone in the library for a private chat.

"You gave me just fleeting information about this lady called Catherine de Kilkelly. I want to hear the whole story now from the beginning."

George saw how important this was for her and obliged, filling in some details that were not entirely factual, but it helped to give more substance and continuity to the story. She listened intently before she spoke again.

"I have made some discreet inquiries and the Kilkelly family has been scattered far and wide, and their wealth and property has been lost over time – Lydican Castle is a ruin. A Moore should have a wife with pedigree, wealth and high society connections – I fear she has very few of those attributes. George, I do not want you to marry below your station in life."

"Mother, I am thirty-five years old, I do not live in Ireland anymore and I do not have to conform to Irish society norms. I live in Spain where I have a thriving business and where society is structured differently. We Irish are respected and admired in Spain, where our Catholic religion is dominant. We are not repressed and discriminated against like here in Ireland – that is the reality of my life. As a matter of fact, Catherine's family has connections to the Spanish Royal Court and should we marry, we will most probably become part of that select grouping."

This statement stopped Jane in her tracks – of course, she had no idea that George had made it up. In truth he had designs on joining the Royal Court after seeing how the O'Reilly clan had managed to do so but doubted that Catherine's family possessed the qualifications. He probably could make a strong case for Royal inclusion based on his own Moore pedigree, but he had not studied it yet. He was tempted to take back his statement but seeing how it changed Jane's entire attitude to Catherine he had to stay the course. Instead, he changed the subject to sea kelp and its importance to him as return cargo. She had a list of six men for him to talk to, three each in County Mayo and County Galway who had the credentials to be middlemen between George's shipping company and the peasants who harvested the kelp. These were rough unpolished men whom George would have to negotiate with and make his own judgements on – she could only say that her contacts knew them as being honest and it was a starting point for him. George decided there was no need for her to know anything about his plans for the importation of brandy and they moved on to other discussion points before Robert joined them. He was winding down his doctor's practice in Galway and getting ready for a full move to Ashbrook House in Mayo where his most important and only patient was about to be his father. Robert told George in hushed tones when Jane was out of the room that the old man's heart was very weak and he probably had only a few months to live, that is, if a stroke didn't get him first.

They moved on to other topics – Robert wanted to hear all about his shipping business in Spain and as a doctor he understood the chemistry of extracting iodine from kelp, and its importance in the medical field. George added that it was a way for him to put money in the hands of some of the poorest peasants who farmed along the seashore, people who had no idea or care about the iodine – they just wanted to make ends meet and keep their families fed. The Penal Laws were still severely impacting Catholics, but there were signs of an impending softening in the laws. It was too early to promise anything, but Robert was hopeful that even the British government saw that the laws were hurting the entire island of Ireland in general; that these laws did not help push more Irish towards Protestantism, and never would.

Next morning George was eager to see the Irish countryside and Robert had horses ready for a ride before breakfast. The route was challenging with some substantial jumps and George was surprised how quickly the memories of the area came flooding back. They checked out the round tower and the holy well and forded the river several times before a sustained gallop through meadows, followed by a leisurely trot the last mile to the house, which was a consideration for the horses. They had passed by many of the tiny cottages of their tenants, where smoke often billowed out the door as well as from a primitive chimney. There were some workers in the fields already and they stopped to look at the horsemen, then waved as they recognized Robert. As they trotted home they talked about their lives.

"Robert, are you excited about becoming the master at Ashbrook?"

"Not at all. I really do not relish being master over the impoverished peasants you saw this morning – I despise this so-called Irish system of tenantry. They are totally illiterate, impoverished, and it is getting worse – having too many children, so many that they are contributing to their own worsening poverty. I wish I could either convince them to reduce family size or could administer some medicine to them that would reduce fertility – alas I can do neither. I am jealous of you in sunny Spain, having left all the troubles of Ireland behind you – tell me about life your life there."

"It was tough at the beginning, being so far away from home and family, not knowing the language or the customs of the people. Thank God for our French schooling and my ability to speak French, because quite a lot of businesspeople in Spain, and especially in the shipping business do speak French. That was my lifeline for communication in the early days before I learned Spanish – I have since managed to learn some Portuguese also."

"Wow, you now speak four languages and Irish. Was it difficult to learn them – I doubt if I could?"

"Needs must – that's what it is. I picked them up because I had to know them to negotiate business, even to deal with the crew members of my ships. I do like Spain, especially the climate but I must also say that I still miss Ireland every day – it's amazing how Ireland has penetrated my bones, my brain."

"Do you think you will stay in Spain forever or will you return to Ireland someday?"

"Forever is a long time – at this stage I really don't know, it depends on what happens with these Penal Laws and a host of other things."

What George did not say was that he had a burning ambition to return to Ireland with wealth enough to buy an estate and build a mansion to dwarf Ashbrook. He despised the system where the oldest son inherited the family estate, a system that forced siblings like him to fend for themselves. This narrative he would keep to himself until the right time came.

"Are you thinking of marrying that lady – Catherine de Kilkelly?"

"In a word, yes – but there are many steps I must go through before I get to that stage."

"Mother is hoping you will settle down soon, yet she frets about you marrying below your station. She is very traditional and thinks one must always marry someone that will bring in more money or land to the family, or indeed both."

"She doesn't understand life in Spain – it is very different than Ireland. For starters, Catholicism is the religion of the King, so I am on the right side and face no hindrances like we do in Ireland. Both the monarchy and the government are very supportive of us in the merchant class, they know they need us to supply Spain's growing colonies in the Americas. As those colonies continue to grow, we all grow with them – it is a good system for me."

After breakfast George spent some time with his father. It was difficult seeing him like this and not being able to have a meaningful conversation with him. Just being there with him was important, holding his hand, so he could look directly into George's face and hopefully understand who he was and that he had returned home. It seemed that sometimes he fully comprehended the situation and then at other times he was lost in a world of his own. George then joined his mother on her daily walk, which she professed was the best form of exercise and she looked very well on it. They talked, or rather George listened while Jane talked – he was fine with that, for he adored his mother.

"My son, I am so very proud of your accomplishments in Spain, and though I did indeed set you forth on your journey there, I give you full credit for your success. I so look forward to your letters and beg you to keep up this tradition we have in place. Ireland is changing ever so slowly and those blasted Penal Laws are soon going to be a thing of the past. When that happens, we Catholics will resume our rightful place in society. Neither have we forgotten our history and our gallant heroes like Sarsfield, despite our defeat at Limerick. Ireland will continue to rebel against the Crown, to try to shake off the yoke of British control, we will never stay quiet for long, and we will break free of their grasp someday – this I truly believe. George, you are the next generation, and you are already showing that you have great potential by your success in Spain. We need men like you in Ireland to lead our people forward – promise me that you will not forget Ireland. There is nothing I would like better than to see you return here with wealth and to buy back the lands of our forefathers, to build an estate with a Big House and establish a second Moore family presence in Connaught that will pave the way for future generations of our family; when the Irish will gain control of their own destiny."

"That was quite a statement, Mother. You have just described my full intentions and at this stage nobody other than you and I know of my plans. Let us keep it that way for now. My shipping interests will mean that I will be back and forth between Spain and Ireland frequently, and I will be keeping a close eye on political developments. I will be ready to take advantage of the situation and I hope that I can indeed achieve the dream that you and I both see – in your lifetime, my dearest Mother."

"God Bless you George."

George then set off on horseback for Westport where he planned to find the sea kelp contacts that Jane had provided. He found only two, the third having been recently drowned at sea. They insisted on taking him to see the piles of dried kelp already saved in several seashore locations. Prices were agreed and George paid half the money up front, the balance to be paid when the kelp was on the dock at Westport for loading onto his ship. George insisted that his middleman pay some of the money to the peasant farmers in his presence, so he knew they were going to benefit. He listened into the conversations in Irish and shocked both parties when he corrected the middleman that there would be more money coming to the peasants when the kelp was loaded, and he stated out loud for all to hear that he would not tolerate any situation where the peasants did not receive all the money due to them. This situation played out several times at various locations and by late afternoon George rode up the avenue to the Browne family estate in Westport. His mother had let them know to expect a visit from George and he was warmly received, fed and invited to stay overnight. By lunchtime the next day he was back at Ashbrook. A few days later a messenger brought word that his ship was in Westport, and he had to say goodbye to everybody.

As he arrived at Westport quay, he saw Pierre inspecting the piles of kelp that were building up there and saw several donkey carts coming and going with their cargo.

"Pierre – did everything go according to plan in Galway?"

"Yes Sir, we unloaded the cargo per your instructions, had visits from the merchants you listed. They collected their allotted cargo and left letters of payment with me that I stored safely in the ship. I quietly presented each of them with two small casks of Spanish brandy which certainly excited their interest and they promised to contact you with orders for future supplies of brandy and wine. Three strange men visited me to talk about kelp supplies. They came back with samples and agreed to the pricing structure details you provided. Supplies were beginning to arrive as we sailed for Westport, and I told them we would return shortly to take the kelp aboard and pay them. Everything is under control, including the repairs on the ship."

"Great work Pierre. What do you think of the quality of the kelp here on the quay, are we good to finish paying them and to load it?"

"Everything I've looked at so far is good. Some men came to the quay earlier and said they will come back later after I told them that you would soon be here."

"Good. Let's continue to inspect and take note of the quantities. Get out the rest of the brandy we have for presents and make space for the cargo. Spread it evenly in the holds for balance, but we need to also know which is Galway kelp and which is Mayo kelp, so we can grade them based on any comments from the French factories after they receive their product. I will pay the middlemen today for what has been delivered and will give them some brandy, which will help both the future kelp and brandy business. We must start loading tonight and I want to set sail for Galway in the morning."

"Yes Sir."

CHAPTER SIX

Everything went smoothly with loading the kelp and the middlemen were very happy to not only get paid but walk away with some free brandy as well. That gesture cemented a long-term deal for George on kelp and assured him of a future lucrative brandy smuggling business. They sailed back to Galway to find another good stockpile of kelp waiting. The material was inspected, the middlemen were paid up, and the product loaded. The feedback on the brandy was excellent, especially as these fellows had already drunk some of it and wanted more as soon as possible. George made tentative plans with them that the next ship coming for kelp would arrive in six weeks. It would have a lot of brandy for both ports, which would be transferred at sea to the local curragh rowboats at specific agreed places along Galway Bay and Clew Bay. The signal plans were made, and cash money payment arrangements agreed. Future ships would be listed as coming for kelp, would carry some legitimate cargo like wine to the ports of Galway and Westport – and between both ports it would be filled with kelp, just like this first ship.

The return voyage to France was pleasant, other than the strong smell of the cargo, and their kelp product was well received at both iodine factories on the French coast. Contracts were agreed and written up for regular shipments and both parties walked away happy. They then proceeded to Bilbao where George planned to stay a week to continue his courtship of Catherine, while the ship's holds were cleaned and the cargo was gathered for the trip back to Alicante, by way of Cadiz. George and Pierre had a planned meeting with the Bilbao warehouse manager to assess local progress in the newly acquired business. There were some issues with operations that were not up to their standards and Pierre began some retraining while George went courting.

He had brought some presents from Ireland for Catherine and something for Dominick. He sent a messenger to them to announce his visit the next day and prepared himself for that important visit with a haircut, a shave and a bath. Next morning, after breakfast and a quick follow-up meeting with Pierre, his carriage set off for the Kilkelly residence. The welcome from Catherine was especially sweet and she allowed him to hold her hand for an extended period as they chatted about Ireland and the voyage. She was very excited when the trunk of presents was unloaded and carried onto the front porch – just like a young girl, George thought to himself, then remembering that she really was a young girl, and he dropped his formality approach to one of celebration. Dominick appeared in due course and joined in the fun. He looked a lot healthier and moved better, a point that George noted to him and his daughter, to their mutual delight.

They spent a lovely day together and George promised to come every afternoon while in Bilbao, carefully avoiding the subject of the length of his stay on this trip. Therefore, George spent the mornings at his facility and his afternoons with Catherine. He wanted Pierre to be based at Bilbao, now that he had a senior position in the business – they had regular ships moving from there to Ireland as well as trips to Alicante with frequent stops to the ports along that route. Pierre was happy to take the new promotion and when he mentioned the need to visit his family in Brest, George suggested to him that he should indeed go there and bring his family back to Bilbao with him. They talked about it and soon Pierre was sold on the idea. They knew they could quickly get cargo to take to northern France and decided that Pierre would undertake a voyage there, returning with his family. Jose, who had gone to Galway with them for training was promoted to captain and would pilot the ship to Alicante along with George.

Every afternoon for the following three days George went to visit Catherine – they rode other routes, took carriage rides to scenic places for picnics and he even took her on a trip to the shipping facility when she expressed a desire to see it. Their relationship was deepening, their temperaments were well suited, and George felt surer every day that he wanted to marry her, if she would have him – that is. His biggest concern was whether she would baulk at the idea of moving to Alicante, and that was further complicated by the health of her father, Dominick. She was his rock and being that her brother was stationed far away, she really had to be there for him. He decided not to broach either subject yet, till he had more time to think about it. On the way back from the wharf she asked when he had to go to Alicante.

"That is indeed a pressing subject, my dear. Our ship will be ready to leave in the next few days and I do need to get back there and attend to business. It had occurred to me to invite you and your father to come along and visit Alicante – is it a possibility or does his health make that trip too risky?"

"I would love to see the place, but I worry that the trip would be too strenuous for him, especially with the risk of bad weather that could affect the voyage – I could never forgive myself if something bad happened."

"I understand and agree. Yes, I must go soon but I promise you that I will be back shortly and will stay a month here on my next trip."

She lamented his departure but understood that his business needed his presence, and she was happy to hear that he would stay longer next time. Catherine had very strong feelings for George by this stage. Yes, she had family issues like an ill father and shrinking wealth but wanted desperately to separate those factors from her real feelings. She thought George and herself were a good match, he was a fine gentleman from a fine Irish Catholic family, and obviously had a substantial and growing wealth from his shipping business. Moreover, he was very kind to her and respectful to her father. Of course, she knew of the complications involved – her being in Bilbao and George being in Alicante. She did not have a solution to that dilemma, so she chose to push the thought of it to the back of her mind.

• • •

Meanwhile back in Ireland, the changing of the guard had taken place. Only days after George departed for Spain his father John had another stroke from which he did not recover. He lingered a few days as Robert gave him expert care and Jane sat with him, holding his hand and speaking softly to him. She retold him the story of George's visit, how successful he had become in Spain and how much it had meant to him to spend time with his father during his recent visit. The priest came several times, administered the last rites and prayed with Jane at the beside. Two days later John died peacefully in his sleep. All the family were present except George and while she wished he had been there she accepted the reality and comforted herself with the recent memories of his visit, and the pleasure the old man derived from George holding his hand and reminiscing with him about growing up in Mayo. After the funeral she wrote a long letter to George, thanked him for visiting in time to see his father alive, and told him not to grieve, that John had enjoyed a long and happy life and died knowing that Ashbrook would be in the good hands of Robert. She told him how much she herself had enjoyed his visit, was thrilled to hear about Catherine and excited and happy for him that he may have found someone to spend his life with. Jane loved to receive his sporadic letters and again encouraged him to respond as soon as possible. George had been back in Alicante several weeks when he received the sad news. He read her letter many times and asked his local priest to say a Mass of remembrance for his father. The news cemented his desire to marry Catherine and start his own family. He was hoping to set sail for Bilbao a few weeks later and promised himself to make real progress on that quest during the next visit.

Alicante Shipping was enjoying continued success. George had Pierre running operations in Bilbao and Raphael was newly in charge in Alicante, helped by Carlos who was happier now that he was relieved of the management responsibilities. All of this meant that George was free to concentrate on overall management and growth of his business, and he could devote more time to his main goal of the moment – to woo and wed Catherine de Kilkelly. A few weeks later he was stepping onto the wharf in Bilbao, being greeted by Pierre, who had moved his family from Brest, and they were settled in a house nearby. George spent a few hours looking over the books and satisfying himself that all was good, then had his trunk moved to the rooms he had retained for the next year in the old city – his home away from home, at least for now. He planned to spend the entire next day at his facility, while sending word to Catherine to expect him the following day. His messenger returned with a letter from her, inviting him to stay over with them as she had quarters prepared for him to use as he pleased. This was good news – he would now have more time there to get to know Dominick and find the opportune moment to ask his permission to speak to Catherine about marriage.

He arrived at the Kilkelly residence mid-morning to find Catherine looking radiant and her father sprightly and talkative. They had received a letter from her brother Michel, informing them that he had been promoted to the rank of Colonel, which was the main reason for Dominick's good humor. After lunch he and Catherine set off in her carriage to visit the nearby river and spend some time alone. She wanted him to again recount his recent trip to Ireland, especially descriptions of Ashbrook and the ports of Galway and Westport, so that she could paint a picture of the place in her mind.

He obliged, "I love sailing along the Irish coast when the weather is good. Approaching Ireland for the first time on my own ship was a thrilling and stressful experience. We could first see the high mountains along the Cork and Kerry coasts as we came round from the channel, into the Atlantic Ocean which buffets the west coast of Ireland – then the green fields came into view, as green as if they were in a painting. A ship must keep its distance from Ireland's southwest shore because of all the small but very tall rocky islets surrounded by dangerous currents. There are thousands of sea birds living on these islands, flying around the rocky outcrops in flocks and making so much noise that we had to calm our Portuguese sailors who thought the birds were a warning of doom. Holy Monks built chapels and round towers from stone on these tiny islands, and they copied and kept the written Gospels safe there during the dark ages. Then we passed the wide estuary of the Shannon River, the largest and longest river in Ireland. Next, we passed County Clare where one can see so much bare rock that it is easy to believe there is no fertile land there at all. Approaching Galway Bay, it is very noticeable that it is a beautiful place – the rectangular bay and the Arainn Islands, positioned as if God had placed them in just the right setting. Spanish ships have been coming to Galway for centuries and the town has a real Spanish feel to it – I had not noticed that in the past, but I notice it now that I know Spain.

After leaving Galway, my native County Mayo is the next county to the north, jutting out into the wild Atlantic like a bull's head, with a rocky coastline sculptured by powerful winter storms. The port of Westport sits in the bottom of the bowl that is Clew Bay, overlooked and guarded by St. Patrick's holy mountain. It is said there are three hundred and sixty-five islands in Clew Bay, one for every day of the year. I have climbed Croagh Patrick, looked down on those islands and tried to count them – there are so many that it is impossible to keep track of what one has already counted. Our family estate of Ashbrook is less than thirty miles from Westport, so it is a relatively short carriage ride, through fields and forests of green and always in sight of the holy mountain."

"It sounds such a wonderful place, why would anyone leave it – although I'm glad you did. Why is it so green in Ireland, and tell me about Ashbrook?"

"Ireland is very green because it rains a lot my dear – we usually see rain at least once in every twenty-four hours, and the grass grows throughout the year – it's a great place to be a cow or a sheep or a horse. However, it is not such a great place to be for all Irish men and women, particularly if you are Roman Catholic and especially if you are a poor Catholic peasant. Ireland is a colony of England, the poor relation one might say. My family came to Mayo in the mid-1600's to accept land granted to them by the Crown, we are part of the aristocracy known as the landed gentry, and as such we are privileged. We ourselves are Catholic while most of our neighboring estates are owned by people who are Church of Ireland Protestants – for the most part they are good people, and we get along well together. All our mutual tenants who lease land from these estates are Catholic peasants and below them are the landless farm workers – who are the poorest of the poor. My family have become totally Irish over the centuries, and we do our best to treat our tenants fairly, but we must operate within the land system that has been devised by the British government – a system that I despise while being helpless to change it at this time; maybe we can do so in the future.

There have been constant rebellions in Ireland for centuries and after each one is defeated; the government brings in more oppressive laws. Several years ago, they enacted the Penal Laws which discriminate against Catholics and were designed to force families like ours to convert to Protestantism. We of course have not converted despite facing the many hardships these laws have inflicted upon us, and one of those was my having to leave Ireland because I could not practice law or buy or lease land or operate a business, or even make a career in the British army – and so I am here in Spain."

"It was the aftermath of one of those rebellions that forced my own father to leave and take me to Spain as a child. In your case Ireland's loss is Spain's gain, and my own personal gain," Catherine said with a blush. "Tell me more about Ashbrook."

"It is a quite a basic house, nothing grand about it – personally I don't like the house, but it is in a very nice setting. I suppose this is as good as any time to tell you the sad news – I received a letter just before coming to Bilbao informing me that my father John Moore died shortly after my recent visit, just after I left to return to Spain."

"Oh my God, I am so sorry to hear that. Was it unexpected?"

"He has been ill for a long time with his heart – he had suffered a stroke and lost the walk, as they say in Ireland. He looked very unwell during my recent visit although he perked up when he saw me. I spent a lot of time with him, recalling stories from when us boys were young which gave him some joy; even though he was unable to express himself due to speech problems caused by the stroke. We all knew he would not be with us for long and I felt sure that I would not see him again. During my visit my brother Robert was already in the process of moving to Ashbrook and he is now the master of the estate, while allowing my mother Jane to retain an important role in everything pertaining to the house and gardens, which mean so much to her. My two younger sisters are married with children and my younger brother is soon to be married. Ireland is quite peaceful at present but that can change as quickly as the weather."

"I worry constantly about my father's health and of course I know that his time is probably short."

"Catherine, I want to speak to your father soon, to ask Dominick's permission and blessing for us to talk about our future together. Are you agreeable for me to approach him on that subject?"

She seemed to be caught unaware and blushed but recovered her composure quickly.

"Yes, I would like for you to speak with him. Why don't we take a boat out on the lake while we are here?"

George nodded and he engaged a young boatman to bring them out. They held hands and made small talk about the scenery and the birds and plants around them. The boatman was quite knowledgeable on these subjects and brought them to secluded spots where they could see colorful birds up close.

George was very encouraged by the happiness he saw on her face this afternoon and resolved to approach Dominick after dinner, now that he himself was staying overnight. When they returned to the residence George found that his trunk was already placed in his rooms and after they spoke briefly with Dominick, George retired to freshen up and change for dinner. He rehearsed his lines and prepared for the most important evening of his life.

Dinner was simple but adequate and they talked mostly about George's recent Irish trip – Dominick had many questions. Once dinner was completed, they retired to a sitting room that also served as a library. Catherine's eyes met George's, she smiled and then excused herself, leaving the men alone – that was her signal to him. After some small talk he got on with his task.

"Mr. Kilkelly, I want to talk to you about your daughter Catherine."

"Please call me Dominick."

"Dominick, thank you for inviting me to stay over at your home. It means we have time like this to talk and get to know each other better. You can probably see that I adore Catherine. I am asking for your permission Sir, to approach her about the subject of marriage."

"George, I am an old man in poor health. I was beginning to worry that you might delay too long, that I might die in the meantime. Yes, you have my permission. I can see how suited you two are and it makes me very happy that you wish to marry her – but I have just one request, if I may. Please do not delay – my time is not long, and I want to be able to enjoy that happy day while I am still relatively well."

"Thank you, – eh, Dominick. Sir, you are looking fit and well to me, but I take your point and assure you that I am not the delaying type. I will speak to her tonight, but there is a point that I wish to raise, if I may."

"Go ahead."

"As you know, my shipping business is based in Alicante, even though we now have quite a presence in Bilbao. Assuming Catherine will have me, we really need to live in Alicante, and I know she worries about your health and will not allow herself to be separated from you. I hope you will consent to come with us to Alicante."

"I knew that subject was likely to come up and I have been giving it some thought. Catherine is everything to me and I will be happy to move to Alicante – I have never been there but have heard many good stories about its climate and people – I am looking forward to it."

The men shook hands warmly and celebrated with glasses of port. George proceeded to tell Dominick of his father's death without dwelling on the subject. Then Dominick announced that he was exhausted, and it was time for him to go to bed. Catherine quickly became aware that her father had retired for the night and joined George in the library shortly afterwards. She smiled knowingly and waited for George to open the conversation.

"Yes, my dear, I did indeed speak with your father, and he has given us both his blessing to talk about our future. Can I pour you a glass of port or sherry or perhaps wine?"

"Sherry, please."

Once reseated George offered a toast to the future, and they clinked their glasses.

"My dearest Catherine, I do not claim to be an orator and I have no speech prepared for this special occasion. Here, place your hands in mine. You know how special you are to me, and I confess that my affection for you has indeed turned to love. I hereby offer you my heart and ask you to consent to marry me, a humble Irishman turned merchant from Alicante, and I present you with this ring to show my love for you."

Catherine began to cry, and George worried that he had messed up the occasion until he saw that the tears were joyful.

"My heart is also filled with love for you, and I am honored to accept you, and to be Mrs. George Moore."

They both stared at each other for what seemed like several moments until they flung their arms around each other, and George stole his first kiss. He proceeded to tell her of Dominick's request to see their union happen very soon, while he was well enough to enjoy the festivities.

"Daddy is always in a hurry, and I am not surprised that he would say such a thing," she laughed.

They chatted happily about their momentous decision and the future. Catherine accepted the reality of needing to live in Alicante and was particularly happy that George had won acceptance from Dominick to move there with them. She wanted to be married in the Cathedral of Santiago by Father Ernesto Torres, which was exactly what George had in mind. Next morning at breakfast Catherine told Dominick the good news, which brought more tears of joy from father and daughter. Soon afterwards they took the carriage to visit Father Ernesto. He was very happy for them and very touched that they wanted him to perform the marriage ceremony. They talked about suitable dates that allowed George time to return to Alicante and get his business in order, prepare a home there for them, write to inform his mother of the good news and then voyage back to Bilbao – there was so much to be done.

CHAPTER SEVEN

In the spring of 1765, the marriage of George Moore and Catherine de Kilkelly took place in Bilbao. Father Ernesto Torres performed the ceremony at the Cathedral of Santiago before a small select group. On Catherine's side she had her father Dominick, her brother Colonel Michel de Kilkelly plus several local friends. On George's side were his senior Captain Pierre and his wife, Jorge O'Reilly and his wife, plus a few dignitaries from other churches and from the city council invited by Father Torres. Nobody came from Ireland – he had informed his mother of the impending marriage in a letter but told her he did not wish for her to travel to Spain because of her advanced age. His brother Robert first thought he may come but later said his Ashbrook commitments and his own poor health would prevent him from travelling.

The day was breezy and sunny, Catherine looked splendid in her white dress while George looked quite the gentleman and Dominick beamed with joy. Father Ernesto had some nice floral decorations placed in the church and gave the happy couple a glowing tribute during his Mass. A banquet followed at the Kilkelly residence. It was during the festivities that Jorge O'Reilly mentioned that he and his wife were members of the Royal Court and regularly attended events in Madrid. This intrigued George and he asked Jorge how they had become members.

"My father supplied the lineage information that was required, and he was accepted."

"Do you think we could do the same, Jorge? I will investigate and make an application as soon as I can – thank you for telling me about this. Now, let's all enjoy this wonderful feast."

A short time before the wedding George had purchased a very nice property within the city of Alicante – it had a large classical Spanish house finished with white plaster, two guest cottages, stables and immaculate gardens. He thought it was ideal for them and Catherine loved it from the first moment she laid eyes on it – which pleased him immensely. The wedding festivities in Bilbao lasted three days and then it was back to work for George while Catherine supervised a staff of workers to get ready for their move to Alicante. They sailed two weeks later, had a calm and pleasant voyage which eased her worries for her father's health – the old man enjoyed the voyage thoroughly. Dominick settled into one of the guest cottages and seemed very happy with his new home and with Alicante. He had made a deal to sell his Bilbao property before sailing to Alicante, so he was totally committed to his new life. Catherine set to work with her staff to put her personal touches on her new home while George went back to work.

Barely a month later, when George met with the O'Reilly's in Seville to deal with ongoing business, he sought their help to begin the process of making application to attend at the Spanish Court. To establish nobility lineage, he asked his brother Robert at Ashbrook to send him the documents pertaining to the granting of the Mayo estate to the Moore ancestors by the British Crown all those years earlier. These documents and other Spanish documents relating to his standing in the community and statements of support from the O'Reilly clan and other members of Court were prepared and sent by special courier to Madrid, and the waiting period began. Meanwhile George's shipping business continued to flourish.

Catherine's father, Dominick died suddenly the following spring – a terrible blow to her during her pregnancy. She was devastated but her strong character shone through, and she continued with her plans for improvements to her new home and integrating the family into Alicante high society.

A few months later they received word that their application to the Spanish Court had been refused – because of George's failure to produce a patent of nobility. He consulted his advisors and during their deliberations George remembered that there was a portrait of Blessed Thomas More hanging at Ashbrook. This revelation had the potential to change the application process if George could claim descent from him, and he told his people he could do it. And so, after the birth of their son John, he travelled to Ireland on the next opportune sailing. While there, he unearthed documentary evidence that his ancestor Captain George Moore, who had relocated from Yorkshire, England to Ballina, County Mayo, was listed in the records of the Ulster King of Arms as Vice-Admiral of Connaught. Utilizing the documents and his claim of being a descendent of Thomas More, who was also from the same area of Yorkshire, George proceeded to register these connections at the office of the Ulster King of Arms in Dublin – in order to prove his family's nobility. On his return to Spain, he re-submitted his application to Madrid, and the waiting began again.

Some months later the Court at Madrid informed them that the Moore family had been accepted into the Spanish Court. George was thrilled with all this good news – he had a son and heir, and with their newly proven nobility the Moore's were eligible to attend at the Spanish Court and could mingle with not only the highest society in Spain but also that of the other European capitals. Life was good. They welcomed another son in 1770 and named him George – followed later by two more sons, Thomas and Peter. As the family continued to grow so did their shipping business. George's ambitions were not confined only to Spain, for he also had his eye on Ireland though he kept his plan to himself, knowing how entrenched Catherine was in Spain. George had always struggled with the summer heat of Spain and as he grew older, he longed to get away from the hot and dusty conditions of Alicante. His mother Jane became deathly ill in 1780 and because he had his own fleet of ships, he was able to go quickly to Mayo and be with her. He took his turn sitting with her for several hours at a time during her final days and he talked to her even though he was not sure that she was able to hear and understand what he was saying. In one of those sessions, he leaned very close to her ear and updated her on his plans.

"Mother – you and I have spoken many times about your desire to see me permanently return to Ireland. I have decided that I am indeed going to return, and soon. In a few short years I will sell my business in Spain for a lot of money and will then retire to Mayo as a country gentleman. Already I am looking for suitable lands to create a new Moore estate and I will build a great house that will dwarf Ashbrook."

Jane seemed to nod her head in agreement, and he was sure he saw an approving smile on her face.

She died early the next morning.

Shortly before Jane's death the Penal Laws had been relaxed with Parliamentary passage of the Acts of Relief, giving Irish Catholics the right to take long-term land leases provided they took the Oath of Allegiance to King George III. After Jane's funeral George Moore took the Oath, and before returning to Spain, he engaged confidential agents with the task of finding suitable land for his plans.

In Spain he continued to build his business and educate his

children. They were sent at a young age to the best Catholic schools in Spain and France. Eventually George's land agents in Mayo found a few properties that met George's strict criteria and he was able to tour them during one of his regular visits to Ireland. That was when he first saw the property at the Hill of Muckloon, overlooking Lough Carra, which captivated him from the moment he stepped foot on it. He walked the property near the lake with his agent, a jolly man called James who professed to be an authority on local history.

"James, tell me the history of these acres as we walk in the footsteps of those who made that history."

"Sir, I am indeed glad that you asked, and I have found that this parcel has a lot of history. In the twelfth century a Welshman named William Barrett set out to conquer the Irish province of Connaught. When he got control of this local area and before advancing south, he became aware that Roderick O'Connor, the High-King of Ireland, was gathering an army to confront him on the plains of Mayo just south of here. Barrett's scouts recommended that his best route south was by water, along the three great lakes of Lough Corrib, Lough Mask and Lough Carra. He took their advice and was so enthralled with Carra that he decided to halt his conquest and not risk a battle with Roderick. Instead, he built a castle fortress on an island off the eastern shore of Lough Carra, that island directly out in front of us as we look over the lake. There he settled in peace and his people controlled the area for two generations, until they were overrun by the Norman invasion. The ruins of the castle are still there to be seen – we can get a boat to take us over there if you would like to see it."

George nodded and a boatman was found to take them to Castle Island. They walked around the small island and the ruins of Barrett's castle – James pointed out the other nearby islands and the view directly across the lake to where they had been earlier.

"What is the headland called that is opposite us, across the lake?"

"That would be Muckloon, Sir, on account of the hill behind it being called Muckloon Hill. The best I can find out about the name is that it was a favorite place of the Druids back before St. Patrick came to convert the people. It's as pretty a piece of land as one could ever see – isn't that right Mr. Moore?"

"It is indeed pretty. I am surprised that nobody before us has seen the same potential and built on it. Why do you think that is, James?"

"Well, I – I don't know Sir. The MacDonalds have owned these 800 acres for a long time, mostly undisturbed woods as you can see, with some cattle grazing and some tillage. Shur, haven't they the other property in Ballygloire with a good house on it, so they have no need to even think about building here."

James neglected to tell everything he knew about the site. The local history of Muckloon deemed it to be an unlucky place, because it had been a Druid site of pagan worship. In

380 A.D. the King of Connaught was Brian Orbsen, who was killed by his enemies that year, the only survivor of the attack being his Druid, Drithliu. He went into hiding around Lough Carra. Eventually these same enemies hunted him down and cornered him at Muckloon Hill. Just before they killed him, Drithliu put a curse on Muckloon and local superstition since then had kept people from building anything there.

George looked at two other properties, but both were less than 200 acres each and didn't hold a candle to Muckloon in his opinion. Being of an impulsive nature he set up a meeting with the owner, Jamie MacDonald, for the next day and bought the Muckloon property from him there and then. Afterwards he gave his agent the task of quietly finding other tracts of land nearby that he could cobble together into a large estate. In a brief visit to Ashbrook before returning to Spain he decided not to mention his purchase to his brother Robert, who was again unwell at the time.

Back in Spain, George busied himself so much that he had little time to dwell on the looming problem he knew was coming – how and when to tell Catherine of his plans to sell out and move the family to Ireland. His two eldest boys, John and George were in school in France, and she was busy caring for the two younger boys, Thomas and Peter. In autumn word came that his brother Robert in Ireland was very ill – he hastily readied a ship and set off to visit him, only to find that Robert had died the week before he arrived. George, as the next son, would now inherit Ashbrook plus the acreage surrounding it and he was presented with both a challenge and an opportunity. He was nowhere close to being ready to leave Spain and had not yet mentioned his advanced plans for Ireland to Catherine – personally he did not feel any attraction to Ashbrook and was sure that Catherine would not like it either. Robert's untimely death did offer him a way of broaching his Ireland plan to her in the guise of continuity of the family lineage in Mayo. While at a remembrance service in Ireland for his brother Robert, George had made the acquaintance of neighboring landlords, including the Blakes of Galway who had known Robert when he was a doctor there, and were distant relatives of his mother Jane Lynch. In their conversations it was mentioned that they had substantial land properties near Lough Carra – at Ballintubber and in Partry, which they were considering selling in the future. Without showing his hand George got descriptions of the properties, liked what he heard and was able to extract a promise that they would contact him when a decision to sell was made and that he would have first refusal on a purchase.

On his return to Spain, he told Catherine of Robert's death, and that he would now inherit the Ashbrook property. She was shocked by his sudden passing and George explained as best that he could how Robert had slipped gradually into bad health at such a young age, before suffering a stroke in the end.

"What are you going to do with the estate?"

"By rights, we should live there and continue the Moore

name and tradition. However, the house is not up to our standards – I would not expect you to live there, nor do I think I would like it."

"Surely you can keep the tenants who are on the land, maybe even sell or lease the house – while we continue to live here in Spain."

"In the short-term yes, but I do want to bring you all back to Ireland in the future – to County Mayo. You have many times expressed the wish to see Ireland again – you are finally going to be able to do it – in style."

"Everything is different now, George; we have four sons to bring up, a large shipping business and a wonderful life in Spain. It is your decision of course, but I beg you to think about what is best for the children. They will get a great education here, and Spain is a land of opportunity, both in the motherland and in its many dominions, especially in the Americas."

"Everything will be staying as it is for several years and I too want the boys educated here, but Ireland is pulling me, and I thought it was pulling you too. Remember your ancestors, the Wild Geese, who were forced to leave after the Treaty of Limerick. They swore they would return to help Ireland. I left Ireland of my own free will, but I also swore an oath to myself that I would return. I want the Moore family to be one of the pre-eminent families of Ireland and I know I can accomplish that. Spain has been good to us but as time passes and I grow older, I find the pull of Ireland even stronger – that oath to myself is one that I must honor."

Catherine fell silent, a silence that became awkward. George knew that she was displeased with what he had just told her. He had hoped she would be more enthusiastic about returning to the land of her birth, to a place she was forced to leave, a place she had expressed the desire to see many times, both before and after they were married. As the head of the family, it was up to him to decide but he had hoped that his wife would be eager to return to Ireland and she apparently was not. He changed the subject to local news and to recent successes in their shipping business. She excused herself shortly after that, saying that she had a headache and was going to bed. George poured himself a brandy and spent the next two hours pacing the floor while he reviewed the events that led him to this position. He had planned to tell her of the Muckloon land purchase this same evening but decided to say nothing when he saw her negative attitude towards the move to Ireland. Somehow, he needed the two older boys to be in favor of the Ireland move, so that they could bring their mother round to his side; he decided to talk-up Ireland and Mayo to them when they were next home from school. Of course, he wanted them to have a well-grounded education before the move, which would push the target date to about 1790 – that gave him ten years to increase his business and his wealth. The younger boys may have to finish their education in Ireland as he couldn't push the relocation much past that – he was getting older himself and would be sixty-one by then.

George had diversified from his shipping business and

owned substantial vineyards and held a significant share in the two iodine operations that he supplied with Irish sea kelp. Between everything he had going on, he was spending a lot of time away from Alicante and that distance from Catherine was both a blessing and a problem. He made a special effort to assure her that Spain was home for the foreseeable future, while he also made time for the two older boys during their school breaks. He took them on short sea voyages on his fleet so they could see the merchant business up close. It became apparent to him that neither young John nor young George had an affinity for this business. George junior was very studious and reserved, while John was more outgoing, with a wild streak that caused frequent discipline issues in school. John was a natural horseman and was constantly winning local races – he was not studious at all; despite being pushed hard by his parents. Young George on the other hand was happiest with a book in his hands and loved to try his hand at poetry and short stories. They were both intrigued about the idea of moving to an estate in the West Coast of Ireland and as time went on George was able to convince them of the excitement and merits of such a move – which gradually brought Catherine round to a position of reluctant acceptance of the inevitable.

George had leased out the Ashbrook lands but not the house, and on his frequent visits to Ireland during the following years he purchased the tracts of land he had been waiting in line for – in the area of Ballintubber and Partry – which together with his Lough Carra and Ashbrook land brought his holdings up to some twelve thousand acres. He then began to plan the mansion he wanted to build overlooking Lough Carra, and to look for the best architect for the project. After several attempts, he convinced John Roberts, one of the top architects in Ireland at the time to take on the contract. Roberts, a Protestant, had designed both the Protestant and Catholic cathedrals in Waterford, as well as some prominent large houses such as Tyrone House in nearby County Galway, and was suitably impressed by George's site at Muckloon Hill, overlooking Lough Carra and its islands.

In preparation for his future move to Ireland, by the late 1780's George had begun to talk seriously to interested buyers for his shipping and other business interests. His longtime shipping partners, the O'Reilly's, wanted the shipping company and were prepared to outbid two other potential buyers. He had several interested parties in the vineyards and his partners in the iodine factories were confident of being able to find new investors to buy George's share of those businesses. As 1790 approached, George confidently expected the accumulated sale of these assets would make him a very rich man. He sought to win Catherine's approval for the move when he asked for her good counsel during preparations for the sale of his assets – instead he found himself at odds with her.

"George, sell your business interests if that is what you want to do, but consider staying here in Spain and live the life of a retired gentleman here. We are members of the Spanish Court and enjoy great privileges because of that. We can visit any of the great cities of Europe and gain access to the highest society there – we can visit Ireland and enjoy all that the city of Dublin has to offer."

"My dear, you are missing the point. We now have the means and status to return to Ireland at the very top of society. I know you left Ireland as a very young child but surely you remember the passion that your father Dominick held for his homeland in Ireland – it is your homeland also. From the day I left those shores I have longed to return, and to be in a position to have the Moore family not only make its mark on Irish society, but to also contribute to the liberation of our country and be part of Irish history going forward. Call it foolish patriotism or whatever you want, but I am unfulfilled until I settle back in Ireland in my rightful place, and I struggle to understand why you do not feel the same way."

Catherine knew she could not change his mind about Ireland and begged him not to sell their house just outside Alicante – a comfortable quaint old building with mature gardens that they used as a weekend retreat and a place she particularly loved. He was happy to agree to keep this property and it fitted in nicely with his plans. It would take a several years to build in Mayo and George thought it was best for his family to stay in Spain until the new house was completed. He had some hasty upgrades carried out on Ashbrook House and he used it as his home away from home during the construction years. He hired local managers to keep his tenants up to date with rent payments – to handle the unpleasantness of eviction and the placing of new tenants. Though his trips during this time only lasted a few weeks at a time George loved to ride out over his property and his willingness to engage the tenants in conversation in their native tongue elevated him to an unusually high level of respect and admiration in the eyes of the tenantry. During those trips he acquired a new fondness for the Ashbrook area that would come into play later in his life.

• • •

Extract from the diaries of Catherine de Kilkelly, Alicante, Spain

Maybe it is selfish or ungrateful, but I prefer to stay in Spain. We are respected members of society's elite here and have a wonderful life, it is the only home the children know, and they are happy in this warm climate. Peter's health issues can be treated better here than in Ireland.

When did George's nostalgic dreams of Ireland turn to repatriation? Was it his frequent business visits to Galway on his own ships that kindled the desire to live there, or was it the inheritance of Ashbrook House? I never met his brother Robert, but I so wish that he had not died. His presence at Ashbrook kept George away from the old estate and kept his Irish dreams where they belong – in the past. Now he has filled the minds of young John and George with exaggerated stories of Ireland, to the point that they are already there in spirit.

Forgive me Daddy, I know that it was your desire that the descendants of Wild Geese return to Ireland, and I did make that promise also. I was so young then and did not fully grasp what that promise meant. Now I know better – Ireland is a land of misery, of deep divisions between Protestants and Catholics, a land that Britain never wants to let go from its grasp. Even as wealthy Catholics, we will be treated as second class citizens by the ruling Protestant ascendancy. I foresee nothing but misfortune and ruin for our family in that situation – and I pray that God will relieve George from his well-meaning but disastrous wish to move there.

Alas – it seems we must go, we must give up sunny Spain for a cold and wet Ireland, must give up the splendors of the Royal Court for a role in a broken and divided society, where even my beloved Catholic religion is backward compared to what it is here in Spain. I will do my duty and go, but I do not go there happily, and I cling to the hope that my husband will have a change of heart.

● ● ●

CHAPTER EIGHT

Building began on the Mayo house in 1791. The design was a three-story country house with thirty-five rooms: a symmetrical floor plan consisting of a detached five-bay building over a raised basement. The walls were made of local cut-limestone, with a hipped roof encircled by a stone balustrade and a pair of limestone central chimneys. At the front, three flights of limestone steps led up to a pillared portico with a heavy oak front door opening into a large hall with a flagstone floor, and a decorative plaster ceiling in the Adam style. The family motto was engraved in a stone slab over the entrance – Fortis Cadere Cedere Non Potest (The Brave May Fall But Cannot Yield). On either side of the front hall were the large dining room and drawing room, and above the hall was the summer drawing room with a balcony which afforded a wonderful view of the lake. A wide corridor ran the length of the ground floor, at the end of which was an ornate staircase for use by family, and two other separate staircases. One was a service staircase for the servants to access the basement; the other was an oak staircase to access the first and second floors which contained a library and several guest apartments. On the second floor there was a suite of family rooms, including a nursery, a billiard room and a private chapel – which later boasted vestments and a Spanish silver chalice gifted to George by Father Ernesto Peres, plus a solid gold crucifix that George acquired from Barcelona in settlement of a shipping debt.

A long driveway led to the house, with a large circular gravel sweep facing the front portico, capable of accommodating several coaches at the same time. The home was designed to be self-sufficient with a bakery, forge, laundry, greenhouses and servant's quarters. Behind the house a collection of sculleries and outbuildings were located, separated from the house by a stone wall, and from here a set of large doors opened to a tunnel that led to the stables, the coach house, the gardens and various other farm outbuildings. Mr. Roberts estimated that it would take three to four years to build the house and all its associated buildings and gardens – and it did take the full four years to complete it. During the construction George took the two eldest boys, John and young George to see the house and estate, before shipping them off to London to complete their studies – they both raved about the setting which pleased their father immensely.

In the summer of 1795 George moved Catherine and their two younger teenage sons to Mayo, aboard a ship that he had just ceased to own – the voyage being a negotiated part of the selling price of the shipping business. This was Catherine's first sight of the house and estate – she had turned down an offer by George to visit six months earlier, to be involved in the selection of furnishings. Therefore, he had proceeded alone on the task of outfitting the entire house, with the help of various designers and agents – including, by his request, the placement of a large iron chest in the front hall that was always locked and promoted stories of Spanish gold The completed house was very impressive, and the two young boys loved it from the first moment, which put pressure on Catherine to add her approval: she eventually did so, but without enthusiasm. There were several other estates nearby owned by notable families such as the Blake's, Lynch Blosse's, Browne's, Russell's and Ruttledge's – people they should befriend and who could help them integrate into the top tiers of Irish society.

Once settled into their new home George threw a party and invited all his neighboring landlords. He had classical musicians playing inside, while around a large outside fire, he had renowned local Mayo musicians – fiddlers and uilleann pipers. By all accounts it was one of the finest parties ever held in Mayo and that led to immediate acceptance, and respect for the Moore's by the neighboring gentry, and accession to their rightful place in high society – while George also managed to win over the native Gaelic population.

George took note of his wife's indifference to the gathering, to Mayo itself and to Ireland in general. She complained of the cold climate, the remoteness of their beautiful new home and even found Ireland's brand of Catholicism less to her liking than what she had enjoyed in Spain. She was reluctant to take up the invitations to visit their neighbors and she had taken little interest in the hiring of the service staff needed to care for the house and her family. The servants told her the story of the Druids of Muckloon and the curse of Drithliu – which further increased her discomfort. She was to carry this fear of the Druids' Curse with her for the rest of her life.

Her immediate attention was mostly consumed by young Peter's health problems and George convinced himself that this unfortunate situation was the reason for her disconsolation. The boy's lack of mental development was worrisome before they left Spain. Now it had deteriorated even more, a fact that Catherine blamed on their stressful relocation. George did not agree with this reasoning, and the opinions of two local doctors were in line with his thinking – but he avoided any confrontation on the matter and let her fuss over the boy while he busied himself with estate matters. Thomas was sent to a finishing school in England prior to him joining the older boys at university in London.

George expanded his regular tenant visitation schedule to include all the Ballintubber and Partry properties, in addition to Ashbrook, and he furthered his unique bond with his tenants by his willingness to speak Gaelic to them and listen to their stories. He gained the reputation of being regarded as one of the best landlords in the region by the poor tenant masses, and that relationship helped him to have the least number of eviction cases of any of his Mayo and Galway neighbors. By the end of their first year in Ireland it appeared necessary to have Peter put under constant supervision and medical care. Catherine wanted him to stay at home with them and devoted most of her time to caring for him, to the point of withdrawing herself from everything else on the estate. John and young George continued with their law studies in London. George was an intellectually gifted young man who knew how to showcase his talents in polite society. He was befriended by members of London's elite and gained entry to the very exclusive Holland House Circle. John, on the other hand, was handsome but directionless, who was more inclined to partying, gambling and womanizing – always overdrawn on his allowance, in the news for all the wrong reasons and a near constant embarrassment to his father. When it was time for Thomas to enter university in London, the parents worried that John may well be a bad influence on him, so George decided that John should leave the distractions of London and return to Mayo. The young man made an impassioned plea to his father to allow him to study in Dublin instead, while promising that he would reform and pass the Irish Bar.

Father and son met in Dublin, where George had some estate trade business to attend to. It was a tense meeting.

"Son, I was younger than you when I went to Spain on my own, with nothing more than a letter of introduction. I parlayed that into a large profitable business because I had a burning ambition to succeed, to make enough money be able to purchase large tracts of land in Ireland as soon as the Penal Laws eased. Why – because I wanted to make the Moore family name something special. Even if my brother Robert had lived a long life, I would still have done it – I wanted a home far grander than Ashbrook – that is why I built Moore Hall. I wanted to create a legacy that would continue for generations, and future members of the Moore family to take honored places in Irish society. For this to happen, my heir must continue to run the estate successfully, marry well and produce healthy intelligent offspring. John, you are almost thirty years old, you are the heir to Moore Hall and estate, yet you continue to disappoint me. When are you going to become the man I expect you to be, to fulfill the obligations I just outlined? Your brother George has made great strides in London, both with his studies and in high society, such that he has been invited to join the exclusive Holland House circle. Meanwhile, you were on the verge of expulsion from Law Studies in London and are lucky that you were not challenged to a duel last month, over your reckless pursuit of Lady McKay, wife to a member of the house of Lords, no less. It is past time for you to grow up John, to uphold the name and honor of our family. I am loathe to change the time-honored tradition of the eldest son being the heir – but I will consider replacing you with George if you don't get your life in order – so help me God. What do you have to say for yourself?"

"Honored Father – I am wholeheartedly sorry for letting

you and my mother down again. George is indeed a brilliant figure in London, and you are justly proud of him – and he will be a good mentor there for Thomas. I am not blessed with similar intelligence, and I have made many youthful errors of judgement which I hereby acknowledge and for which I feel mortal regret. London was too much for me Sir, and I know I will be better suited to a smaller town like Dublin. Since you summoned me to this meeting, I have spent much time in quiet reflection and much time on my knees in prayer – I know I can do better and I promise you that I have now emerged from the darkness into the light, and I am ready to make you proud. How is dearest Mother, and I pray every day for Peter – is he doing better?"

"Your mother has so much to contend with as she cares for Peter, and she is a pillar of strength – she loves you dearly and does not deserve to have to worry about you all the time as well. Assuming we can get you enrolled here in Dublin to read Law, you must understand that this is your final chance to redeem yourself – you cannot afford to fail this time, for yourself or for the family honor. Ireland is constantly full of rebellious rumors and Dublin is the usual hub of these rumors, especially among the educated classes. John, you must stay clear of all this rancor – promise me here and now that you will."

"I totally understand, Father – and I am ready to devote every hour of every day to my studies for the Irish Bar. I will not allow anything or anybody to deflect me from my task ahead."

"Good, I was hoping for this outcome. Yesterday I was able to use my good offices to get this letter of introduction that I hold up in my hand – it is to the Dean of the Law School. Take the letter and go meet with him tomorrow morning to get enrolled. I have also secured lodgings for you within sight of the law school – details are enclosed in this envelope."

"Thank you, Father, I will act immediately. Sir, I am also in need of money to accomplish all of this."

"Take this third envelope to Mr. Peters at the law offices of Peters and Chaplin at The Green. I have retained him to be your financial advisor, he will administer your allowances. I warn you now that you will not be able to exceed these allowances, so you must live within your means – do you understand all of this?"

"Yes Father, loud and clear."

• • •

Extract from the diaries of Catherine de Kilkelly, Moore Hall, Ireland

What is it about this place that heaps misfortune upon our family? I have read my earlier entries with trepidation – I am shocked at how much of my prophecy has come true. The servants have told me the stories linking the ghosts of the Druids with Muckloon Hill – stories that George dismisses as fairytales. I hope and pray that we have turned the corner, now that father and John were able to resolve their differences – and John will complete his law studies in Dublin. He is a dear boy with a good heart – I believe that he has changed for the better and will finally get on a good path. Young George will do even better in London without the distractions created by John and will watch over Thomas as he begins his studies there.

As much as I hate myself for saying it, I must agree that George and the doctors are correct – that it is best for Peter to live in a closed community where he will be safe and get constant medical help. The lake is too dangerous for him and next time there may not be anybody nearby to save him – and nearly every servant here cannot swim. All the boys will be home for a family Easter – then we will move Peter to the abbey in Galway – may God forgive me for this.

• • •

A few short years earlier, The French Revolution had shocked everyone in Ireland, an event that resulted in the removal of 'Louis the Last' and was followed by the establishment of a Republic. This cataclysmic event was viewed with great interest by many sectors of Irish society. In Dublin, Roman Catholics redoubled their efforts to campaign for full civil rights and formed unlikely alliances with Presbyterians to press the government on these issues. The Catholic Committee got totally re-energized and appointed a young Protestant barrister called

Theobald Wolfe Tone as their paid secretary. Tone's avowed aim was to bring Irishmen of all creeds together to push for a radical reform of parliament and to establish complete religious equality. He formed close ties with the Presbyterians of Ulster and in 1791 in Belfast he co-founded the Society of United Irishmen, as the instrument to carry out his stated aims. Similar societies were quickly established throughout the country, including a very active one in Dublin, which was Wolfe Tone's home base.

By the time that John Moore settled in Dublin and began his studies for the Irish Bar the United Irishmen were a force to be reckoned with, and were particularly well represented among the educated classes, among Catholics and Protestants. John, ever the impressionable type, was blown away at his first encounter with Wolfe Tone, accompanied by James Napper Tandy. They claimed to be in close touch with the 'Directory' in Paris, the body that governed policy for the revolutionary leaders of the French Republic. The Directory were sworn enemies of Britain and were willing to help Ireland to get what had been achieved in France – namely a Republic. John took the oath to join the United Irishmen and became a low level but active member. The promises he had made to his father were soon forgotten and his energies were directed more towards the Society activities than to his studies – despite Tone himself telling him that he would be of more help to them as a member of the Irish Bar and urging him to keep up his studies. With the outbreak of war between Britain and France the

United Irishmen society moved steadily towards becoming an armed force, who hoped that military aid from France would be the spark to ignite a nationwide rebellion. In 1796 Wolfe Tone was threatened with arrest for his activities – he was later allowed to leave Ireland for exile in America under a deal with the government. He quickly moved on from there to Paris, which immediately raised hopes in Ireland for an impending large French military expedition to Ireland to support a full-scale rebellion by the United Irishmen, in conjunction with the 'Defenders' who were an agrarian protection force that was particularly strong in Ulster. Tone convinced the Directory to send an expedition to Ireland – in December the following year a French armada of over forty ships and some fifteen thousand soldiers led by General Hoche was sent to Ireland, with Wolfe Tone aboard. The armada approached the County Cork coast, but terrible storms prevented them from landing, and after five days of waiting they returned to France, worried that they were about to be confronted by a British Navy fleet.

John Moore had first met Lord Edward Fitzgerald in the company of Wolfe Tone, and after Tone's departure for America he became an ardent follower of Lord Edward. They were close in age, both handsome, from aristocratic backgrounds and both womanizers. The British administration was very attuned to signs of rebellion and Dublin Castle had a very efficient system of informers. Fearing an imminent outbreak of rebellion, they decided to embark on a policy of military repression to break the United Irishmen and its parallel agrarian society, the Defenders – in the spring of 1798. On the day in March when most of the conspiring leaders were arrested, John Moore was with Lord Edward and a select group in a safe house just outside Dublin. After a messenger brought news of the arrests to them, Edward took charge of the situation and calmed everyone down. When John got the opportunity to speak, he was ready to offer his services.

"Lord Edward, tell me what I can do to best serve the cause and I will gladly do it, at whatever cost."

"Thank you, John. Lucky for you that your name is not on the list of persons being sought by the Castle. We must convene a new emergency leadership Directory and you can help me in this quest – I know you have your trusty steed with you in the barn. Take this list of four names and addresses and go to each person, use my secret code word 'LEFUI' and tell them they must join me here as soon as possible. Once you have completed your mission dispose of this list and do not come back here, for your own safety. I urge you to leave Dublin and head west towards your family home in Mayo, you will be safer there than anywhere in Leinster. Once we decide on a date for the insurrection, I will send word to you. Go now and God Speed."

John did his bidding – he alerted each of the named individuals and disposed of the written addresses after delivering his message. He then picked up some clothes and some of his law study books from a secret hideaway without going to his lodgings and rode west to Lucan where he stayed the night with a fellow law student friend. He concocted a story that he had a family illness and asked his friend to excuse his absence to his professors. Going home for Easter too early would arouse suspicion that he was neglecting his studies, so John needed to use up a week before arriving at Mayo. During his London days he had been a friend of Stephen Hanratty, whose family trained horses on the plains of Kildare, and John knew he had a standing invitation to visit the family any time. Luckily, he found Hanratty (they always called each other by last name only) was present at the family estate and he stayed with him for six days, got to learn about the business of horse training and helped with the exercise riding of several of their best horses. It also gave him the chance to lie low while listening for any big news from Dublin – there was none – he concluded that no news was good news.

"Moore, you need to break your journey by calling at Preston Hall in Longford," Hanratty said, "Preston's daughter Elizabeth is a stunning beauty and just your type. I happen to know she is at home at present and this letter of introduction I have written for you will get you dinner and a night of lodging, if not more, eh, me bucko."

John took up the offer, headed west and after presenting his letter of introduction he was invited to have dinner with the family and to stay overnight. Elizabeth was present for dinner and was quite taken with John, his Mayo family and his law studies. She was not the beauty that Hanratty had promised – instead she was a pleasant girl, plain and plump. Hanratty, always the joker, had pinned a good one on him this time. John smiled inwardly, enjoyed the hospitality and dutifully set off on the road the next morning.

Though he was still a little early for Easter his excuses seemed to satisfy his mother, especially when he produced the books that he said he brought home for study purposes, and he spent time talking and tending to Peter, which gave Catherine a much-needed break. His father was away at the further reaches of the estate and did not return until the next day – and was surprised to find him home.

"Welcome – but you are a little bit early. I trust everything is well with your studies and your professors are not looking for you."

"No indeed father – they wanted to take advantage of the good spell of weather we are having and allowed us to leave early. I did of course bring my books with me and have already had study time this morning, after Peter and I took a walk down along the lake."

"Good, I'm sure he enjoyed seeing a new face, did he remember you?"

"Ah, yes of course he did, father. How is everything with the estate?"

"Good – all things considered and compared to neighboring estates. There have been some agrarian incidents near Ballintubber that resulted in minor property damage, and we have lost some cattle to poachers in Partry. The good news is that the crops have come in good over the past year and the tenants have been keeping up with rents. We have had no recent evictions and as we approach Easter, we don't plan to turn anybody out onto the road. Ride out with me tomorrow and see the estate up close – this is a good opportunity for you to see the workings of the estate and you have two days before George and Thomas arrive. You should also squeeze in some fishing on the lake – Michael Connolly is a fine ghillie and will bring you to the best spots for the big trout and pike."

"I look forward to both activities."

It had been arranged that young George would meet up with his brother Thomas at his college and they would travel home for Easter together. The pair arrived home via the Dublin mail coach the day before Good Friday, in time for the entire family to celebrate the holy feast of Easter together, where they attended services at the local church in Carnacon. The weather co-operated for most of the time and during the following week they enjoyed family outdoor activities in the orchards and meadows beside the lake, picnicking and playing games that brought smiles to everyone's face – even Peter's spirits were lifted, and he looked the happiest that Catherine had seen him for years.

John and young George got to ride out over the meadows alone, their first meeting since parting in London. George opened one of their conversations with the big question.

"Have you given much thought to the reality that in a

relatively short time you will be master of this Mayo Estate? How would you run things differently than father?"

"It may surprise you to know that I have not thought about that at all. Father is in great health and has many years left. I have other things to occupy my mind."

"Like what?"

"My law studies, I am not as clever as you so I must really study. Then there are women to think about, and Dublin has a great many beautiful specimens to occupy my time."

"Anybody special?"

"Of course not, you know me – we are not the type to be tied down, we must share our time with as many of the ladies as possible. Are you not doing the same in London?"

"Yes, I must confess that I am indeed doing just that, and it is wonderful. I also have some excellent male friends at Holland House and elsewhere, men who are the gifted thinkers of our time and we have stimulating debates and discussions – many of them heated, I should add, but kept within the realm of the spoken word only. Have you made good friends during your time in Dublin?"

"Indeed, I have – barristers and people of property and good standing in the city, plus fellow students of course. Ireland is a more volatile place than England, we are a country of friction between Catholics and Protestants, joined at the hip to the government in London despite having our own parliament. Rumors of rebellion and revolution are always in the air, especially since the recent events in France, and now the ongoing war between Britain and France. If I may make the analogy of a chess game, Ireland represents the pawns, with Britain and France controlling all the powerful pieces. We are the breadbasket that feeds the Empire yet most of the Irish go to bed hungry at night."

"John, that sounds like revolutionary talk. I hope you have not caught any of the germs of rebellion in Dublin – even in London I hear rumors all the time of imminent trouble in Dublin."

"I keep company with educated Catholic and Protestant friends alike. My aim is to reduce and eliminate the friction that has been bred into us. I believe that we are all equal human beings under God, and that includes the poverty-stricken peasants of this country. We, the Irish gentry are all 'just Irish' in the eyes of the average English gentleman or lady – you and I have both experienced that tut-tut in London where high society is reluctant to put us Irish on an equal footing with our English counterparts. Those of us in the top tier of Irish society are guilty of aiding and abetting the Crown in keeping the Irish peasant population ignorant and under the heel. This situation cannot continue forever, and we may all burn in hell for this crime against our fellow Irish and may even burn here on this island first if we do not remedy these wrongs."

"John, that is revolutionary talk for sure – you must rectify your thinking before you become master of Moore Hall. Please do not repeat those words in front of Father or Mother.

I cannot listen to any more of this – tell you what, I'll race you back to the house."

He urged his horse forward in a gallop as he finished his words, and quickly opened a big lead on John. However, John was the superior horseman and before they hit the tree-lined avenue he was ahead and stretched that lead all the way to the stables.

George and Thomas took the mail coach to Dublin a week later, the plan being for George to deliver Thomas to his college before continuing to London. John stayed home a few extra days, to comfort his mother in her loneliness and to curry favor with his father by joining him on his rounds of the estate. On one of his walks with his mother she openly confessed to him her plans for Peter.

"Your father and I have decided that Peter will be best cared for in an institution. I am unable to cope with him here and I am failing in my duties to your father and to the estate by trying to keep him here. Next week he will be moved to the Abbey in Galway where he will be housed with similar patients and receive the best medical care to keep him safe. Obviously, we will pay for his upkeep there and will visit with him on a regular basis. Please forgive me for this – but we have no choice."

"I totally understand and agree with your decision, Mother. We all have difficult decisions to make in life – I can see that he is incapable of taking care of himself and I also see the strain it has put on you and on Father. Now let's talk about more pleasant things, like spring flowers and new-born lambs."

By the time they walked back from the lake Catherine was in much better spirits.

John set off for Dublin the next day.

• • •

Extract from the Diaries of Catherine de Kilkelly, Moore Hall, County Mayo

We had a lovely family Easter together. It is probably the last one where we are all together – Peter will be moving to a care home and John and George will be wanting to travel or spend Easter with friends, or maybe with the families of ladies they may be courting (they tell me nothing). I have high hopes that John is getting his life on track in Dublin and will soon be called to the Irish Bar – and yet, I am haunted by worries brought on by his past transgressions. He and young George looked magnificent riding at speed down our avenue – tall and handsome – very eligible bachelors. I long for the day we celebrate their weddings and have grandchildren to fuss over. Maybe that will brighten life here in this dour and desolate parish.

Father Torres sent a letter in time for Easter – so nice to have Spanish to read and I shall send him a long letter in reply.

His letter makes me homesick for Spain, I can almost smell the flowers in the garden in Alicante and feel the warmth of the sunshine that is bathing the city this time of year – better than yesterday's hailstones here. My brother Michel has not written for so long; I hope my last letters did find their way to him – I shall ask Father Torres to try to contact him and I pray that he returned safely from his posting in the American colonies. I cannot bear to dwell on the wonderful spring and early summer activities that are about to take place at the Royal Court in Madrid – to think that we could be there instead of here fills my heart with longing and regret.

George seems content to be out among his tenants – 'the unwashed masses' he calls them. He seems to have aged considerably since we moved to Mayo – I remember how he looked so tanned and carefree in Spain, just a few short years ago. I think I also have aged too quickly in this place. Nobody looks good in an overcoat and muffler in the rain, and we always have coughs that do not sound good. John's behavior for several years past has been a great disappointment to his father, and his waywardness continues to weigh on him – he loves him so much.

Hoping for better times for us all before we hit the new century in a little over a year.

CHAPTER NINE

Athlone was the first stop on John's return journey to Dublin, where he inquired about Patrick Corcoran, a college friend who had recently passed the Irish Bar and was in practice there. He duly found the address, where he was met with less than a warm welcome when he asked for Patrick. After introducing himself as a friend and fellow law student he was ushered into a room where he was greeted by a Mr. Steele who identified himself as Patrick's partner in the practice. The man seemed nervous, then opened and checked the door before locking it and showing John to an empty chair.

"Forgive me for my cautious welcome but we live in dangerous times. I have heard your name mentioned by Patrick and I wanted to make sure it was indeed yourself. He is not here and frankly I have no idea of his whereabouts – I was hoping you might have some news."

"I have not seen him for a few months, and I am confused – please enlighten me, Sir."

"You have heard the news of Lord Edward Fitzgerald, have you not?"

"No."

"Then let me tell you what I know to date. Lord Edward was severely wounded four days ago while resisting arrest in Dublin. Two associates with him at the time were killed outright and Lord Edward was taken away by Dublin Castle forces. I fear that Patrick may have been with him at the time for he had journeyed to Dublin the previous day and told me that his first meeting was with Lord Edward. There are rumors that Lord Edward has died from his wounds and rumors that he has escaped – that is all I know."

John sank in his chair and put his face in his hands. "On my God, what dreadful news – I have been with my family in Mayo since before Easter and have heard nothing of this. I am on my way to Dublin to continue my law studies – do you know if it is safe for me to travel there currently?"

"From what travelers on the mail coach told my assistant this morning there is no general unrest in Dublin. However, I suggest that you proceed with the greatest caution, especially once you approach the outskirts of Dublin – you know the trickery that the Castle gets up to. Take this letterhead sheet with my address – I would be indebted to you if you can make inquiries and advise me of the actual situation there – both in respect to Patrick and to Lord Edward."

John slid the sheet into his satchel, they shook hands and he departed immediately. The longer evenings of early summer afforded him extra daylight to make good progress and he found lodgings at a coach house in Maynooth just after dark. He had planned to surprise Hanratty in Kildare and boast of his new relationship with their mutual friend Elizabeth, but he was now in no mood for frivolity and decided to omit that visit.

Next day he approached the city of Dublin with trepidation. Without incident, he rode past small groups of marching redcoats with military hardware in tow, and saw similar movements going the other way, concluding it was nothing more than normal rotation of soldiers and supplies to and from the Curragh camps which the military had in that area for many years. He did not attempt to go into the university, instead lingered nearby and waited to spot some class associates that he could approach and talk to. This plan told him all he needed to know. Sadly, Lord Edward Fitzgerald had died from his wounds, and Patrick was one of the casualties along with Joe Foster, whom he did not know. No agents from the Castle had visited either the law school classrooms or dormitories – they were not searching for him by all accounts, so he thought it safe to go to his rooms. He delivered his horse to his usual stable, went to his lodgings and slept in his own bed and resumed lectures the next day – all without incident. He dispatched off a letter to Athlone with the sad news – keeping the content very short and saying nothing that could incriminate himself or anybody else.

Over the course of the following weeks, he was able to

contact some members of the Society who were still free and going about their business. He found out that the Directory of the United Irishmen had set a date of May 23rd for a countrywide rising, but it was very unclear what exactly was to happen on that day and whether any French force was to arrive to aid the United Irishmen – and he received no orders requiring his participation. Out of an abundance of caution, John decided to continue with his studies and did reasonably well in his tests, all of which kept his mind occupied and he stayed away from the regular United Irishmen society haunts that he knew were likely to be monitored by Dublin Castle agents.

On the appointed day there were a few isolated small uprisings near Dublin that were quickly put down by government forces, nothing at all occurred in the city center area – and neither John nor any members that he personally knew took part in any rebellious activity. No French military forces or aid arrived, and County Wexford was the only place where a substantial insurrection took place – under the command of Bagenal Harvey, a Protestant barrister, and Father John Murphy, a Catholic priest. The rebels took control of most of that county including the towns of Wexford and Enniscorthy, but were unable to advance further, and once the government brought in reinforcements the rebellion was quickly put down with much loss of life on the rebel side – and all the leaders were summarily hanged. The depleted leadership of the Dublin directory took no action and John helplessly witnessed the Wexford defeat unfold. This was followed by a similar failed June rising in the Ulster County of Antrim led by Henry Joy McCracken, one of the founders of the United Irishmen movement. John was burdened with a great shame for his lack of action, even though the blame was squarely on the Directory leadership of the movement rather than him personally.

The news of a French expeditionary force landing at Killala, County Mayo on August 22nd reached John a few days later. He was both amazed and energized, as he rushed to tell his close friend and fellow United society member, William Wilson.

"Willy, the French have finally come to free Ireland. We must go immediately to Mayo and do our part to serve our country. How soon can you be ready to leave?"

"John, we both have final exams starting in ten days – I must stay and pass these exams. I understand your excitement at hearing this news, you being from Mayo and all, but please take time to digest this information and its implications. Our principal Directory leaders have all either been killed or arrested. You saw with your own eyes how the intended rising in May never happened here, nor did it happen in most of the country. The gallant men in Wexford and in Antrim never stood a chance and were wiped out on the battlefield and all their leaders executed – Harvey, McCracken and Murphy are all dead. Even Edward Crosbie, a member of parliament and a man known to my family was falsely accused of treason and hanged in Wexford – I know for a fact that he was not a member of the society. I beg you to stay, do not rush to Mayo. It is probably a very small French force – even a large force has no chance of success, now that there will not be a countrywide rising and the Crown forces have already smashed our leadership. The opportunity for a successful rebellion has eluded us, we must regroup and rebuild – this French invasion force is doomed to failure and every Irishman who joins their ranks is doomed to die with them. Please, please don't go, John."

"I cannot believe what I am hearing from you. Wolfe Tone has been in Paris arguing the case for Ireland with the Directory and has finally convinced them to send an expedition – he is probably with them now in Mayo, and you will not rise to do your part. What about the oath we took? This is Ireland's hour of need, our chance to do what we promised – we must take it, failure is not an option. I am going to do my part – Willy, you will have to live with your guilt if you turn your back on Ireland at this time."

With that, John walked out, mounted his horse and set off. Willy rushed out behind him, begging him to change his mind but got no reply. He watched him ride away till he was out of sight, hoping to catch his attention when he turned around in the saddle – John never looked around.

As he rode west in anger, John thought at first that he should make for Moore Hall and rally a force of their tenants to lead towards Killala. By the time he crossed the Shannon he had decided against that plan. His father had taken the Oath of

Allegiance some years earlier; involving the family estate in any way could harm father's standing among his fellow landlords, which in turn could bring the wrath of the government and military forces down on him. This would have to be John Moore's war on his own terms; he would go it alone and not drag his family into it – his dear mother did not need another burden of worry. He found meagre lodgings at an inn near Longford, giving his horse a deserved feeding and rest, and set off for Mayo at first light dressed in a fresh set of clothes that bore all the hallmark of an aristocrat gentleman.

As he approached Ballina, he knew something was different. He saw two coaches heading his way on the road ahead and they waved him down as he approached them. A Church of Ireland clergyman stepped from the carriage, leaving behind several women and children peering out at John.

"Good sir, I am Pastor Smith of St. Peter's Church – I must warn you that the town of Ballina has been overrun by French soldiers and local rebels. Many of our local Yeomanry and government soldiers have been killed trying to defend the town, many good citizens have been injured or killed – I am compelled to warn you not the go there. We are fleeing for our lives, and I beg you to turn around and come with us."

"Reverend, thank you for stopping and telling me this. Who is the French commander – I must go there and speak with him."

"General Humbert is his name. You are indeed a brave man Sir to attempt to engage the enemy in such a way. I will pray for your safe passage and pray that you will be able to negotiate an end to this bloodshed. We must go now in order to reach Castlebar before nightfall. To whom do I have the pleasure of speaking?"

John began to ride away and shouted back, "I am John – Apostle John, good day to you."

At the edge of the town, he rode along a dirt track that he remembered was called Rosserk Road, noticing that there were soldiers' encampments on either side. One side was the French camp, and on the other side was the Irish rebel camp – he headed into the French side. A sentry stepped before him and ordered him in French to identify himself and his business. John replied in French, announcing himself as Citizen John Moore and that he was on his way to meet with General Humbert. The sentry saluted and waved him through, telling him that the general was at the house at the end of the tree-lined avenue. He proceeded without incident to the house, a nice-looking residence that was no doubt abandoned by a Loyalist landowner, dismounted and approached the open door. Just then a French officer exited the door, a man who when he turned around was also wearing a priest's collar.

Assuming him to be the chaplain John spoke to him in French, "Pardon me, I am in search of General Humbert."

The man answered him in French, with an Irish accent, "I am Captain Henry O'Keane, a member of General Jean Joseph Humbert's staff. Who is it that I have the pleasure of talking to, Sir?"

"Citizen John Moore of Moore Hall, Ballintubber, County Mayo. I am an acquaintance of Theobald Wolfe Tone and a proud member of the United Irishmen. I have come to offer my services to the General in this great mission."

"You are welcome indeed, Citizen Moore. You command excellent French – might I ask where you were taught?"

"I attended College des Grands Anglaise, in Douai, Flanders – and later attended Liege and the University of Paris. What is your own background if I may ask?"

"I was born here locally in Killala and was ordained a priest here in the diocese. Then I went to France to study at the Irish College of Nantes. At the outbreak of the Revolution, I was a curate in that area, I took the constitutional oath and joined the French army. I am a Captain in the 65th Regiment and I came with the expedition to Ireland to serve as the local liaison officer because I also speak Irish. Follow me, I will introduce you to the General."

John followed him back into the house and to a room where several French officers stood around a table, upon which there was a map of Ireland and one of County Mayo. In the center of the group stood a large swarthy man, aged about mid-thirties John guessed, in a uniform that was pulled tight across his expansive stomach. The captain asked permission to intervene and spoke in French directly to the man at the center of the group.

"General Humbert, we have an honored visitor, an emissary from the Society of United Irishmen and an acquaintance of Citizen Wolfe Tone – I have the pleasure of introducing you to Citizen John Moore of Moore Hall, Ballintubber County Mayo, and a fluent French speaker."

General Humbert began speaking to John in French even before he turned away from the maps.

"We have been looking forward to welcoming our United Irishmen friends from the Irish aristocracy to lead their countrymen in this expedition. You are the first to come forward and we make you most welcome. I see you have already met Captain O'Keane – these gentlemen at my side are General Sarrazin, General Fontaine and Major Azemar."

John burst out, "Vive la Republique."

"Vive la Republique," they all responded and raised their wine glasses in a salute. Humbert saw that John did not have a glass, apologized and gestured that someone find wine for their visitor. Once John was in possession of a glass of wine Humbert led them in a fresh salute to the Republique, then shook John's hand warmly.

"Citizen John, I assume you have brought a force of Irish fighters with you; we need to grow our army in preparation for the upcoming battles."

John saw that all the French officers were waiting for his reply, and he quickly improvised, "I expect that your plan is to attack Castlebar and in anticipation of that I have a promise of three hundred armed men to join us there for that battle."

They all cheered his reply, and Humbert said, "You are very astute. We are indeed reviewing our plans before advancing towards Castlebar, the leading town of this county, right? Come look at the map with us – your local knowledge will be a big help in our preparations."

On the map of County Mayo, the main road between Ballina and Castlebar was highlighted.

"Irish roads are very rough, based on what we have experienced so far. What is the condition of this road to Castlebar and where do you think the English forces will assemble to engage us in battle?"

"I apologize for our roads, Monsieur General – this one is reasonably good by Mayo standards. Just to the north of the town and alongside the road there is an elevated area called Sion Hill which I would expect the English to have selected for the encounter. There are some small lakes off to both sides which will prevent either force from spreading very wide. I have come directly here from Dublin and did not travel near Castlebar, so I do not have first-hand knowledge of the situation today. Even so, I saw some mobilization activity in Mayo and spoke to fellow travelers who told me about British troop and Yeomen militia movements. It is a garrisoned town and they have been bringing in troops from the wider region for the past few days and continue to do so. I would advise that you advance immediately, to surprise them and disrupt their preparations – and attack them before their top generals have time to arrive from other parts of Ireland."

Humbert stroked his chin and mumbled a few words to Sarrazin that John didn't catch. The other officers nodded in agreement and Humbert turned to John.

"We hear what you say and agree with you in principle. However, we are still arming and training the Irish recruits and resting our men – we need several more days before we are ready. Do you think they will try to advance further from Castlebar – to meet us on the road somewhere?"

"No, I do not – they want their top commanders to arrive before doing anything much. Lord Cornwallis is the Viceroy of Ireland and Commander in chief of British forces in Ireland, but it will take him quite some time to journey from Dublin – he is old and fat and suffers from severe gout. General Lake and General Trench are the more likely field generals that will be arriving in Castlebar first – it would be great to get to Castlebar ahead of them."

"Monsieur John, I like your fire and energy and I would love to move immediately – however, that is not possible. We have much preparation to do before we march but I promise you we will speed up as much as possible and we will be ready to set out the day after tomorrow."

His officers were taken aback by this haste and raised their hands to the sky while shaking their heads and protesting to Humbert. His tone became very stern, and he ordered them to go and redouble their efforts to get ready for a march on Castlebar. They filed out and gave John frosty looks as they left – they seemed to blame him for this change of plan. Once they left, Humbert gestured him to a chair, poured them both a refill of wine and sat down opposite him.

"You must have lived in France for some years to speak the language so well. Why did you come back to Ireland?"

"Family reasons. My father emigrated from Ireland to Spain as a very young man – because of religious persecution – we are Catholics and Britain has decided we are to be treated as second class citizens to the Protestants that they want to be in the ascendency. He became a wine merchant for many years in Alicante, where he also ran a fleet of cargo ships. I was born in Spain, but my father wanted myself and my younger brothers educated in France – which is how I learned to speak French. When father's older brother in Ireland died suddenly, he inherited the Moore estate in Mayo and returned here with his family, me included. He had to take an Oath of Allegiance to the English King to be able to own land in Ireland – he lives at the family estate in Ballintubber, twenty miles south of Castlebar, with my mother and younger brothers. I am reading law in Dublin and hope to become a barrister by the new year."

"I have had no such education and became a soldier early in life. The revolution propelled my career in The Vendee, and I was asked by the Directory to lead one of the expeditions to help your rebellion in Ireland – and so here I am. C'est la vie."

"What other expeditions are coming and when?"

"My information is that a larger force under General Hardy is on the water and due here very soon. General Kilmaine is coming with an even larger force. We sailed separately to evade the British fleet. Are you going to ride with us to Castlebar?"

"Of course. General, I confess that have no military training – my experience with guns has been totally derived from hunting. My forte is organizing and planning and rallying support for our cause."

"You will ride with me as my liaison officer in place of Captain O'Keane, who will be staying behind in Ballina to command our joint force of French and Irish defenders here, to hold the town against any attempt by the enemy to take it back. Come, ride with me now as I make a final inspection of our encampment before retiring for the night."

The sentries stood to attention as the General and John exited the house. Humbert called for his horse and for two mounted guards to accompany him, while John fetched his own horse. In minutes they were entering the Irish camp on the other side of the road. Unlike the French camp where soldiers were resting, this side was a hive of activity. Humbert told John they had taken possession of this vacant estate – he and his officers were in the farmhouse and outbuildings across the road, while the Irish had occupied these orchards and fields. John saw several fires where entire cows were being roasted and men were milling about like a market fair day at night, gnawing on big hunks of roasted beef. Everybody noticed as Humbert's party approached and all became quieter. Some Irish commanding officers came forward and John was introduced to them – Colonel Bartholomew Teeling, Mathew Tone, Austin O'Malley, James O'Dowd and their overall commander, General George Blake. Blake said he knew John's father, George Moore, and enquired of his health. After some banter Humbert gestured to Blake to follow them away a distance from the crowd. He then gave him a series of orders – there was to be no more looting, men were to finish their meals within half an hour and the entire camp was then to bed down for the night.

"We have much to do tomorrow to prepare for our march on Castlebar. Men need to get some sleep if they are to be fit and ready to march and to fight – this is not a party."

"Yes General, I will attend to it immediately."

With that, Humbert wheeled his horse around and they rode back to the house. He then took his leave and retired to an upstairs room. John was offered some food, a place to sleep and he was allowed to have his horse taken care of by the stableboys caring for the French officer's horses.

CHAPTER TEN

Meanwhile, in Ballintubber, a friendly tenant came to Moore Hall steps with his brother, who had been visiting a relative in Killala and saw the French ships and soldiers with his own eyes. George quizzed the man about the number of French soldiers, what Irish squireens (local Irish small landowners) and peasant rebels had joined them, and on the events that happened in Killala – all spoken in Irish.

"Sir, there must have been thousands of them French soldiers coming ashore at Kilcummin strand, and they unloaded crates of guns to hand out to all the Irish who would join them. Then they marched towards Killala where there was thousands of our fellas coming in from the surrounding hills, armed with homemade pikes and ready to join the French – I watched it all from a hill, I never saw anything like it, Sir. I was told there were some Irish generals came on the ships with the French – all dressed in the same French uniforms."

"Go on."

"Well, Micheal told me they were going to take over the whole place, and I had best leave before all the trouble started and that's what I did Sir. I hitched up my donkey and cart and headed home right then and there, so I did; and I prayed all the way home. What is going to happen now, what is to become of us all, Sir?"

"Thank you for your information. Go on home now and tell all your neighbors to continue their lives just as they did before – that is the way to stay safe. French soldiers have no reason to bother us – it's the garrisons at Ballina and Castlebar they will be after, or maybe Sligo. I will find out more and will pass the word to you all as I make my rounds of the estate."

As soon as the tenants left, Catherine came to see George and he told her what he knew to date.

She was shaking with worry – "Thank God that John and George and Thomas are safely away from here, and that Peter is already settled at the Abbey in Galway. What are you going to do?"

"In the morning I will ride over to the Russell's to inquire what they know – their son is one of the leaders of the local militia. Depending on what I find out there, I may ride on to Ballintubber. It's important for you to keep the household calm."

Privately George was excited in some strange way by the developments and felt his nationalist Irish blood rush through his veins. He was aware of the recent rising in Wexford and of the rumors that the French were going to send expeditions to help the Irish mount a rebellion, but he never expected it to happen, especially in these rural backwaters of Mayo.

The morning brought a thick mist, not the sort of day to ride many miles. He had his coach made ready and set off – he would remain dry while his driver felt the sting of the rain on his face. They pulled up in front of Russell Hall an hour later. William Russell was a dour sort of old fellow, a Protestant landowner who gave George the respect due to a fellow landowner, but who may have had different private feelings about his Catholic neighbor – George never felt fully at ease in this man's company.

"Welcome to you George Moore, what brings you out on such a dreary morning. Mary, come take his wet coat and get it drying in the kitchen. Come join me by the fire while you and I talk."

"Thank you, I'm sorry to barge in unannounced but –"

"Moore, I know why you are here. It's this dreadful business with the French invading our peaceful County Mayo shores – blast them."

"I just heard the news from a traveler – thought you might be able to tell me more details, no doubt Joseph and the militia will have been mobilized."

"He left out of here in the early hours with twenty men while it was still dark, bound for Castlebar. Information is very sketchy, suffice to say that we have a rebellion on our hands and there will be a major battle fought in the Castlebar area in the coming days. Generals Lake, Trench and Hutchinson are gathering their forces as we speak and making their way to Castlebar – all are experienced leaders and they will snuff this out quickly, and the perpetrators will get their just rewards. I am going to prevent any of my tenants from joining up with the invaders and forming a rebel army to support them – under fear of immediate eviction. It is imperative that you do the same, especially with you being – how should I say it – that you dig with the other foot as it were."

"Me being a Catholic landlord, a papist – is what you are trying not the say."

"Yes – I, I didn't want to offend you by saying it. These peasants will take more notice of you than they will take of me."

"Thank you for your time, Sir – I should be off now."

"Will you not stay for tea while your coat is drying?"

"No thank you, I have much to do – I must digest your words of wisdom and figure out how a papist should treat his papist tenants ahead of this impending war. Good day to you Sir. I will see myself out."

George went to the kitchen to retrieve his coat and left Russell open-mouthed at his fireplace.

• • •

John was up early the next morning, after a restless night's sleep – partly caused by the uncomfortable cot he slept in and partly because he had so much on his mind. He went to the stables to check on his horse and thank the attendants. He chatted freely with them, noting their indifference to their Irish surroundings while seeing their unwavering loyalty to their commander. Arriving back at the house he saw General Humbert seated alone at the table eating breakfast and was about to divert away when Humbert called out to him, inviting him to join him. Once seated there was no time lost on small talk.

"Citizen John, I have a problem with the road to Castlebar that has bothered me all night."

"What is the nature of your problem General?"

"That the British forces possess the advantage of knowing our approach route and will have strong defensive positions prepared."

"The very reason why I suggested last night that we march there at the soonest possible moment, to catch them by surprise."

"We are speeding up our departure, but I would like to surprise them in another way also."

"How is that General?"

"By arriving by a different route. I have been looking over the map and I see the main route runs to the east of this lake called Conn. What about the western side of the lake? From my experience the land on the western side should also be passable."

"As far as I know, the land along the western shore of Lough Conn is composed of mountains and rough moorland – I am not aware of it having any roads."

"We have been joined by men from all around this area, and surely some of them are from this land west of the lake. I want you to talk to the Irish commanders, find some men from that area and bring them here to me – after you eat some breakfast, Mon Ami."

John asked Captain O'Keane to help him find a leader from Nephin area called O'Hara, who had come with a dozen men. He and O'Keane spoke quietly to O'Hara in Irish and then led him and five of his men across the road to where Humbert was still poring over his maps. He asked them how they got here to Ballina, and they described the goat paths they used through the mountains. Then he asked if these paths extended south along the lake and whether they would be able to reach Castlebar via these paths. Their answer was yes, but it was a much more treacherous route than the main road. Humbert thanked them, swore then to silence and sent them back to their camp – then addressed John and O'Keane.

"Not a word about this to anyone. I will be giving orders to move out this evening and we will proceed on the main route to the point that these men told us about. Then we will divert onto the goat path route and make our way under cover of darkness to Castlebar."

O'Keane protested, "General, that will be a very difficult route Sir, and we will not be able to take artillery along that route."

"We will try, and I think we will succeed. This route will bring us into Castlebar along the flank of the strong British defense positions and give us a much-needed advantage of surprise. I will talk to my French commanders and will tell General Blake to get his Irish soldiers ready to depart by six in the evening. Have O'Hara and his same five rebels here at six to march beside my guard detail. At the appropriate time we will have them lead us along our new route to Castlebar. Go to it Captain."

After Captain O'Keane took his leave, General Humbert and John were alone in front of the table with the maps spread out. The General walked to a credenza and returned with a sword attached to an elaborate belt, plus two pistols and a supply of ammunition.

He presented the sword to John – "I bestow on Citizen John Moore the title of Special Delegate, from the Society of United Irishmen to the Army of the Republique of France. This officer's sword and brace of pistols have been in my family for several years. I want you to wear them proudly tomorrow as we march on the British forces in Castlebar, and we will defeat them. Vive la Republique de Connaught."

"Vive la Republique de Connaught," John replied, "I am honored beyond belief, General Humbert."

Humbert took out two wine glasses and filled each with red wine from a freshly opened bottle.

"To victory and to Ireland. I could not imagine going to war without a supply of good French wine – I wish that your father, 'The Wine Merchant of Alicante' was here with us to celebrate. He would be justly proud of you John, I am sure."

"Eh, yes, it would be quite something if he was here with us now. General, tell me what to expect tomorrow – this is my first battle in my first war."

"I have been in many campaigns. A battle is the ultimate rush of blood to the head – the bedding of a hot-blooded woman is a distant second, in my estimation. There are similarities in the execution of both – every detail must be planned, every contingency prepared for, never bow to the odds against success, show total determination to win at all costs, complete submission of the adversary is the aim – and keeping one's head in the climax of victory."

"Wow. I never thought of war like that, and I do like the idea of wine before battle. What worries me most is getting this army over the pathways that run through the bogs between here and Castlebar."

"Before I became a soldier, I was a trader of goat skins and rabbit skins. I spent years walking such pathways as we will travel tonight. The only thing that can stop us is ourselves. Yes, it will be a difficult journey, but it is better to sneak up on the lion's den from behind than to walk into the lion's jaws."

They savored their wine for several long minutes, each deep in their own thoughts, without any more words being spoken. After his last sip, Humbert rose from his chair.

"I must go to speak with my French officers before they take rest ahead of our departure. You should visit with your General Blake and ask him to encourage his men to get at least a few hours of rest – we gather at five o'clock and leave at six."

John found the Irish camp in high spirits, literally – much whiskey had been appropriated from taverns in the town. Its consumption had led to a party-like atmosphere in the camp, with much noise and even music being played on crude uilleann pipes and wooden flutes. Blake said he could do little to stop this type of Irish celebration and resorted to telling his commanders that they would all muster at five o'clock, drunk or sober. John then returned via the stables and sat on his bed for the afternoon, trying to calm himself, to little avail. Within twenty-four hours he would experience the thrill of battle for the first, and maybe the last time. Humbert had about 700 French infantry, plus 100 cavalrymen, aided by over 600 Irish rebel fighters armed by the French, and upwards of another 1,000 rebel volunteers – armed with pikes, old swords, pitchforks and knives – and whiskey. The enemy probably would have a force of over 10,000 waiting for them in Castlebar, a substantial number of them being experienced British infantry, cavalry and artillery, plus a large group of Irish Yeomanry with a mixed bag of weapons and experience. On paper Humbert's army didn't stand a chance but they were the ones attacking and Humbert was not fazed by the numbers on the other side or by their decorated commanders. There was no turning back now, John and everyone in Humberts army were all-in and had to play the cards they had been dealt.

At five o'clock John was startled by the sound of a bugle – he had indeed dozed off at some stage. Now, he rushed to gather up his belongings, pull on his boots, and strap on his new sword and pistols. He saw the stable attendants bring out General Humbert's horse, followed by his own stallion. The French cavalry and infantry were being assembled, as were the teams pulling artillery guns and supply wagons. There was much commotion in the Irish camp but little sign of any orderly assembly. The buglers blasted another volley and finally the Irish began to gather. O'Hara and his band of frieze-clad rebels looked totally out of place among the French officers. John didn't know where to position himself until Humbert called him up to ride beside the General, much to the consternation of the top French commanders. Humbert sternly told them of John's newly appointed position – they saluted and fell into line with their troops. The Irish commanders were bemused by John's appointment, especially as they had been there before him, from the very beginning. Captain O'Keane looked demoralized at being left behind to defend Ballina but accepted his orders and used his men to get the last of the stragglers up and moving. Miraculously, the army started to move out at six – despite signs of many drunken Irish being pushed and shoved into marching groups.

They marched south on the main route towards Foxford for a few miles, then the column turned westward towards Crossmolina. They reached the town just as the daylight began to fade, and then the column turned southwards over the rough mountain and bog track – watched only by curious locals standing around their cabin doors, and from above by flocks of birds heading to roost in scarce stands of trees in this barren wasteland. The Irish contingent was befuddled by this turn and their commanders rode forward and protested in loud and disbelieving Irish to Humbert's staff. He had expected this protest and was well prepared to quell their protests immediately.

His French was translated into Irish by Teeling – "tell them the British generals are thinking just like them, and they have their artillery and troops ready to face an enemy advancing south along the Foxford road. Instead of being cannon fodder for the British forces we are going to disappoint them and deceive them. After a night march along the western shore of Lough Conn guided by O'Hara's local fighters, we will fall upon the lightly defended British flank. I am here to lead you to victory in this battle and we will win it if you follow my plans to the letter. Vive la Republique de Connaught."

John had a bird's eye view of these stirring words, which were translated and passed down through the ranks of the grumbling Irish rebels. The rebels saw that the French soldiers had their heads down and trusted their general's leadership. A ripple of loud cheers rang out through the mass of bodies struggling along the bog road, and even the half sober wretches helping with the artillery redoubled their efforts to drag the guns through the bog.

The forced march continued in the darkness, mercifully

lit by a decent moon and the clear sky meant there was no rain to worsen their struggle. Men fell into bog holes and were dragged out by comrades, when artillery wheels buckled, they were either left behind, or quickly pulled apart and the separate pieces strapped onto the donkeys and even carried in turns by these hardy men. The Irish commanders rode up and down the line exhorting their men to keep up the pace. John was amazed how relaxed Humbert was – he chatted with Sarrizen and Fontaine, often involving John in the conversations, made several jokes and laughed out loud. At midnight there was confusion over which direction to take at a fork in the pathway. Humbert stopped the column and called for a rest while scouts moved ahead to check both paths, to resolve the situation. O'Hara found a man amongst his group who lived nearby and after forty-five minutes the column resumed its trek. Even this delay didn't faze Humbert – he dismounted and ate some food which he washed down with his customary wine, in a glass of course. John had no stomach for food or wine and had to force himself to drink some water.

As the first wisps of light came their way from the east there was momentary panic when some riders were spotted in the distance. The riders made no effort to come closer and Humbert dismissed it as part of the usual pre-battle preparations – scouts were spying on them.

He shouted to his commanders and to the Irish commanders – "The enemy scouts have become aware of our change of plan. We must press on with greater haste now, before they can re-arrange their battle formations."

Next, he sent out a company of cavalry under the command of Captain Jobert to repulse any efforts by the British to outflank the column. Some minor contact occurred between the opposing cavalry just after dawn before the British retreated. The column safely descended the last steep section of the trail and entered flat countryside that John estimated put them within five miles of Castlebar – information he conveyed to General Humbert, as he huddled with his French commanders to review their plans. John was able to listen in on their conversations – animated now but lacking any sign of panic, even as they could see the telltale flurry of redcoat activity in the distant mists of early morning. Humbert was figuring what hurried changes were possible on the British side – consulting with Sarrizen and Fontaine, with Teeling observing for the Irish side.

John reminded the General of the two lakes that he knew were on the left and right of the battlefield that was now shaping up in front of them.

"Merci", he snapped and after some final words with his commanders – Sarrazin, Fontaine and Azemar moved away to put their new strategy into action. He called out to John – "Citizen John, stay close to me and my guards as the battle progresses. Vive la Republique."

Humbert halted the column, and then he moved a short distance to one side, to a patch of high ground that allowed him a commanding view of the terrain ahead. Sarrazin led a large group of French infantry soldiers straight down the main road towards the enemy, immediately coming under artillery fire and forcing them to take cover behind a ditch. Two French artillery guns opened up with supporting fire. Another French contingent moved out to create a right-side line while a large body of Irish rebels armed with muskets and pikes were urged forward by a French commander named Dufont, and the Irish General Blake. They came under musket fire and suffered many casualties which halted their advance, as well as the advance of the French group on the right, while other Irish formations used the diversion to move forward on the British left flank – using field hedges for cover. Humbert contemplated the scene for several minutes, then signaled for all three groups to charge forward simultaneously.

John saw Sarrazin lead his grenadiers forward, while Colonel Teeling's men rushed in from the left and Dufont's group went forward and in from the right. Humbert was using a special eye glass to zero in on specific parts of the battlefield below them. The entire area was dissolved in large pockets of smoke from artillery and musket fire, and John struggled to see much clear detail of the French Irish assault taking place in front of him. The noise of battle was terrifying – musket fire and screams filled the air. He could see that the Irish front line was taking heavy losses, but it did not stop this mass of shrieking men from charging forward towards the British infantry line that was protecting their artillery – wild men rushed onward in a frenzied rage, slashing and hooking at the enemy with their pikes and swords. The British line broke and their artillery was overrun, then the second and third lines broke and fled from this onslaught, stumbling into their own cavalry and leaving them no room to maneuver. Humbert saw this and launched his cavalry in quick pursuit resulting in a complete scattering of thousands of British forces. The vaunted British cavalry left the field and galloped away south towards Tuam.

The narrow streets of Castlebar were thronged with British infantry, artillery and support wagons, all in headlong panic retreat and pursued by the French and Irish forces. A small force of British infantry regrouped around the bridge in the center of the town – were joined by one or two artillery guns and mounted an attempt to halt the French Irish pursuit. French infantry commandeered some nearby houses and pinned down the gunners on the bridge. The French cavalry and General Fontaine's Chasseurs then came in support and quickly killed off the remaining gunners to complete the rout.

Victory belonged to General Humbert and his disciplined French forces, supported by a raggle-taggle of Irish rebels. John Moore saw this victory unfold before his very eyes, sitting astride his horse beside General Humbert and witnessing him directing the battle with great skill. The only time John raised his sword was to clash it with General Humbert's sword when he raised his own in salute to his victorious army.

Humbert turned to him as the battle remnants disappeared

into the town – "Citizen John, Vive la Republique de Connaught. We have scored a wonderful victory today for France, for Ireland and especially for Connaught."

He then sent a messenger to his commanders, congratulating them on their victory and asked for updates on securing the town prior to his entry. He asked John to ride ahead and scout a suitable residence for use as his headquarters, while he remained behind with his entourage. As he rode away John saw the general dismount and his aides began to set up a temporary tent for him to use. By the time John reached the town it was obvious that Humberts army had defeated a British force that far outnumbered them. There were dead redcoats strewn all over the place and muskets that had been dropped by the retreating British littered the streets. The Irish in the town were in jubilant mood and there was loud shouting and cheering coming from all directions. He saw Colonel Teeling talking with Sarrazin, and approached them, shouting his congratulations in French and English.

"Vive la Republique de Connaught. I have been sent forward by General Humbert to find suitable headquarters for him – perhaps the defeated British have left us a nice place for our victorious general."

"I know just the place," Teeling said – "General Hutchinson had commandeered a large house at the edge of the town for himself and General Lake. They have run away to Tuam now and I'm sure they will have no objection to passing the keys to General Humbert. Come, let us ride over there to make sure it is safe, and I'll show you the place."

At the house there were several French infantrymen surveying the grounds, who confirmed that it was clear of any enemy soldiers, and they even tried to make John and Teeling believe that they were already scouting it for their General. It was a fine two-story house with a walled garden around it and stables at the rear. A party of Irish rebels with looting intentions then showed up and were ordered away by Teeling. He told the French soldiers to secure the house and grounds and wait for the arrival of their General. John thanked Teeling and set off back to report to Humbert. On the way he came across a group of Irish rebels who were celebrating the victory, recognizing commanders O'Daly and O'Dowd from meeting them in Ballina. He stopped briefly to speak with them. O'Daly was telling the others that it was General Lake himself and the entire army of Connaught that they defeated.

"We bet Lake, and Hutchinson, and their Connaught Army – they all hightailed it to Tuam at such speed that they would have won the Castlebar races," referring to the annual horse racing event that occurred in Castlebar. All this fighting and shouting has given me a ferocious thirst, lads – let's find a tavern and wet our whistles, what do ye all say to that idea, me boys."

"Hip Hurrah for Humbert and our croppies," they all shouted.

John declined their invitation to join them and rode back to the General's tent.

"Sir, with the help of Colonel Teeling I have found a nice big house that the departing Generals Lake and Hutchinson vacated, and they had no objection to you taking it over for your headquarters – isn't that very kind of them."

Humbert chuckled at John's irreverence and told his stewards to pack up in readiness to enter the town. Just then General Fontaine rode up with a dozen of his cavalry.

"General, we have secured the town. What is left of the British that we have not killed or captured have run away towards Galway, including their commanding generals. I have a guard of grenadiers waiting in town to escort you on for your triumphant entrance and victory parade through the Main Street."

Humbert congratulated his general on their victory and praised the bravery of the French and Irish soldiers in the face of overwhelming odds. Twenty minutes later the cavalry led Humbert's entourage towards the town, with John riding just behind him. He had described the house and its location to the head steward, and knew they would pass by the place on their way in. As they approached the house John pointed it out to Humbert, who seemed very pleased with it. John led the steward and his wagons to the gate and spoke briefly with the French guards after they saluted and applauded their general, as he passed in front of them. John caught up with the general's group when they stopped to reassemble with the waiting grenadiers, with Sarrazin at their head for the victory parade. Next was the cavalry led by Fontaine, with General Humbert riding on his own in the center of the street, the obvious leader in full visibility to the throngs of soldiers and onlookers who lined the sides. John got back to his earlier position behind Humbert, where he was joined by Teeling and Blake, both on horseback. This is how they paraded through Main Street, then onto Spencer Street and Castle Street, in a loop that brought them back to Main Street.

It was an amazing sight, this foreign army being given a hero's welcome by the Irish rebels and the townspeople – packed into the alleyways, perched on the walls of the river bridge and with heads sticking out all the open doorways and windows. Humbert sat very erect in his saddle, a large commanding figure, not showing any outward emotion but John knew how much he savored it on the inside. Teeling and Blake waved their arms and John followed their lead, even removed his hat to wave and acknowledge the cheering crowds. The entire parade lasted about an hour from the time they passed the general's house to the time they returned there.

Humbert dismounted in front of the house and climbed the three steps to the open front door, where he turned, acknowledged his troops, motioned to his French generals to enter, then gestured to John and Teeling and Blake to also enter. By the time John dismounted and entered he found a much-relaxed Humbert ready to enjoy a final 'Vive la Republique' and toast his victory with his beloved red wine.

There were glasses ready for them all and John managed to get a few moments of quiet time to formally welcome General Humbert to Castlebar.

CHAPTER ELEVEN

General Humbert spent less than an hour at the celebration before making a brief announcement and retiring to his quarters for the night.

He told them that he had already sent one of his aides to Westport who was disguised as a sailor and would carry a dispatch to Paris to inform the Directory of their great victory. This news would speed up the arrival of additional French troops to reinforce their ranks and continue their mission to establish a "Republique d'Irlande."

John was not a man for hard liquor, and after a few glasses of wine he selected a bedroom in the house and left the party to the remaining crowd that were moving outside to a blazing bonfire in the courtyard. Once he sat down on the bed, he immediately realized how exhausting it was to partake in a battle. He was still wondering how soon the news of their victory at Castlebar and his participation in it would reach Moore Hall, when he fell asleep. It was not a restful sleep – his dreams had him fighting on the front lines alongside Lord Edward, Wolfe Tone and his own dear father. Sometime in the early morning he awoke in a cold sweat, realized where he was and peered out the window. There were several sleeping bodies near the embers of the bonfire, and it was eerily quiet – he went back to bed.

There was no sign of General Humbert when John ate breakfast in the morning. He decided to ride around the town to assess the situation. The dead redcoats lay where they had fallen, with grossly disfigured faces and congealed blood staining their uniforms. Some French soldiers were gathering up the fallen muskets and other weapons, while another group alongside some locals were beginning to collect the dead by tossing them into open carts pulled by donkeys. Limp bodies of many Irish rebels were also to be seen and John worried about their own losses. When one of those bodies stirred and rolled over – he realized with relief that most of the Irish bodies were casualties of whiskey rather than casualties of battle. Townspeople were going about their usual tasks – carts moving produce to market and small groups of sheep and cattle being herded towards a slaughterhouse. Smoke rose from most chimneys and the smell of bacon being cooked hung in the air. He almost ran down a young man who rushed out of a door carrying loaves of fresh bread. The man apologized and then recognized who was on the horse and insisted that John accept a large bag of loaves in gratitude.

"Thank you for the bread, I will share it with our great General and his officers, what is your name?"

"Sir, I am James Murphy, my father Brian Murphy owns Murphy's Bakery."

"Thank you both for the bread, it smells delicious."

John had given no thought as to what he should do next, now that Castlebar and most of Mayo was in the hands of the French Irish victors. Should he ride home to Ballintubber and tell his parents of the great victory? They were of the belief that he was safely in Dublin studying for the Bar, and he would have great difficulty convincing his father of the wisdom of his rushed trip to Mayo to participate in the battle of Castlebar with General Humbert. He was in so deep now that he had little choice other than see what Humbert had in store for the victorious army and for John Moore – 'Special Delegate of the Society of United Irishmen to the Army of the Republique of France.'

The General was up and busy with paperwork when John returned with his bread.

"Citizen John, I see you have been out on an early reconnoiter, and you have come with fresh bread. We French love bread, and I am going to sample it right away. What did you find out on your early morning rounds?"

"General, we beat the British bad and the evidence is everywhere. There are lots of dead redcoats, and the rest who ran away left everything in their panic. There are muskets and other weapons scattered everywhere and your French soldiers are gathering up those for distribution to our new recruits. The British generals retreated so fast that their luggage is still here – General Lake's luggage is here in Castlebar, but he probably didn't stop running until he got to Tuam or maybe Athlone."

Humbert found that amusing, then his tone changed. "I am preparing the details of a decree that I want to have read out tomorrow when we have a victory ceremony in front of the courthouse. I could use the help of an educated man like yourself in this endeavor."

"I am happy to be of assistance."

For the next few hours, the two men worked on the decree: Humbert dictating in French while consulting with John on much of the details. John wrote down the details in French, helping to perfect the language needed to convey what the General wished to say. Afterwards, while John was translating the decree into English and Irish, Humbert instructed his aides to alert his French commanders to prepare for the ceremony. A band was needed, the main French and Irish commanders were to be present, the flags of France and of the United Irishmen were to be raised, and a tree of freedom was to be planted. John later sent word asking the Irish commanders, asking them to be present and to pass the word to the entire rebel forces and to the townspeople of Castlebar.

At precisely three o'clock the following afternoon a troop of French guards escorted General Humbert to a stage that had been erected in front of the steps of the courthouse, where everyone had assembled. The band played suitable music, General Humbert acknowledged the crowd, the two flags were raised and an aide to Humbert read the seven-point proclamation in French, one item at a time, allowing Colonel Teeling to follow with the English version, and Captain O'Keane who had come over from Ballina for the event, to read the Irish version.

Decree – August 31st, 1798 – Republic of Ireland, Province of Connaught

Army of Ireland – Castlebar

Headquartered at Castlebar, County Mayo – 14th Fructidor, year six of the French Republic.

General Jean Joseph Humbert, Commander-in-Chief of the Army of Ireland, desirous of organizing with the least delay, an administrative power for the Province of Connaught, decrees as follows:

1. The Government of the Province of Connaught shall reside at Castlebar till further notice.
2. The Government Council shall be composed of twelve members who shall be named by the Commander-in-Chief of the Army.
3. Citizen John Moore is named President of the Government of the Province of Connaught and is

entrusted with the nomination of the members of the Government Council.
4. The Government shall occupy itself immediately with organizing the military power of the Province of Connaught and with providing subsistence to the French and Irish armies.
5. There shall be created eight regiments of infantry with each containing twelve hundred men, and four regiments of cavalry with each containing six hundred men.
6. All those who have received clothing and arms must join the army within four and twenty hours.
7. Every male between the ages of sixteen and forty must betake himself immediately to the French camp, to march in-masse against the common enemy, the tyrant of Anglicized Ireland, whose destruction alone can establish the independence and happiness of Ireland

— General Jean Joseph Humbert,
Commander-in-Chief.

A rousing cheer went up from the crowd when the last of the decrees was read out. John had prior knowledge of his appointment to be President, because he was with Humbert when the decrees were composed. There were many in leadership positions in the Irish forces who were shocked and dismayed by John's appointment – but after a murmur of discontent they accepted it because they were not about to disagree with General Humbert. John had modestly asked Humbert at the time if he was sure of his choice – he said he was sure, and John thanked him. It was strange to hear it read out in public, and the sound of it made the hair on his neck stand up. While many of the French and Irish commanders looked at John with surprise, the vast majority of the Irish rebels and locals present cheered the announcement. John was almost overcome with emotion and deep pride, as he acknowledged the cheers of the people. At the time of the decree announcement, only a few of the twelve local gentlemen that were needed to serve on the Government Council had been selected.

That evening Humbert demanded that John enact a levy for an immediate contribution of one thousand guineas to be raised from the inhabitants of Castlebar. Assignats were issued and signed by John, whereby goods were requisitioned for use by the army, with payment promised upon the establishment of a Republic of Ireland and guaranteed by the Republique de France.

• • •

George Moore was in a foul mood when he returned from his visit with Russell – a man whom he neither liked nor trusted. The information to date was scarce and was a few days old – a French expeditionary force had landed at Killala, had quickly taken the town and followed that by overpowering the small garrison at Ballina. Castlebar, as the seat of power in Mayo was the obvious next target for their army which was swelling with thousands of

Irish rebels joining their ranks every day. The Castlebar garrison was being strengthened by British soldiers and militia being pulled in from Sligo and other surrounding areas. The word was that General Lake was in route to the town to take command of a substantial British army that would stop the invasion in its tracks. George told Catherine the bare outline of the story – he didn't want to scare her unnecessarily and he fully expected that it would all end very quickly. He knew that some of his tenants would be inclined to join the rebels and he spent every waking hour exhorting them to stay on the estate and continue with the harvest – they would be safe here, the rebellion would be put down quickly and anyone who helped the rebels would be punished severely by the British forces. The gates of the estate were locked, and everyone inside waited for this all to pass.

Scarcely a day later came the shocking news that a large British army under General Lake had been routed by the French and Irish forces at Castlebar. The remnants of the retreating British and loyalist militias passed by the local roads on their way south to Tuam – luckily, they were in such haste that they caused no damage to any buildings or crops on the estate, and the French stopped chasing them a few miles south of Castlebar and turned back to the town. Once the news of the French victory spread, dozens of his tenants did leave the estate to join the victorious French Irish forces, in the belief that the French were going to liberate the entire country.

Pat Murphy, one of his tenants who came back to Moore Hall, began to spread the news that the French had declared the Republic of Connaught, and had appointed its new President to be none other than John Moore of Ballintubber. George rushed to interview the man as soon as he heard this.

"You are safe here Pat, and nobody will be told you ever left. Now, you must tell me in detail what you have heard and seen – take your time."

"Sir, I was with the group what left here and we was in town to join up with the army. A fella in a French uniform came and spoke to us – he was Irish, and he was speaking Irish just like us. They were glad to have us, and we would be given muskets and pikes once we was assembled into a regiment. Somebody asked this man if the English were all gone. Yes, he said all of them that were not killed or taken prisoner had run away to Tuam. We were now all part of the Republic of Connaught, and Castlebar was where the new government was to be – John Moore was the new President and was the leader of a council of twelve that would run the government. That's what he said, on me oath, I heard it with me own ears."

"Good man Pat. Did you see John Moore or General Humbert – tell me what you yourself saw."

"The town was quiet when we got there but we could see that there had been a battle – with all the stuff that was laying around. There was men digging graves, one area for the Irish and French that was killed, and a bigger area for the dead redcoats. From what we heard there was hundreds of redcoats killed and a lot less of the French or Irish. Everyone was celebrating the victory and there was a lot of drink being taken. I didn't see John or any of the leaders – we was told they were using a big house on Foxford Road as their headquarters. Once I heard that it was John Moore of Ballintubber that was President, I decided to come back and tell you, Sir."

"You did the right thing. Did you hear anything about what Humbert is going to do next?"

"Our lads wanted to know before they joined up where was the next battle going to be. The word is that there are more French ships coming any day and while they waited for them, they were training up the Irish so they will have a big army. I think some were saying that there was a big rising happened in the midlands and once Humbert's army met up with them fellas, they would be able to take over all of Ireland."

That was all that George was able to glean from Pat and he thanked him, gave him a few shillings and sent him back to his family. Then he sat at his desk to absorb what he had just been told and to brainstorm – what could be done to rescue John from the clutches of Humbert before it was too late. Several minutes passed while he ran the details through his head – then Catherine came in and she was in a mess.

"Tell me it's not true George, tell me that our John is not in Castlebar but in Dublin studying for his final exams. Please God, let this news I just heard not be true."

George embraced her and she sank against him, sobbing uncontrollably.

"I wish I could tell you that my dear, but I have just received an eyewitness account of what is going on in Castlebar, from a tenant who was there yesterday. The French Irish army has defeated

General Lake and has taken over Castlebar and everywhere between there and Killala. The French commander, General Humbert has declared a Republic and set up a Government of the Province of Connaught. John Moore was named as President. My tenant did not see John in person, but I have no doubt that his information is correct – John is there, is part of the rebellion and is acting President of this new Government. What on earth has got into the boy to do such a thing?"

"Oh my God, this is the worst moment of my life. The British will come back and defeat them and take revenge on everyone who is part of this – they will – they will hang anyone who is not killed in the battle. What are you going to do – how are you going to save our boy, our John?"

"I don't know yet what I can do – I am trying to think of what my best plan is. John has really done it this time – why on earth did he travel down from Dublin to throw in with this lot who are doomed to failure. He is a grown man, and he will have to bear the consequences of his actions, I am _____"

Catherine interrupted him – "Don't say that – he must have been lured into this, by those United Irishmen who were scheming with the French and forced him into this position. He is not a soldier or a politician or a rebel – he is just a boy, about to pass the Bar, he has his whole life ahead of him – we must find a way to save him George, please, please, please – oh, my baby, my _____," she broke down sobbing.

• • •

The day after the decrees were issued at Castlebar, John Moore awoke to someone knocking on his bedroom door. The person at the door said that John was required to meet General Humbert immediately in the downstairs dining room. Five minutes later he stumbled into the room where Humbert was poring over maps with his French commanders and Colonel Teeling of the Irish troops.

Humbert looked up as John entered, "Ah, Mr. President, thank you for joining us. We have much work to do in preparation for the next phase of military operations and you must pull the financial business side of the new government together."

"Yes, indeed General – I thought you were in a holding pattern while waiting for the arrival of Hardy's expedition. In the meantime, I am in the process of selecting our council of government – we have six members at present and today I am hoping to add six more to complete the council."

"That's of secondary importance – those people are there just to rubber-stamp your decisions. We need urgent supplies for our forces and the Irish forces also need the same, from what Colonel Teeling tells me. The food and other supplies are here in the local merchants' shops and stores, but they want payment for them. You must issue paper money immediately in the name of the Republic of Connaught, backed of course by the French Government. They will accept that money and we can get on with feeding and equipping the soldiers. We have information that the British forces are gathering in Sligo and Athlone – we must hasten all our preparations. Can you get this money issued within the next few hours?"

"I will get right on it General. Send two guards with me to the town hall and we will start immediately."

Colonel Teeling watched this encounter and nodded his head at John, – "I have two men here ready to accompany you right now, Mr. President, and I will go with you myself."

Once they had left the room Humbert resumed his deliberations.

"We have received no new instructions from the Directory. I must assume that General Hardy's expedition has not yet sailed, and time is now becoming our enemy, along with the British. We must get ready to march out of here before the British have time to close in on us. With a little luck we can thread our way between their approaching forces and join up with the rebel army that is taking the field in the midlands. Then we will have enough numbers to march on Dublin."

General Sarrazin spoke – "I think we need a lot of luck, but I agree that we cannot stay here. We must take the fight to Cornwallis and his commanders before they have time to regroup – I can have my soldiers ready to move in four and twenty hours – I am not so confident that the Irish will be ready."

"What about you Fontaine?"

"My cavalry can be ready in a similar time frame Sir, and I too am concerned about our effective numbers. We have lots of rebel volunteers, but they are not soldiers and they may not hold up against strong opponents."

"Gentlemen, if we were to work on training this mob for a full month, we would not be able to make them into soldiers. They must be used as they were at Castlebar, to draw and absorb the enemy fire in the center, so that our veteran French soldiers can attack from the flanks."

"Agreed."

"Pass the word that we will march in four and twenty hours, make sure your French troops are rested, well supplied and ready. Do the best you can with the Irish rebels – don't tell Blake and Teeling too much but encourage them to gather their best fighters into groups and have the rest as a support mob to terrorize the enemy as we did before. You are dismissed. Vive la Republique."

• • •

George Moore paced the floor of his office late into the night. He agonized over whether he should attempt to inform his younger son, George, in London about the situation in Castlebar – deciding that news of the French invasion would have already reached London by now. Therefore, he penned a letter to George advising him of the developments in Mayo since the French invasion, and the folly that John had got himself into – intimating without offering evidence that he believed that John had somehow been tricked by General Humbert into taking the position of 'President of this Government of Connaught'. He specifically told George to stay in London and asked him to start developing a list of influential people known to him that may be approached in due course to plead for clemency for John, should that become necessary. Then he made the decision that he himself must travel to Castlebar the next morning, find John and talk him out of this foolishness before it was too late.

He elected to ride rather than go in a carriage and took his estate manager James O'Donnell with him – a big imposing man, both as companion and protection. The morning was clear as they set out at eight, with the plan to head for the town hall, on the assumption that John would be in that vicinity as head of the new government. The road was quiet as they reached the outskirts of the town without incident. Suddenly they were approached by a group of about a dozen rebels armed with pikes, travelling on foot but with two donkey carts laden with such quality household items that were obviously looted from some loyalist household. George took control of the situation with authority and in his native Irish – and addressed the rebel group.

"John Moore, President of the Republic of Connaught is my son and has requested my presence to meet with him and General Humbert. Thank you for guarding the road and protecting us from any roaming loyalist militias. God Bless you all, we must hurry to our meeting."

His pronouncement took the rebels by surprise, but they were suitably impressed by his mention of President John and General Humbert by name. One of them who seemed to be the leader spoke up.

"Mr. Moore and the General are great men to be sure, and we are proud to serve them. Sure, didn't they send us out here to search for the yeomen and to guard the road, and that's what we're doing – isn't that right lads. Ride on through Sir and tell them that the lads from Swinford are out doing their job."

"Thank you. I will indeed tell them."

After that they were almost immediately in the town itself and quickly reached the town hall. There were a few French soldiers standing guard – George spoke to them in French telling them they had come to meet with President John Moore. One of the soldiers told him that the President had left a short time earlier, but they were told that he would be back very soon.

They waited and sure enough saw John riding in their direction not long afterwards – his long golden hair flowing in the wind as he rode his stallion, the horse George had presented to him a year earlier. As John approached and recognized his father he slowed noticeably and reined in beside them.

"Hello John, nice horse."

"Yes indeed. Good day to you Father. It is great to see you."

"John, we need to talk privately."

"Yes – I am very busy with my duties. Please follow me inside, Father."

James offered to mind the horses and the two men walked into the building – he wanted to give them their privacy and he didn't wish to leave the horses unattended.

Inside the building John led the way to an office where lots of papers were lying on a desk, much of it resembling paper money. John motioned to empty chairs, but George was not interested in sitting.

"John, for God's sake tell me what is going on."

"Well, as I am sure you know, General Humbert's army has won a great victory here. The first steps have been taken to create an Irish Republic and Connaught is in the forefront. I have been chosen as President of the Republic of Connaught."

"Your mother and I thought you were in Dublin studying for the Irish Bar – the final exams are next week if I remember correctly – and you have come here instead. Why?"

"Father, Ireland is in the middle of a massive revolt and a revolution – we are following in the footsteps of the American Revolution and the French Revolution. The Society of the United Irishmen has united Catholics and Protestants in a common cause to liberate Ireland and create a new Republic based on equality and justice."

"Who filled your head with all of this – was it Wolfe Tone, or maybe Lord Edward Fitzgerald? Ireland is not ready for revolution – remember that the recent rising in Wexford was defeated quickly by General Lake with great bloodshed on the Irish side. Most of the Irish rebels were slaughtered at Vinegar Hill and all the leaders like Bagenal Harvey and Father Murphy were hanged. This is exactly what will happen here – Lord Cornwallis is probably on his way west right now with a huge army."

"We defeated General Lake's army here in Castlebar, he and the other commanders ran away so fast that he left all his luggage behind. This is different than Wexford, we have battle hardened French troops that are more than a match for the British."

"That may be the case John, man to man – but the French force is very few and the British are mustering an army that will outnumber the French five to one, with superior artillery and cavalry. The Irish rebels with their pikes that we saw here on the way into town are no match for the British infantry. This is suicide, John, and you are caught in the middle of it. Let us together figure a way to extricate you from this before it is too late."

"Father, I have accepted the position of President, I have given my word of honor – I believe that our cause is just and that we will emerge victorious."

"Allow me to tell you what will happen. The French Irish army will be defeated in the next battle. General Humbert will surrender and get terms for himself and his French officers. The Irish will get no such terms, they will be slaughtered in revenge for what has happened here at Castlebar, and any surviving leaders of the Irish will be court martialed for treason and hanged. In that outcome you will either be killed on the battlefield or be hanged afterwards – do you understand?"

"Father, I know that I have disappointed you, while George in London has made you proud. I am not cut out to be a barrister and would fail the Bar exams if I took them. In Dublin

I found my calling, I have studied Irish history, I truly believe the United Irishmen can carry the day and I know that this is what I must do – this is Ireland's hour of need, and I cannot let her down. I have heard you yourself expressing the desire to see Ireland freed from the yoke of England – surely you understand and can sympathize."

"Son, I was talking about peaceful transition to change laws over a long period of time. Freedom cannot be achieved by the force of arms – no Irish rebel army can rival the might of the British forces, as history has shown. I have worked very hard all my life to elevate the Moore name and family to a position of wealth and respectability. My hope and ambition for you is to carry that name forward to the next generation; your actions in this rebellion will destroy this plan – you are going to destroy everything I have striven for and will ruin our family – you are a disgrace."

"I do not possess your business skills, nor do I possess the academic skills of my brother. This is my highest achievement – to fight for Ireland's freedom and to die for it if that is God's will."

"What of your mother's hour of need? Last night she cried in my arms, she pleaded with me to rescue you from the clutches of this French folly – from this certain death. What am I to tell her?"

"Please tell her that I love her and that I love Ireland. Tell her that I have at last found my calling and ask her to pray for me and my comrades, pray that we and Ireland will be victorious. Father, I have urgent work to do here today, to provide financial instruments to our new government so they can secure the supplies our soldiers need to proceed with the rebellion and the revolution."

"John, I hope this is not our final goodbye. I will return to your mother at Moore Hall and try to prepare her for what is about to happen, try to console her. May God be with you in this endeavor."

They stood facing each other, and instinctively both moved to embrace the other. One last look through watery eyes – then George turned and walked out. He thanked James for staying guard, mounted his horse and they headed back to Ballintubber in silence.

Extract from the diaries of Catherine de Kilkelly, Moore Hall, County Mayo

My pages are stained with tears as I write this.

I have never seen George cry until yesterday after he returned from Castlebar. He met John at the town hall but was unable to convince him to give up his escapade of participation in this ill-timed and ill-fated rebellion. He is steadfast in his belief that what he is doing is right and just – maybe it is but he is blinded by youth and idealism, and does not realize the danger he is in.

I cried all last night and I have no tears left.

Why-oh-why did we come back to this Godforsaken country? If only George had listened to me, we would be warm and safe in Spain, and John would be a doing what he loved best – working with horses. Alas, we moved to Ireland, ignored the curses of the Druids and built this house on Muckloon Hill. Every possible misfortune seems to have befallen us since then.

Daddy, laying in your grave in Spain – the ancient Irish poets that you loved to recite – they spent years composing their epic poems, recounting the defeats of Ireland's many rebellions and always ended their poems with the promise of future success and glory.

I see no sign of that success and glory, just more misery and death – and now the same fate is bearing down on our family, on our handsome and fearless John.

May God protect him and may God forgive us for carrying our sons to this land of war and death.

CHAPTER TWELVE

John made sure that the 'Government of the Republic of Connaught' delivered on his promises to General Humbert – a large batch of paper money was issued, and the soldiers received provisions of food plus all and any other supplies as were available in Castlebar. He added enough local names to complete his list of twelve members for the governing council. Despite his efforts he could not persuade any Catholic clergy to join the council, being that the Irish Roman Catholic Hierarchy were totally opposed to French republicanism and its ideals. His list consisted mostly of local merchants who had a vested interest in the enterprise because they had taken the newly printed money in exchange for provisions.

He was invited to eat supper at the house of one of these merchants, Mr. Murphy the baker, and he accepted the invitation – visiting and talking with the family kept his mind off the unpleasantness of his earlier meeting with his father. Returning late to the house that he was sharing with the

French officers he found Humbert sitting alone at the table with his maps before him, and an almost empty bottle of brandy in front of him.

"General, I wanted to bid you good night before I retire."

"Sit, sit – Citizen John, pardon me – Mr. President, talk to me – tell me how goes the business of the new Government."

"Very good, Sir. I got the paper money printed and Colonel Teeling confirmed to me that both the Irish and French soldiers were able to get all their needed supplies. I have appointed a magistrate to deal with local judicial matters like looting and bar brawls, and we have gathered up fifty head of roaming cattle into a secure pasture where they will be kept for the exclusive use and food for our government and defenders. I have here a list of twelve candidates for our Government Council, all vetted by me – I would be obliged if you would sign off on the list."

"Give me a pen and I will sign it now and get yourself a glass to join me in a brandy."

Humbert scratched his name at the bottom of the list while John got a glass and poured some wine.

"I am not able for brandy, Sir; I am happy to drink your health with this excellent French red wine."

They tipped glasses and John proposed the toast, – "Vive la Republique."

"Vive la Republique de Connaught. Tomorrow we must make final preparations – we march from Castlebar the following morning."

"What about Hardy who is due to arrive any day – are you not waiting for him?"

"No, because he has not yet departed Brest. The Directory have delayed any decision to send more ships without giving me an explanation, or giving me any new orders, but I know what they are doing, and I know what I must do next."

"What do you mean, General?"

"Let me tell you what is really going on. Bonepart has a very large expedition in-route to Egypt and plans to push the British out of the Nile region. In the minds of the Directory our expedition to Ireland is a diversionary tactic to tie up major portions of the British fleet and increase Bonepart's prospects for success. Meanwhile the British forces on the ground here are regrouping and gathering a large army to our east and south – under Cornwallis, he who surrendered and was defeated in America by the American revolutionary patriots. We must surprise them and break through their lines before they gain too much strength – and so we march out the day after tomorrow."

"Have you told your commanders this?"

"They have been told on a 'need to know basis,' and will be ready."

"Which direction will you go?"

"I have a plan, that is all you need to know for now."

"What are your plans for Castlebar?"

"We will leave a garrison of French and Irish soldiers to hold the town. Our wounded are recovering and will strengthen the garrison very soon. The British and loyalists have run away to Galway."

"Part of me wants to go with you and part of me wants to stay here."

"Citizen John, you must stay. This is your home, you are the President, you must govern the Province of Connaught in preparation to take your place alongside the other provinces, as part of the Republic of Ireland that is coming very soon. France has helped you on your path to freedom – you and your fellow Irish must take the reins from here. Remember – our conversation details are not for everyone's ears, not yet – you must lead your people, but you must always know more than they know. Now, I must retire to my chamber and rest. Vive la Republique."

The next day brought rain showers while the soldiers, both French and Irish appeared to John to be busy cleaning weapons, getting supply wagons loaded and readying wheeled artillery guns for hitching to horses. John spent most of the day at the town hall after notifying his new council members of their first meeting the following day. He saw Humbert's scout riders coming back in, and all visitors coming into the town were questioned about what they had seen on the roads. Colonel Teeling came to visit with him at the town hall in the afternoon.

"Come in Colonel, have a seat. Your men seemed very busy today, are you at liberty to tell me what is in the works?"

"Well, I know that you already know we are leaving in the morning, and that you are staying in Castlebar after we leave. I came to say goodbye and to thank you for all that you have done to help us. We are going off to war and the next few weeks will determine our fate and that of the 'Republic of Ireland' that we crave."

"General Humbert is a skillful commander and I'm sure he has a plan to achieve more victories. I hope you rout Cornwallis just as you did Lake, and that the rest of Ireland rises up in rebellion to swell your ranks. In the meantime, I will do everything I can to lead the new government of Connaught to a position of economic strength, and we will start raising the regiments asked for in the decrees."

"Can you take possession of this letter from me, addressed to my wife in Ulster. If I fall in the upcoming battles, please see that she gets this letter."

"You have my assurance of that – but I have confidence that you will do just fine."

They shook hands warmly and Teeling departed. John received another sealed letter in a dry box from a peasant messenger in the late afternoon – it was from his mother.

'Dearest John – Your father and I are praying that you will reconsider his offer to come home before the situation becomes more dangerous in Castlebar. You are the heir to Moore Hall and the estate – your father has spent his entire life planning for this and building a magnificent legacy for you and the other boys. After your father, you are the most precious being in my life – a life that will have no meaning should any harm happen to you.

Please, for God's sake leave Castlebar the instant you read this letter.

Come home John and soothe my aching heart.

Your loving Mother.'

John re-read the letter several times and sat there in tearful meditation for quite some time. He was so very sorry for afflicting such anguish and pain on his mother, and the thought did cross his mind to ride home and leave this all behind. Connaught was on the verge of freedom and needed for him to stay at the helm. Once a final victory was achieved, she would understand why he could not leave his post – she would be proud of him then, and happy. His thoughts were interrupted by his aides needing his signature on government documents, and he got absorbed in work for another two hours. It was almost dark when John came out onto the open square and called for his horse. There was a heavy mist that reduced visibility, but he sensed something was different as he made his way through the town, towards the big house on Foxford Road. As he got closer, he saw lines of men gathering up into formation, with the distinct look of getting ready for departure. He saw Colonel Teeling and reined in beside him.

"Colonel, I was told that you were leaving in the morning, but what I am witnessing here leads me to believe that your army is getting ready to leave now."

"General Humbert has received new information on the movement of enemy forces. He has decided to march out tonight using the mist and the darkness to our advantage. We are leaving a group of Irish defenders under the command of Adam O'Daly along with some French soldiers to garrison the town – and it is my understanding that they will have two or three cannons plus their gunners – that should be plenty of protection for the town. Pardon me but I must move on – I have much to do to get my forces ready to leave. Goodbye again and good luck – remember to keep safe the letter I left with you."

"I will indeed. Good luck and God speed."

The road near the house was clogged with French infantry, horses hitched to supply wagons and artillery, with the cavalry of General Fontaine off to the side being fed and watered. John searched out General Humbert who was still inside the house – he found him finishing a plate of food with his customary glass of red wine.

"Come in Mr. President – I had just sent for you, but you must have already been on the way here to arrive so soon. Please excuse me for eating, I may not have time to eat again for some time."

"Your plans seem to have changed – what is happening, General?"

"Based on new information I received this afternoon; I have decided to move out sooner to get our forces into a superior position with reference to the advancing enemy. We are leaving Irish and French soldiers here to defend the town – under Major Ruffie, plus a few cannons and gunners to guard the approaches to the town."

"Do you think the town will be in much danger after your army leaves?"

"No, I do not. The British and their militias will be consumed by their efforts to engage my army and should stay well away from Castlebar."

"Which route are you taking when you leave?"

"Citizen John, that is one question that you should not ask a General in my position – I forgive you and politely refuse to answer. I think you will make a fine leader of the Republic of Connaught. I must go and check the progress of departure with my commanders. A tout a l'heure, Mon Ami."

"Abientot."

John retreated to his rooms upstairs as the sounds of the army's final preparations filled the damp air. A steady rain soon began to fall, and he could hear it drumming against the window. His heart was beating in his chest, he could feel his anxiety level rising. Despite General Humbert's assurances and the defense forces he was leaving behind, John worried about the safety of the town. He knew there were loyalists still hiding out in the area and they would probably alert the British as soon as Humbert marched out. John did not share the view that the town would be spared. As the county seat of government, it was a prize that the British would be itching to regain control of, as soon as the French army vacated it. Despite all the activity and his busy mind, John dozed off. The buglers startled him when they called the column to attention. His lamp was still burning, and his watch was at three o'clock. Peering out the window into the courtyard he saw the column starting to move out, lit up with rows of flaming torches and full of the noise of straining animals and men marching. John came down to the front steps of the house and stood to attention as they passed in front of him. General Humbert saluted and John returned the salute. Several of the other commanders acknowledged his presence as they passed – Colonel Teeling rode past with his cavalry and saluted. It took more than an hour for the entire column to pass and after that, the noise they made hung in the damp dark air – as they headed out onto the Sligo Road.

John went back to bed for a few hours of restless sleep – waking with a start as daylight streamed through the window. Downstairs was totally empty except for the old cook who was poking the fire to boil a kettle. She poured him a streaming mug of strong tea and he sat at the big table eating two slices of buttered bread, the table on which General Humbert had spread out his maps. Now he was alone, and his anxiety returned. He quickly finished the tea and went to the stables where he found a few French soldiers getting up from their cots. They directed him to the other barn where he found Major Ruffie, introduced himself and began asking questions about their defense plan.

"Monsieur President, we do not expect any attack from the British or their loyalist supporters. General Humbert could spare only a dozen of us and there is about twenty-five Irish under O'Daly."

"Where are they all; I see just a few soldiers here – I am deeply concerned that the town will be attacked by the British and I worry that we are vulnerable. Please show me our defenses – can we take a ride."

They got their horses and headed towards the two bridges that guarded the entrance to the town. As they approached the first bridge, John could see an artillery gun but there were no soldiers attending it. Nearby, they found the French gunner and several Irish rebel soldiers – all asleep. John was horrified, not just by the unreadiness but also by the lack of concern by the Major, who was oblivious to the danger of attack. At the other bridge, they found O'Daly with about six men and the other field gun – up and awake but with little urgency. John asked Major Ruffie and Colonel O'Daly to move with him out of earshot of the men where he attempted to convince them of the need for action – John acting as interpreter between the Irish and the French.

"Gentlemen, we must organize our defenses immediately and prepare for the inevitable attack from loyalist yeoman militia or even a raiding force of British troops."

O'Daly, who was obviously under the effects of too much whiskey the previous night, spoke up –

"Mr. Moore – Sur don't we know the British and their

militia ran away to Tuam. They probably went on to Athlone from there and will not bother us in Castlebar – you heard General Humbert himself say that. They will all be sucked into Cornwallis's army in Athlone, and they are only interested in General Humberts army, who is headed to meet them in battle. They have no interest in Castlebar, there's nothing here for them. Our lads have sacked Swinford and Foxford and Westport and Newport – we control the whole of Mayo by now."

"With all due respect to you and Major Ruffie – I demand that we take the defense of Castlebar more seriously, that we keep the two guns always manned, and that we patrol the perimeter of the town. We must remember that there are a lot of loyalists here in Castlebar and General Humbert released his prisoners before he left – I worry that some of them will send word to the British that Castlebar is under-defended and vulnerable enough to be retaken."

Major Ruffie accepted John's concerns and was okay with the idea of upping their defenses – O'Daly then agreed to follow suit. A plan was hastily put together – they would rotate shifts of five men at each artillery gun position and begin town perimeter patrols of five men – and O'Daly promised that he would instruct his men to reduce their alcohol intake to no more than what was needed for medicinal purposes – whatever level that meant was lost in translation and not contested by John. With that, John told the two commanders to put the plan into action and he rode to the town hall to prepare for the first meeting of the Government Council at noon.

The noon meeting time came and only four of the twelve showed up – Murphy the baker, and three provisions merchants – Burke, Joyce and Tuohy – who were mainly concerned about how to get new supplies delivered from Galway and when they could convert the 'Province of Connaught' promissory notes into currency they could use for trade – British Pounds, or Gold or Silver. John did not know but he pretended that he did, and promptly told them that another French fleet would be arriving in Killala within a week or two, and they would be carrying gold and silver to exchange for the promissory notes. The other main concern was local law and order – there had been a substantial amount of whiskey and porter stolen from taverns and warehouses since the Castlebar victory. The merchants wanted compensation and they wanted the thieves to be prosecuted, and protection against future thefts. All the looting of loyalist houses that had occurred in the area did not greatly concern them despite some loss of life and destruction of property. John was already out of his depth in his first government assignment – he made promises that he felt would calm their concerns while buying time to figure out a solution. The council members departed, and John sank into a chair – the enormity of the task he had undertaken was now plain and he was filled with doubt. His newly appointed magistrate had been waiting outside – he now entered and wanted to talk about how they were going to appoint new police constables to replace those that had deserted their posts when Humbert's army took the town. These questions he deflected for future consideration using the excuse that he needed to inspect the town defenses, and he set off to do just that.

Both bridges were being manned when John rode through and he complimented O'Daly and Ruffie on their progress. Then he continued to his lodgings.

At ten o'clock that night John was re-reading his mother's letter when he heard artillery and musket fire. He dropped the letter and rushed outside and determined that an attack of some type was under way. He mounted his horse and carefully headed towards the bridge, slowly, keeping off the main road. Some men came running in his direction – he asked them what was happening.

"The British are back. There are a hundred dragoons riding through the town Sir, they've killed our fellas who were defending the bridges with the big guns, and they are cutting down anybody they come across – run for your life."

John made an instant decision – he would ride around the outskirts to get to the Ballintubber road and would then head for Moore Hall. He made it around the trouble and gained the road, thinking he was free and clear.

Suddenly, as the moonlight lit up the road ahead of him there was a row of four horsemen blocking his path.

A man shouted in English, "Who goes there? Identify yourself in the name of the King."

"Moore of Moore Hall in Ballintubber. I am heading home after visiting a sick relative – I am a gentleman and unarmed as you can see. I am speaking the King's English. Let me pass."

One of the men spoke up in a strong Scottish accent – "Colonel Crawford has given orders to stop anybody leaving the area. You must accompany us back to the town."

With that one of the men took the reins of John's horse and led the way in the direction of Castlebar, two other riders were on either side of him, ignoring his continued protests, and the group leader was at the back – the was no chance of escape for John. On the way they passed over one of the bridges where several dead bodies of Irish defenders lay around the artillery gun. As they approached the town hall, they were met by four riders, one of which was a civilian and immediately pointed to John and spoke to the British commander next to him.

"Colonel Crawford, that's him, that's John Moore, the man appointed as President of Connaught."

John heard the men at his side draw their swords and felt the tip of a blade against his back. They came to a halt in front of Colonel Crawford, who addressed John is a sarcastic tone.

"So, here we have John Moore, welcome back Mr. President. Where did you lads find him?"

"We stopped him on the road as he was attempting to ride out of town, Sir. When he identified himself as Moore, I just knew he was the one you told us to be watching out for, and we took him into custody and here he is Sir."

"Well done, Sergeant, you have just earned yourself a promotion. Dismount Mr. President."

John dismounted and so did Colonel Crawford, a large man who glared at John as he walked around him a few times.

"Even in your nice gentry clothes you don't look very presidential to me, does he look presidential to you lads?"

"No Sir," they all shouted.

Crawford then grabbed John's collars and pulled his face in front of his own – "Let me show you what we do with rebels like you." He frog-marched John around the corner of the building to where two men were dangling from ropes – one of them John recognized as O'Daly.

"We killed the ones at the gun as we rode over them and rode down these two trying to run away. That one on the right claimed to be an officer in the French army but couldn't speak French – bloody rebel – got what he deserved. How would you like to join him?"

The man who had fingered John then came up. "Colonel, I am a medical doctor and a Christian and I deplore this summary execution of prisoners, as God is my witness. This man may be a rebel, but he is from a good family whose father is a loyal subject of the King. I demand that you respect his position as a civilian leader even though he is your prisoner. You must confine him to the gaol, inform Lord Cornwallis of his capture and he must be tried in a court of law. You will be rewarded for your service Colonel and your adherence to the principles of justice, I will see to that."

Crawford was so taken aback by this interjection that he released his hold on John and dusted off John's crumpled jacket.

"You are correct, Doctor Ellis, and I'm sure Lord Cornwallis will want to interview this prisoner himself. Now, Mr. President – tell us where Humbert's army is headed, it will be in your interest to tell us everything you know."

John recovered enough composure to answer. "General Humbert did not tell me where he was going. His army went out the Sligo Road as I am sure the doctor has already told you – that is all I know."

"Sergeant Knox, search this man's person now, in front of the good doctor who was kind enough to meet us on the Hollymount Road, inform us of the French army's desertion of Castlebar and lead us into the town. Maybe the President has evidence on him to show where Humbert is headed."

Knox opened John's waistcoat and moments later pulled out an envelope, which he handed to Colonel Crawford, who immediately opened it.

"We have here a letter of commission signed by General Humbert, appointing Citizen John Moore as President of the Province of Connaught. Doctor, verify this letter before I put it away for safekeeping. This will indeed be of great interest to His Lordship and will help convict this man of treason – then he will be hanged in accordance with the laws that you refer to."

John was marched the short distance to the gaol, a bleak featureless building that the previous week been emptied of all prisoners when the French captured Castlebar. General Humbert had arrested dozens of suspected loyalists and imprisoned them in the same cells but decided to free them all before his departure from the town. John had seen these different gaol situations play out and knew that the place had a reputation of damp and death – now it was his turn to occupy one of its filthy cells.

Colonel Crawford appointed a gaoler and ordered several of his soldiers to act as temporary guards – giving strict orders to keep the prisoners safe and fed until such time as new permanent guards could be appointed. Then he rode out of town with his dragoons to rejoin the forces being amassed by Lord Cornwallis for the upcoming battle with the French Irish forces led by General Humbert.

• • •

During the occupation of Castlebar by the French Irish forces there was a sizeable contingent of Irish rebels that were bent on revenge against all local Protestant loyalists and even against any Catholics who were deemed to be loyal to the King. The estate of Lord Lucan who literally owned Castlebar was attacked, partially plundered and vandalized, even though Lucan had done much good for the local community. Lord Altamont in Westport and his brother Dennis Browne were perceived as exploiters of the peasant population and enemies of Ireland – their properties were mostly destroyed by rebel mobs. Furniture and valuables were carried off to adorn the mud cottages of these looters, whose interest was self-gain and not the liberation of their country.

George Moore of Moore Hall in Ballintubber, south of Castlebar, was a Catholic landlord and was highly respected not only by the other landlords but also by his tenants, and the various entities that agitated for peasant rights. That respect, or the fact that his son was a prominent member of the rebellion did not guarantee safety from the marauding mobs. George and his managers spent every waking hour exhorting their tenants to remain in their homes and reject any attempts by the rebels to entice them into committing violence against their landlord, or his property. He posted guards at the main entrance to the House and had mounted patrols monitoring the boundaries of the estate twenty-four hours a day, since the Castlebar victory of General Humbert's army and the influx of rebels into the area. Their vigilance paid off, as only a few of their tenants went off to join the rebels, and no serious attacks were made on the estate.

Inside their Big House, Mr. and Mrs. Moore worried and fretted about the safety of their son John. First, news came of the departure of General Humbert and the main army from Castlebar – who thankfully marched north, in the opposite direction from the estate. Next came the news that British dragoons had recaptured the town, had slain most of its rebel defenders, and had taken the French soldiers as captives. Finally, the news came to them that John had been captured and lodged in the town gaol. After briefly rejoicing for his safety, they were overcome by the realization that their son was being held captive in the squalor of the that old gaol – possibly wounded and suffering.

George and Catherine were exploring the possibility of engaging the services of local attorney Alexander O'Donnell in the defense of John, cousin of his estate manager, James – when they were notified that there was a Doctor Ellis from Castlebar at the gate who wished to talk with George urgently. He knew the name of this man, a Protestant and loyalist but had never met him personally – he invited him to ride up to the house and he greeted the man from the porch steps.

"You are welcome, Doctor Ellis, please come inside. To what do I owe this visit, Sir."

The man entered, a boney tall man in his middle years, "Thank you, Mr. and Mrs. Moore for your welcome – I bring you good and bad news. Your son John has been arrested by the returning British forces in Castlebar and is confined to the gaol there. I myself interceded with Colonel Crawford and succeeded in preventing any harm befalling the young man – I can assure you that he is in good health and is safe for now, guarded by Crawford's dragoons. He has a cell all to himself and the French prisoners are in the next building – as far as I know all the Irish rebel defenders were either killed in Crawford's attack or were captured and hanged soon afterwards – forgive me dear lady for my oversight in including such graphic detail."

Catherine sobbed while George replied, "Thank you for your action in securing John's safety. We have been discussing the avenues open to us to save the life of our son, a dear boy who has somehow been sucked into this rebellion and has been appointed by General Humbert to a government leadership position that he should have declined."

"Mr. Moore, I know that you and I are on different sides of the religious divide, but I also know that we are both Christians who believe in the same true God, and we believe in law and order. You have a reputation as a righteous man and that is why I have come here today to offer my profound regrets for the position your son has found himself in, and to offer to help in any way I can, to keep him safe and to get fair treatment for him in a court of law. Unfortunately, by his actions and association with the leaders of this rebellion he is seen as an enemy of the British government, and he will face serious charges. I have made inquiries and I am quite sure that he did not take up arms in the Castlebar defeat of General Lake's forces – his only crime has been his participation in the illegal Connaught government that General Humbert set up. However, once Humbert's force is defeated there will be many seeking revenge on all who have in any way supported the rebels. General Lake did not take his defeat well and I happen to know that he has a cruel and vengeful streak and dislikes the system of habeas corpus – he supported drumhead court-martials in Wexford after the rebels were defeated at Vinegar Hill, and he meted out summary justice immediately in the battlefield. I expect the same from him after Humbert's defeat and he will then turn his sights on Castlebar."

"I thank you again for what you have done for John. What do you suggest we do now?"

"Engage the best attorneys you can get and task them with getting him moved to a gaol outside of Mayo. The coming revenge will be most severely felt in Mayo – particularly in Castlebar and Killala, but in all the nearby towns which supported the rebel cause. Sir, he is not going to get off free, but he does not deserve the kind of summary justice that court-martials will be dealing out in Mayo very soon – I apologize my dear woman, I do not mean to frighten you, but the reality is that Mayo will see a lot of death before this is over. You should try to get him moved out of this county – to Clare or Limerick, south and away from here and away from the developing battleground in the midlands."

"We intend to engage attorney Alex O'Donnell – do you suggest anybody else?"

"I would suggest you engage Thomas Burke also; he is well connected with Lord Lucan's people, and they have sway over everything that happens in Castlebar. I assume you will talk to Denis Browne, High Sheriff of Mayo, who may be your best contact for getting John moved to a safer location."

"Yes, indeed we will. The Moore's and Browne's go back a long way."

"Sir, I will take my leave. I intend to check on the prisoner's welfare daily. Is there any message you would like me to pass along to John?"

Catherine was already in the other room writing a letter to John in anticipation of sending it with Dr. Ellis. She finished it and handed the envelope to him, "Thank you Doctor, you have shown yourself to be a Christian man of great compassion, even at such a trying time for your family and your town. Please give this letter to John and tell him to keep his spirits up as we try to help him."

George spoke again – "Do you think we would be allowed to visit with John at the gaol and could meet with the two attorneys at the same time?"

"Sir, Castlebar is not a safe place to visit at this moment and the temporary gaol guards are rather coarse Scottish highlanders who are easily provoked. I suggest that you send a note with me that I will gladly pass to both attorneys, informing them of your desire to engage them and asking them to come visit with you at your home – they are both young men and it is easier for them to come here. In the coming days there is going to be a battle between Humbert's and Cornwallis's armies somewhere in the midlands. There is great uncertainty until that battle is decided and normality returns to Castlebar – in the meantime no prisoners will be moved anywhere else. You are safer here and John will be safe there – I will see to it."

George quickly wrote two notes for the attorneys and rode with Ellis to the main gate of the estate, where he again thanked him for his kindness. James O'Donnell approached and spoke to George once the doctor had departed.

"Sir, I know that Alexander will come as soon as he receives the note. I have just heard news that some rebels almost caught Denis Browne as the Castlebar battle unfolded and would have killed him for sure. He escaped to his home in Claremorris and later had to run to Galway when rebels overran his Claremount House, which they damaged severely after he eluded them again. Another mob attacked and ransacked his Mount Browne House in Westport, and they then attacked his brother's residence, Westport House – Lord Altamont and his family were not at the estate during all of this."

"This is going to make it more difficult for me to convince Denis to use his good offices to have John moved. He is not a pleasant man to start with and he will be fit to be tied after the destruction of his two homes. As soon as Cornwallis's army is victorious, and that is a given considering his vast superiority in numbers, Denis will be running behind the army as they reclaim Westport and consolidate their hold on Castlebar. Then he will claim victory and as high sheriff of Mayo will exact his revenge on everyone he perceives as having helped the rebels and any way – and that includes John. I will swallow my pride and put myself before him at the first opportunity, but it will be a tall task to convince him to give John the fair treatment that habeas corpus lays out – even more difficult to get favorable treatment for him. For now, I must comfort Catherine in her grief, and we must all wait for the next chapter of the rebellion to play out on the battlefield. I have gained new respect today for Dr. Ellis and I hope he can keep John safe until we can mount a defense."

• • •

Extract from the diaries of Catherine de Kilkelly, Moore Hall, County Mayo

I am distraught and so is George. John's foolhardiness has put his life in danger. We thought moving him to Dublin would be best but now I realize it put him in close contact with the Society of United Irishmen, and John's personality is such that he was drawn to their ideals and to their misguided rebellion. If only we could turn back the clock.

Now he languishes in Castlebar gaol, having been pushed into the position of President of Connaught, which is but a fleeting dream – and he was so beguiled by his post that he carried the proclamation on his person – the foolish boy. George is burdened by enormous stress over this matter, and I worry for his health. I wish young George was here to comfort him, but I dare not suggest it – he is safer in London and hopefully his contacts there can help us in our hour of need.

We must await the outcome of the battle in the midlands while we hope and pray that John remains safe in Castlebar. I am thankful that he did not march from the town with Humbert – that expedition will end in certain defeat and the Irish contingent will be shown no mercy by the British.

Lord God – protect us all and deliver John back to his family from the jaws of death.

• • •

CHAPTER THIRTEEN

The plan that General Humbert had in mind after leaving Castlebar was to slip through the net that the British forces were laying for him, cross the River Shannon, and join up with the large army of rebels that he believed were waiting for him in the Midlands. His army was harassed by British forces who marched out from Sligo under Colonel Verecker, and he was drawn into battle in Collooney – a battle that was quickly and decisively won by the French. It didn't help that his army was being constantly depleted by desertions of Irish rebels – some were bent on looting nearby loyalist properties, and some were losing the stomach for the upcoming decisive battle. The Collooney encounter and continued harassment of his rearguard convinced Humbert to change direction more than once during the following days, he gradually turned southeast towards Longford and unfortunately into the trap that Lord Cornwallis was laying for him. Once in the net it was a matter of hours before the French Irish army was surrounded and attacked from all sides in a place called Ballinamuck, County Longford. A brief flurry of combat ensued before Humbert surrendered to General Lake, and negotiated honorable terms for himself, his officers and French troops. The Irish forces were not offered the same chance to surrender – the British repeatedly charged into them and despite gallant defending they were overwhelmed. Hundreds were killed on the spot and those that took flight were pursued and either killed in the local bogs or dragged back to the battlefield. There they were hauled before drumhead court-martials and hanged immediately. It was reported that rebels were being hanged by the twenty – including officers of the rebel forces like Blake, O'Dowd and O'Malley.

The British accepted the French surrender and moved among them noting names and ranks, allowing Humbert's commanders to keep their horses and personal weapons. Humbert made little effort to gain honorable terms for his Irish officers and men, even those that were officers in the French army and wore French uniforms. Men like Colonel Teeling and Matthew Tone were not afforded the normal protection that prisoners of war are entitled to, and they were hauled off the battlefield separately from the French prisoners – to be later tried for treason in Dublin, convicted and publicly executed.

The news of Humbert's defeat, just days after Dr. Ellis's visit, reached Moore Hall at the same time as attorney Alexander

O'Donnell was visiting George and Catherine to plan a defense for John – attorney Burke, a staunch loyalist, had declined the offer to be part of John's defense. News of the defeat hit Catherine very hard, and she felt too unwell to participate in the discussions. They had no inkling at that time that such wanton reprisal killings had taken place at Ballinamuck but were convinced that John was in imminent danger and the need to get him moved out of Castlebar was urgent. Alexander told George that civil courts were supposedly still in operation, and they decided that the best course of action was to push for John's case to be handled by the civil authorities and keep him away from the upcoming military courts.

"Sir, I suggest we file immediately for John's release under the writ of habeas corpus. It will probably be denied, but it will establish doubt with reference to which type of court should oversee his case, and that will buy us time. Let us also appeal directly to Lord Cornwallis on this issue; he has the reputation of being a reasonable man and he may be merciful after his victory. We need him to rein in General Lake and other diehard loyalists and we should ask that he direct them to omit John's name from the lists of rebels that will be subject to drumhead court-martials in Castlebar, as they hunt down rebels over the coming weeks. I want to give Cornwallis an obvious route that would entice him to order that John to be moved from Castlebar – they do need to make space in the gaol for all the new prisoners that will be hauled in."

Despite the chaos that ensued over the following weeks

O'Donnell entered his pleadings at Castlebar. Everything was tabled until the local security situation was deemed to be under control. They also sent the planned letter to Lord Cornwallis but received no reply – it was unknown if he had received the letter into his own hands and read it. John remained in gaol, and the danger of him getting lumped in with the other rebels was very real – in which case he was in grave danger of being executed.

• • •

Denis Browne returned to the Mayo area after he learned of Cornwallis's victory at Longford; he inspected his damaged home in Claremorris and proceeded to Westport to do the same at his house there, as well as inspect Westport House for his brother who remained in Dublin. He was consumed with rage and offered to serve as chief prosecutor for the government during the upcoming trials in Mayo – a position he was able to garner, as High Sheriff of Mayo and brother of Lord Altamont, the most powerful figure in Mayo. By the middle of September these trials had begun, and he wasted no time in starting the hangings. Some of the first hangings included two Catholic priests, James Conroy and Manus Sweeney – not for rebellion but simply for acting as interpreters between the French soldiers and Irish rebels. During his Castlebar stay Denis was the guest of Lord Lucan and stayed at one of the lodges on his estate which had escaped damage by the rebel mobs. George had sent a letter to him asking for a meeting but had received no reply. He was getting more concerned by the day for John's safety, and Catherine was almost a basket case – he decided that he had to force the issue by going uninvited and hoping that he could get in front of Denis.

He rode there on a Sunday afternoon thinking that even Denis Browne would observe The Lord's Day. His butler answered the door and told him that his master was expected shortly but he didn't have the authority to invite him in, so George sat outside, astride his horse in the September sunshine. While waiting he found himself replaying the history of the Moore and Browne families in his head. During the years of the Penal Laws the Moore's held onto their Catholic faith despite the persecution meted out to them. The Browne's renounced their Catholic faith early on, swore allegiance to King George and were received into the Protestant Church – they were what was called Turncoats. They wanted to hold onto their lands and their power and decided to step over to the winning Protestant side, as they saw it. Over time they built up an even bigger power base by their willingness to be go-betweens and negotiators. In the present age Denis was MP for Mayo and High Sheriff of Mayo as well, while his older brother was Lord Altamont, the owner of the huge Westport House estate and the most powerful man in Mayo – the turncoats had done very well for themselves. Denis Browne had the reputation of getting things done that others could not – and so George Moore was here to prostrate himself in front of this beastly man.

Twenty minutes later Denis arrived in a carriage escorted by two militia guards. George removed his hat so that he was easier to recognize, and Denis waved off the guards who had become nervous of this lone horseman waiting outside the front door.

"Moore, it's good to see you. I do apologize for not replying to your letter – I have been a busy man. Follow me inside and let's talk. I trust your dear wife is well."

"Hello Denis. She is as well as could be expected under the circumstances."

Denis was a pudgy man in his forties, with sandy colored hair and big jowls. Once inside and having dispatched their coats and hats to the butler, Denis led the way into a parlor room that had been repurposed as an office with a desk. He motioned George to a comfortable chair by the fireplace and went immediately to a cupboard, removed a decanter of brandy and two glasses. He poured two large measures and handed one to George who was still standing by the chairs.

"This Spanish brandy came from your good self – casks quietly shipped by the Merchant of Alicante into Clew Bay some years ago, when you and my father did business outside of the bounds of the excise man – much better than any of the parliamentary brandy. It has improved with age in my opinion, just like you George – you are looking very well. To the Moore's and the Browne's."

They both sipped the brandy and sat down as the warmth of Spain trickled down their throats.

George broke the silence – "That was a long time ago and much has changed in our lives since then. Your father was a good man, a man that would always stand by his friends, and I am sure that his son has inherited those same qualities. I am here to talk about John – no doubt you know that."

"Terrible business this French invasion. The rebel mobs attacked my properties of Claremount House and Mountbrowne House – rendering them both uninhabitable until major repairs are undertaken. Westport House also suffered. Thank God that I was able to elude the rebels and Lord Altamont was away at the time, or we would surely have been set upon by the mob. Now that Humbert's army has been defeated and the rebellion has been neutralized it is time to restore law and order to Mayo, and I intend to instill the fear of God and of the Crown into every peasant in Mayo – after the rebels are rooted out and dealt with."

"I sympathize wholeheartedly with your property loss – you have every right to be angry and to be fully compensated for your losses. As High Sheriff of Mayo you are in the position to say who goes to trial and who does not. I am not here to debate the rights or wrongs of what has happened. You know that John is a high spirited and impressionable boy, he is not a soldier and did not take up arms against the British forces in this rebellion. He was in the wrong place at the wrong time and because of his proficiency in French he got sucked into Humbert's circle and was appointed President of Connaught without any prior knowledge – he was overawed by the title and didn't have enough sense to walk away. He is guilty of youthful stupidity, but he is not guilty of treason."

"He is over thirty years old, long past his youth, and as Lord Cornwallis said – he acted and exercised authority under the enemy, being at war with our Sovereign Lord the King, and he continued to so act until he was made a prisoner."

"As I said already, he took no part in the fighting and was at no time in charge of any body of fighting men. If you asked the average rebel who he was they would have no idea. Humbert simply used him, or should I say used his family name – my name, to further his own ambitions. John is a scapegoat caught up in this nasty situation and hanging him will do nothing to help the Crown to pacify Mayo, or Ireland. Move him to a gaol in another part of the country until this area is pacified to your satisfaction – ship him off to America or Spain, and he was indeed born a Spanish subject. Denis – pure and simple – I want his life saved."

Denis refilled their glasses.

"Blake, and O'Dowd and other rebel leaders have already been court-martialed on the field of battle, found guilty and were hanged in Longford. Many more like Teeling and Tone will face the same fate when they are tried in Dublin. Is John Moore, with his title of President of the Republic of Connaught less guilty than them in the eyes of the Crown?"

"Yes. He is a civilian, not a soldier who put any member of the King's army in danger. I am not arguing the bigger question of the rights and wrongs of rebellion or those of the drumhead court-martials you just described – I have only one mission here today and that is to save the life of my son John. What must I do to achieve that – pray tell me."

"You have been a very successful merchant and no doubt you are skilled in the art of bargaining. I am going to tell you something that nobody yet knows in Ireland. This rebellion is the straw that has broken the camel's back – the camel in this case being the Irish Parliament. When the smoke clears the Irish Parliament will be abolished, the Kingdom of Ireland will become one with the rest of Britain and henceforth Ireland will be governed by the London Parliament."

"Until a few short years ago, I myself as a Catholic did not even have a vote, and the people who govern Ireland now are so corrupt that a change like this may turn out to be better for all us Papists – who, as you know, comprise the vast majority of the population of Ireland. I don't care what happens to the Irish Parliament – we digress – what must I do to get John moved away from Castlebar gaol, and soon thereafter get him out of Ireland?"

"George, let me finish what I was getting to. When the Irish Parliament is abolished, I will lose my position of MP for Mayo. I want to be elected to serve as one of the two MPs for Mayo in the London Parliament, when this new arrangement comes to pass, and I want your support to achieve that aim."

"I don't see how a powerless Papist landlord like me can do very much to help your cause."

"George, you are underselling yourself. To quote your own

words from the past – we Browne's are turncoat Protestants. I will need the support of the Catholic gentry when the time comes, and your words will be listened to better than mine – I want you to promise me that you will throw your weight behind me. Let us say that I will do my best to help John in the way you have asked for, and you will help me when parliamentary union is passed – in my election to the London parliament as MP for Mayo."

"So, we have a deal? You will work to get John moved away from Castlebar gaol."

"Of course. The Browne's and Moore's go back a long way – you said so yourself."

• • •

The remaining rebel forces holding out in Killala had been defeated by the end of September, with much revenge bloodletting and more prisoners pushed through the courts, found guilty of treason and other offences. Most were sentenced to death and the rest were sentenced to transportation to the Far East colonies. It was said that Denis Browne insisted on having at least one man hanged every day in Castlebar for several weeks stretching into late October – earning himself the title of 'Denis of the Rope' among the local population. He planned to continue this policy of 'White Terror' into the winter of 1798 and fumed at the delay in finding some of the rebels who had gone into hiding in the remote mountains of Connemara.

All the while, John sat in a filthy prison cell in Castlebar, his window view being that of the gallows.

• • •

Extract from the diaries of Catherine de Kilkelly, Moore Hall, County Mayo

I cannot bear to look at myself in the mirror – I know I have aged terribly during this ordeal, just as George has – I can see it in him every day. At least he has the day-to-day needs of the estate to occupy him and that helps keep his mind busy. We are almost glad that we are not allowed to visit John as I am sure I could not cope with seeing him in such conditions, but I worry every day about his health. Luckily the other boys are away from here – Thomas and Young George studying in London and Peter, God Bless him is safe and cared for in Galway. I cannot imagine what kind of Christmas we will have, and I don't want to think about it. Attorney McDonnell's legal charges continue to mount while we seem to be making no progress. George met with Denis Browne last Sunday – God forgive me but I despise that man. If that Devil is the only one who can help us, then we must deal with the Devil. George recounted details of his difficult meeting with him, and the 'bargain' they made. Mayo is in a continued frenzy of revenge and killings and Denis Browne is the main hangman. Nobody is safe and John is in mortal danger from that man. I dread the long winter nights that are almost upon us – I cannot eat or sleep or read without thinking of John.

We wait and we wait, and we wait _____

• • •

Initially, George had wanted a speedy trial for John, but he was persuaded by attorney McDonnell to wait for the 'revenge fever' to subside. Their court pleadings had been filed without any response and their letter to Lord Cornwallis had not been answered. George's face-to-face meeting with Denis Browne had gone about as well as he could have expected – now it was a waiting game and the stress that George endured every hour of every day was weighing him down; both he and Catherine had lost weight. Their time together used to be full of laughter but now they could only manage small talk as they poked at the food on their plates.

Then the news came – John had been moved to Athlone – with Denis Browne claiming credit for this move. They rejoiced so much they almost forgot that he was still in gaol, but anything was better than Castlebar. Attorney O'Donnell brought news that his attempt to free John under the writ of habeas corpus had been unsuccessful. However, it had been indicated to him that Lord Cornwallis was concerned over the continued high number of weekly hangings and the added deaths of many more peasants by marauding loyalist militias in the name of pacifying the County. He was beginning to rein in Denis Browne and openly chastised him, saying that killing every peasant in Mayo was a self-defeatist policy – the landlords would have no tenants to pay rents. He espoused a new policy of 'lenity' towards individuals that had only minor roles in the rebellion, many of whom were goaded into helping the French.

Next came word of a trial date for John in Athlone. Attorney O'Donnell and his assistant marshalled their defense to take advantage of the jurisdiction struggle between civil and military authorities, a strategy so successful that the trial was aborted after just hours of proceedings. Shortly after that John was moved again, this time to Dublin and he remained there through the winter and into the New Year of 1799. At least this situation allowed the Moore family to have some semblance of Christmas when the other three boys came home to Moore Hall. Young George managed to get a short visit with John at the gaol in Dublin and was allowed to bring him some personal hygiene items and some books. This visit not only cheered up John – it brought some measure of relief to his grieving parents.

George later confided to a friend that he lied to his parents about John's condition because he didn't want to upset them ahead of Christmas – John was very emaciated, depressed and suffered from both respiratory and stomach ailments. During their meeting at the gaol John told George of the Dublin meeting with his father a year earlier, when father had threatened to overstep him and make young George the heir to Moore Hall. He urged him to have his father go ahead and do this – he didn't want his father's worst succession fears to happen. At best, he himself would be exiled in the Far East colonies for most of his life and he wanted his brother to prepare for taking control of the estate so that he could make it the success his father wanted. The brothers hugged and cried when time was called on their meeting. On his way back to England George had tried to visit John again but was told at the prison entrance that due to a disturbance no visitors were allowed – they would only let him leave a written message for John via the guard office. The following spring Denis Browne took credit for presenting a memorial for John's pardon to Viceroy Cornwallis – at first it seemed like it was going to be successful but later it was denied without an explanation.

During the summer of 1799 the plans to abolish the parliament of Ireland and merge with the London parliament gathered momentum. Denis Browne had no qualms about visiting George at Moore Hall to remind him of his promise of support for the 'Union' – Catherine refused to meet him. George duly reminded Denis of his own promise to work for John's freedom – he was unapologetic in his answer.

"Sur haven't I been working on that quietly behind the scenes and it was me who got him moved from Castlebar in the first place."

"I am grateful for that move, but the fact remains that he is still imprisoned – Athlone and Dublin are only a step up from Castlebar. Good God man – can't you see that his continued imprisonment is killing him slowly and torturing his mother and myself at the same time. I'll say publicly whatever you want me to say about your bloody act of union even though I care nothing about it, and I will help you to get elected. You must find a way to get John out of gaol before another winter sets in."

"This has been a very delicate situation where I have had to work around diehards who want the President of Connaught made an example of. Privately I have been given a pledge from the highest authority that John and some other selected prisoners will very soon be offered a plea arrangement whereby they will accept transportation to the colonies. Do you think John will accept that?"

"He is getting so weak that he is almost beyond caring – I will see to it that this arrangement is accepted. Make it happen Denis, and soon, before it breaks John and breaks me."

"I know you have spent a lot of money on his defense, and I commend you for your efforts."

"Unlike you Denis, money is of no importance to me. That boy has suffered enough, so has his mother and so have I."

The summer dragged on with no sign of an official plea agreement for John being put on the table. The stress on George and Catherine's health increased – even more so on John, from the limited information they had access to. Then in mid-September, John was sent back to Castlebar gaol, which added insult to injury. Denis Browne sent a message that he had to do it this way in order to move things toward a positive outcome. It was mid-October when the transportation offer came through – John Moore, two priests named Cannon and Molloney, a farmer named Jordan and an innkeeper named Fergus were listed together in the plea. Attorney O'Donnell completed all the paperwork requirements immediately and they were told to wait, again. George was now seventy years old, a tired man, feeling and looking old for his age. Just a week later his own health failed him, and he became blind in his sleep. The doctors struggled to diagnose the cause, advised complete rest and said they were confident that his sight would return.

Catherine nursed him and comforted him – she knew his breakdown was brought on by the stress of the past year. She now became the contact person for attorney O'Donnell as he continued to push the authorities to complete the plea deal. At the beginning of November John and the other prisoners of the group were moved out of Castlebar, supposedly to Waterford in preparation for transportation abroad. Catherine told George the good news that evening after his nurse bathed his eyes.

"My dear, I have been thinking a lot while trapped in this dark world. I remember how opposed you were to my plans to leave our life in sunny Spain and return to Ireland. You didn't want to move, I knew that, but you did your duty and came to live at Moore Hall. You were right, I know that now, and I apologize for not listening to you."

"You built us a wonderful house on a beautiful lake – the kids loved it from the start and over time I have grown to love it also. You have nothing to regret, my dear."

"Oh yes, I have. I allowed my romantic memories of Ireland to cloud my better judgement. Ireland had not changed enough to merit my faith in her, it has continued to be a festering mess and this rebellion that ensnared John is proof of that fact. We have managed to save his life, but at what cost – he will be confined to exile for the rest of his life, and I blame myself. Dearest Catherine, forgive me for bringing this tragedy upon you and our family. Please ask for John's forgiveness for me when you write to him in exile, and ask the same from George, Thomas and Peter – poor Peter, locked in his own world. I would gladly give my life to undo the wrongs that I have wrought upon you all. May God forgive me for these sins." He sobbed uncontrollably as Catherine tried to comfort him.

"You will recover from this and regain your eyesight – the doctors have promised me."

"Alas, the doctors don't understand the underlying problem – my heart is broken."

"You must rest now my dear – getting upset like this is no good for you. Tomorrow is a new day, and we will face the road together, renew our faith in God and ask His help. Good night my dearest."

That same night George Moore the First, the merchant of Alicante, suffered a paralytic stroke and was in very poor condition when Catherine saw him next morning. While she waited for the doctor, she sent off a letter to Young George in London telling him to collect Thomas and come home.

• • •

Meanwhile, the cavalry guards and their group of prisoners from Castlebar approached the city of Waterford. The nearby abandoned Swiss settlement of New Geneva had been taken over by the government and repurposed as a barracks to process prisoners who were being shipped into exile in the far-off colonies. Near Waterford the prisoners were allowed to lodge at a tavern called the Royal Oak, because of John's weakened condition. He had to be carried into the tavern and he was permitted to remain there the next day to be treated by local doctors, while the rest of the party continued to New Geneva.

CHAPTER FOURTEEN

Extract from the diaries of Catherine de Kilkelly, Moore Hall, County Mayo

George is deathly ill, and my heart is broken. The story of the Druids Curse on Muckloon Hill seems even more real to me now.

I saw George last night in my dream – we were in Spain, and we were so happy. Now, in the cold light of morning I wish I could get back into my dream. George could do no wrong in Spain – everything he touched turned to gold – he had vineyards, and his ships were busy carrying wine and brandy to Ireland, returning with sea kelp for the iodine factories. Our children were born in Alicante and grew up happy, far away from this war-torn land of Ireland. I tried so hard to convince him to stay in warm sunny Spain – how did I fail, could I have done more? I freely admit that I had not possessed any great desire to return to Ireland, unlike George who had that flame burning deep in his heart. Just as he promised, he built us a beautiful house overlooking Lough Carra – a lake shrouded in mist and rain for most of the year – unlike Lake Albufera, which was near us in Spain and was always bathed in sunshine. George later transported us to Ireland on one of his ships, and we started our new life. He seemed happy here and so were our boys – and I came to accept it as home. The terrible poverty of the Irish peasants has always upset me, and even though we are landed gentry and are at the top of society, I have never felt comfortable. I have put up with it for the sake of our family.

It is hardly five years now since the house was finished and we moved to Mayo, lock, stock and barrel. George has got only five years as a retired country gentleman – that is a cruel reward for a man who worked so hard for so many years to earn that position – why God, why?

Young Peter's condition did not improve as we had hoped, and reluctantly we had to move him into a care home. Young George settled into law studies in London and has become the darling of high society there – I am so proud of him. Thomas is a sweet and clever boy and is doing well at his London college – he will be a fine young man.

John was an impressionable and wayward boy from the moment he left Spain, as a youngster for schooling in France. His personality is totally unsuited for a country like Ireland – a divided and depraved land simmering with the constant threat of rebellion. If only we could have fast-forwarded his maturity levels. Everywhere he went he fell in with the wrong company and his father loved him too much to punish him – and then, suddenly it was too late. Why did the French pick Mayo to land their expedition – of all the Godforsaken places in this wretched country, they had to put themselves in front of our John, our wandering lost soul.

As soon as Humbert heard John speak French, he filled his head with big ideas of the soon-to-be Irish Republic – something the British government would never allow. John was always in awe of fancy titles and was enthralled with being appointed 'President of the Province of Connaught'. The mobs were ecstatic after their Castlebar victory and in the heat of the moment there was no voice of reason there to dissuade him from accepting this fleeting and foolish title. Then Humbert marched out of town with all his best soldiers, seeking his next glory, while leaving John with just a handful of French soldiers and some rebels to hold the town. If only the boy had taken the advice from my letter that I know he read – if he had come home to Moore Hall before the British returned to Castlebar, he would have been safe, and George would not be an invalid.

What a cruel, cruel hand has been dealt to us by fate.

• • •

It had been back in the summer that young George received a letter from his father, telling him the news of a government plea offer that would get his brother John out of gaol – the bad part was that it meant he would be exiled to the far-away penal colonies. It was a shock, but he understood and accepted that it was the best that could be expected, and he knew that it was the only way to save John's life – he hoped it would happen quickly before John's health deteriorated further. When a letter came from his mother in early November, he was a little surprised and assumed his father was just too busy. It contained the sad news of his father's sudden blindness, another great shock for the young man. His mother told him to stay in London for the moment – she said that the doctors were doing everything they could for his father, and she wanted him to continue to cultivate contacts in high society who may be able to help the family effort to get his brother John moved from Castlebar gaol.

Then the letter came telling him of his father's stroke, and she asked him to collect Thomas and come home immediately. Thomas was even more shocked, having been unaware of his father's recent health issues and of his blindness. George comforted his brother as best he could as they made their way to Dublin on the ferry boat and caught the first coach to Mayo. Their mother was distraught and wept uncontrollably when the boys arrived. In due course, she was able to gather herself and tell him the details.

"The doctors said he was making great progress in regaining his sight. As you know, attorney O'Donnell had been working to finalize the plea bargain that was to get John moved to Waterford ahead of his transportation overseas. We received word that the six prisoners, including John, had indeed departed Castlebar for the New Geneva barracks. This was good news in that he was finally out of Castlebar gaol, and I told your father the details as his nurse was bathing his eyes before he retired for the night. He seemed pleased with this news, and I kissed him good night. Very early next morning I was awakened by a commotion outside my bedroom – to find the nurse in a panic over George having suffered what she called a 'strong weakness'. I went with her to his bedside. He was in obvious distress and unable to speak despite his lips moving – I immediately sent a rider to fetch the doctor, while we did what we could to comfort him. He never regained full consciousness and when the doctor arrived, his diagnosis was a paralytic stroke. Oh, George, as God is my witness, I think this has all been brought on by the stress of John's imprisonment – the thought of him being sent away for life to the far east colonies was just too much for his father to bear. Your father is such a good man; he deserved a long and happy retirement, he was so content here till this rebellion came down on us and John got sucked into it by the French; I cannot bear to see him like this – worra, worra, worra _____."

Catherine was overcome again by emotion and young George put his arms around her and led her to a chair, where he was able to get her to drink some water and gather herself.

"Mother, I don't think we should attempt to send news of Father's condition to John, wherever he might be – and there is nothing he can do. He cannot be here, and he needs to focus all his strength to get through his confinement at the barracks while he awaits a ship. Let us concentrate our efforts in comforting father and helping him to recover."

Catherine nodded – "Mary, his nurse, has organized a rotation among the servants so that someone is always present to attend to him and pray at his side. Thomas is going through a growth spurt and has gone to the kitchen for a snack; go find him and we will all go upstairs to visit your father."

Presently, Catherine and the two boys went up to the bedroom where George was being cared for. There were two servants present, praying a rosary in Irish – they stopped and left the room. Catherine held George's hand and told him that Thomas and Young George had returned from London to visit him and help him get well. His breathing was shallow and there was no indication that he was aware of their presence. Catherine asked the boys to speak to their father in turn, tell him how their studies were progressing and what else they were doing – each of them did this. Young George was the more eloquent of the pair. As he spoke, the realization hit him that Moore Hall may need a new master soon. John was the heir to the estate, and obviously absent and about to be transported overseas for a long time. If their father died, John would be the heir but could not take possession of the estate. His thoughts were interrupted when Catherine nudged him and began to lead them in prayers.

Later in the day the doctor came again. After attending to the patient, he spoke quietly to Catherine – George's heart was getting weaker, and he feared that he had very little time left. She shared this with the boys after the doctor left, and before Father Conolly was due to arrive. They decided that one of the three of them should always be in the room with George, in addition to the rotation of attending servants that was already in place. Father Connolly arrived later and after talking with Catherine he administered the Last Rites to George. Then began a long and sad night, which ended at six o'clock in the morning when George Moore, Merchant of Alicante, builder of the magnificent Moore Hall and creator of one of the largest landed estates in Ireland – died – during the watch of young George. He asked the house maid not to disturb his mother and brother, who were sleeping, but to send for the doctor and the priest at first light. Catherine was told at nine when she was getting ready for her shift, and Thomas a little later when he heard the commotion. The curtains remained drawn, and the family and servants grieved and prayed together until the doctor arrived. He confirmed the death of George Moore, offered his condolences to the family and said he would take care of the death certificate paperwork. Catherine fretted over this, and the impending visit from Father Connolly, till young George assured her that he would be there to comfort her and help her with the funeral arrangements.

The Irish custom during a 'Wake' was to never leave the dead person alone while laid out at the home and to pray beside the body of the dead person. The nurse washed the body and prepared it for the Wake, and two hours later George

Moore the First lay dressed in his finest suit, with a set of rosary beads entwined in his hands. James O'Donnell had taken the initiative to send a wagon to town in order to pick up a coffin. By late afternoon George's body was lifted into the coffin, and the coffin was placed in the parlor just off the main entrance hall – convenient to the front door. Father Conolly arrived to do a blessing and discuss funeral arrangements – a thin pale man who regularly recited the Mass at the local church that George and Catherine attended. He sympathized with Catherine and the two boys and then, as Thomas went off to the forge to relay a message to get all their carriages in good working order, he opened funeral discussions with Catherine and young George.

"I assume you will want the Requiem Mass to be held here at our church in Carnacon, presided over by Father Moran, the parish priest – I would expect several other priests to come and concelebrate along with myself. What were Mr. Moore's wishes for a burial?"

Catherine answered, "George expressed the desire to be buried at Ashbrook beside his ancestors, but we did not get into the thorny details – the family was Protestant back then and were buried in the local Protestant cemetery. After that, the family became Catholic when George's father, John, married Jane Lynch and we have continued being Catholics since. I want to bury him near Ashbrook, but it must be in a Catholic cemetery; can you do that for us, Father?"

"I had expected this difficulty and have already spoken to

Father Moran about it. There is a ruined Catholic Abbey site nearby at Straide, which has a cemetery that is consecrated ground – we suggest that he is buried there."

"Thank you, Father, we will have the Mass locally as you suggested, and graciously accept your offer for burial at Straide. What timetable have you got in mind?"

"I assume you will hold a Wake here tonight. Tomorrow the coffin will be removed to the church, and we will celebrate Mass at ten o'clock the day after that, with burial the following afternoon to give time for everyone to get over to Straide."

"Thank you, Father."

The priest had barely departed when visitors began to trickle in. The word of George's death spread quickly throughout the estate, and such was the respect for him among his tenants that they came in droves throughout the night. James had expected this outpouring of sympathy and had a large outside fire burning, surrounded by wooden benches, where he organized to have generous amounts of whiskey and brandy for the mourners – everybody was anxious to drink a toast to their departed landlord. Two women who were full-time 'Keeners' arrived early and took turns 'Keening' – loud wailing for the departed soul, beating their breasts, tearing at their hair and dramatically waiving their hands up to the sky, to signify the soul of George Moore going to heaven. Mourners arrived at the benches, were given a drink and tobacco, then joined a steady solemn procession through the house, to view George in the open coffin and offer sympathy to the family. It was a shock to Thomas and young George to see so many of their father's 'Unwashed Masses' coming to pay their respects, and especially the Keeners in full cry – all dressed in what the boys would call rags but were obviously the best rags these people had. After viewing the body, the procession of mourners stopped again at the outside benches to have a drink for the road.

In the morning there was still a trickle of tenants, plus shop keepers from the local villages who were suppliers to the estate. By afternoon local gentry from nearby estates began to visit. One of them was Mr. Russell, who had had the testy exchange with George some time earlier. Catherine was courteous but did not encourage him to linger; after he departed, she told young George about his father's distain for the man. Doctor Lewis, the loyalist who had saved John from summary judgement, came all the way from Castlebar; Catherine received him graciously and later told the boys the details of the protection he provided to John after his arrest, and his previous visit to inform them of the arrest.

Late in the afternoon the coffin was closed, amid more loud 'Keening', prior to it being transported to the local church where a short ceremony took place. The Mass next day was a sad affair, well attended by locals from both the peasant class and the gentry. Mayo High Sheriff Denis Browne showed up, and Catherine managed to be civil, for the family's sake, despite her revulsion for him. Denis then spoke privately to young George when Catherine walked away to speak to other mourners.

"George, I want you to know that I have worked very hard on your brother John's case over the past year. His position as 'President of Connaught', though short lived, brought about enormous pressure for revenge from the loyalist diehards, and from the military leaders who lost a substantial number of soldiers against the French – Irish rebel army in Castlebar. I had to tread very carefully to finally achieve the plea bargain – to save John's life in return for transportation to the colonies."

"Mr. Browne, this is our first meeting and it is occurring in difficult circumstances. I have heard much about you, and I will tell you frankly Sir, that those stories do not portray you as a popular individual. However, I will reserve my judgement for now, until I see how John's case proceeds. John's long incarceration has taken a tremendous toll on his health, and it surely has been a factor in the untimely death of my dear father. I trust that you are doing all that you can to make John's transportation overseas as speedy and as comfortable as possible."

"I have never sought popularity and I will not take issue with your statement at this difficult time for you, while I assure you of my intention to get John moved through the justice system as quickly as possible. Your father had promised to help me in my upcoming election for the position of Mayo MP to the London Parliament, in return for my assistance in getting a plea bargain for John. I would hope that you would stand in for him in that promise."

"My father is dead, and his promises died with him."

"It is not as simple as that in Ireland, but we can talk about it at another time. I believe you are acquainted with my niece, Miss Louisa Browne, whom you have met a few times in London. She has spoken highly of you."

"That is very kind of her. I must take your leave now as my mother needs my attention. Good day to you Mr. Browne."

• • •

They buried George Moore, The Merchant of Alicante, the next day – it was a private burial attended by family members. Obviously, John was absent, Peter had to be supervised by a nurse, and Thomas was just a young lad overwhelmed by the loss of his father. That put all the pressure on Young George – he needed to be a rock for his mother, who was overcome with grief.

The next few days were difficult for everybody. Peter was returned to the care home while George comforted his mother and younger brother. The weather turned wintry, and it was made worse by darkness setting in by mid-afternoon. Catherine wanted to get Thomas back to school so he could prepare for his end-of-year exams. That forced Young George to leave also since he needed to accompany Thomas on his journey, though he was reluctant to leave his mother alone at such a time. She insisted that she would be fine and would busy herself running the place, with the help of James O'Donnell, their estate manager. Back in England, young George met with Mr. Smith, the principal at Thomas's school, who promised that Thomas would be given favorable treatment during such a difficult time – then he continued to London. On the journey he mulled over the family conundrum – John, as the heir should become the Master of the estate now, but due to his forced exile overseas, he would not be able to fulfill that role. George had no idea what process should happen in this complicated situation but decided not to broach the subject with his mother at this time.

• • •

In Waterford, John Moore had been allowed to remain at the Royal Oak tavern for several weeks while doctors treated him for what they called an obstinate disorder of his stomach. His condition showed little improvement despite this care, and Denis Browne was in panic mode in Mayo – he wanted the 'President of Connaught' exiled far away from Ireland and this delay did not fit well with his plans to put this entire episode behind him. He didn't much care whether John lived or died, he just didn't want him to die before he got him shipped out of the country – let him die on the voyage and be buried at sea, he said to one of the administrators in charge of prisoner exile. He decided to send one of his agents from Mayo to Waterford, to check on John's condition, with explicit instructions to do whatever was necessary to get him aboard a ship as soon as possible. Denis forgot to tell the man to keep news of the death of his father a secret from John. Later, in the course of his evaluation of the prisoner, the agent inadvertently told John that his father had suffered a stroke and died. This news had a profound effect on John, and despite his weakened condition he questioned the man to verify that the news was correct – to the point of extracting details from him of George Moore's burial.

Next morning, December 6th, John Moore was found dead in his bed at the tavern. The attending doctor said he had succumbed to his illness; he was thirty-two years old. The tavern owner wanted Denis's agent to take possession of the body. He refused, and after consultations it was decided that the money draft of one hundred pounds in John's possession, and other items of value that he had on his person were to be given to the tavern owner for his services to date – in return for his agreement to have John Moore buried quietly and quickly in a local cemetery. That was done the next day, and nothing more than a simple stone marker was placed on the grave. The agent then journeyed to New Geneva to rendezvous with a merchant ship from Liverpool that was stopping in route to Van Dieman's Land, to collect three prisoners bound for exile there. He met privately with the captain of the ship, 'The North Star,' and after their encounter he left with a copy of the ship's manifesto listing four prisoners – the name of John Moore having been added to the list.

Nobody in authority notified the Moore family of John's death.

CHAPTER FIFTEEN

Young George Moore was happy to be back in London and to renew acquaintances with his circle of friends ahead of the fast-approaching Christmas season. These high society people knew of his father's death and expressed sympathy, but they did not know about John's predicament and George decided it was unwise to broach a subject like that with such people. He attended several social events as he tried to overcome the sadness he felt over the death of his father and of John's banishment. It was a struggle to keep up appearances while holding all this grief bottled up inside. At one of those events, he met again with Louisa Browne of Mayo – niece of Denis Browne, Mayo High Sherrif and niece of his very influential brother, Lord Altamont – a pretty girl, slender, with long dark hair and a pale complexion. She offered her condolences on the death of his father and asked about John.

"Miss Browne, you must not speak a word to any of these people of John or his current status, please."

"They will not hear any such news from me, I assure you. These people around us now are privileged and know little of Ireland, and nothing of Mayo. They tolerate us because we have money and titles. Frankly, I am getting bored with this entire London charade and am thinking of relocating back to Ireland – to Dublin or maybe even to Mayo."

"Forgive me for asking, but I was under the impression that you were on the verge of getting married to the son of Lord Dunmore."

"Thank you for putting it so delicately. I know that you have been busy with your writings, and I congratulate you on your recent publication – you have also been in Ireland and missed the gossip story of his betrayal. I must confess that my decision to leave London is influenced by these events; other than that, I have nothing to say on the subject. What is your next writing project?"

"I have always been fascinated by the English revolution, and by French history – currently I am doing research in preparation for books on those subjects."

"I prefer poetry and romance novels; I don't profess to be clever enough for history. If I remember correctly, you speak French fluently – it must be so nice to speak other languages."

"I was born in Spain and was educated in France, so I was lucky to have the opportunity to learn those languages as a child. What will you do in Ireland, in Mayo?"

"At this stage I don't honestly know but Lord Altamont has kindly invited me to Westport House and says he has a project in mind for me – I never get tired of its majestic location overlooking the islands of Clew Bay; it is my ideal therapy. I need to leave London and will use the time in Mayo to regroup – maybe I will join the nuns – I was educated by them."

"I did not know that. I assumed you were of the same persuasion as your uncles, Lord Altamont and Denis Browne. Surely you jest about joining the nuns."

"Yes, but I am indeed a product of convent education. It is a complicated story, for another time perhaps, but yes indeed I am a Catholic like yourself, and I will be at St. Anne's for 9 o'clock Mass tomorrow as usual."

"I know that church and often attend there myself."

They parted and made their rounds among other guests. A week later he saw her as he attended Mass and made it his business to speak to her afterwards at the rectory. During the conversation he mentioned that he was about to return to Ireland for Christmas, by way of Thomas's school to collect his brother. "I promised my mother that we would be home in good time, being that it is only a month since we lost my father, and she is still in deep mourning. What are your plans for Christmas?"

"I am packed and ready to go to Westport but have been delaying, waiting for a companion as I don't wish to take on the journey on my own. Would you mind if I was to invite myself along with you and Thomas?"

"Not at all, provided you know that we have to collect Thomas on route."

She was fine with that, and they coordinated their travel plans over tea at the rectory. They met as arranged at Kings Cross Station several days later and continued to get to know each other as the train steamed out of London. It was mostly polite conversation until she asked him a direct question.

"George, who takes control of Moore Hall now, being that John cannot do so, despite being the heir?"

"Frankly I do not know, and I don't want to think about it. My mother is a very capable lady, and James, their estate manager has been with them many years – he can shoulder the everyday stuff, dealing with tenant issues and such."

"I am pleased that you are an open-minded man who sees nothing wrong with a woman taking charge of an estate. It is past time for the old rules to be changed and for the place of women in society to be upgraded to parity with men."

"Those are indeed strong sentiments that you express. Is there a movement afoot to press for changes like this to occur – if so then I have not heard of such a thing?"

"No, those opinions are my own. What are your plans for Christmas?"

"I have none, other than to comfort my mother and help her through this very trying time for the family. Thomas and I will do some riding and some shooting, weather permitting."

"Perhaps you may find time to visit me in Westport, I would like that."

"Perhaps."

Thomas was waiting at the station with other students, accompanied by a teacher from the school. He was surprised to find that they were sharing a carriage with Miss Louisa Browne but was polite about it. The Browne family name was well known to him, but he had not met Louisa or any of them personally. She engaged him in conversation, – "What year of school are you in?"

"Miss, this is my final year, I will complete my final exams next summer."

"What are your plans then?"

"To move to university in Dublin and study law, just like my older brother George – except, I'm cleverer than he is," he added with a wink.

"I heard that," George interrupted, "you probably are cleverer, but you don't need to say that in polite company – you're making me look bad."

They all laughed at that, then George moved the conversation on to other subjects. They ate a meal at a hotel in Anglesea while they waited for the ship ferry – it was better than mixing with the crowds near the quay. On arrival in Dublin, they stayed overnight at another hotel at Louisa's request, before boarding the coach after breakfast the next morning for their journey west – she wanted to complete the coach ride in daylight hours. It was a dreary damp trip but uneventful, and they kept upbeat by playing games and talking about the countryside they passed. The boys got off in Ballintubber and said their goodbyes, while Louisa continued to Westport with two other passengers. George reminded Thomas not to mention to his mother that they had made the trip with Louisa Browne, for obvious reasons.

Catherine was delighted to see them and to fuss over them. The house was all lit up, warm and inviting and the boys were greeted by the staff. It was like other previous Christmas's, but with two empty seats this time – those of George and John. Young George complimented his mother on how well she looked but privately he noticed that she looked tired – his guess was that she had not been sleeping. At supper that night she picked at her food while the boys ate heartily. It was after dinner before the first mention of the obvious missing guests by Catherine.

"I visited your father's grave last week. The setting at Straide Abbey is very peaceful, I think George would be pleased with the choice."

"I felt a true peace there myself when we had the service. Thomas and I will visit him in the next few days – right, Thomas?"

"Yes indeed."

"Your college report is very encouraging, Thomas," Catherine said to him, "How did the exams go?"

"Very well Mother. The principal allowed me extra study time and gave me some work sheets that really helped me to concentrate on the important subjects. Mother, has there been any word from John since I went back to school?"

"Yes and no, my dear. He was moved to Waterford and was allowed to rest there under doctor's care to build up his strength before boarding the ship. I assume he is now under voyage, but I have not had confirmation of that – the authorities are so inefficient and slow at sending out communications."

Young George added, – "I will make inquiries this week. How is everything with the estate?"

"Good. We are lucky to have James O'Donnell, he knows the ways of the tenants and can coax them to honor their rent commitments before it gets to a problem stage. We have the least evictions of any estate in Connaught."

Next day George rode into Castlebar and went to the office of the High Sheriff. Denis Browne was away in another county, so he spoke to an assistant who could only promise to have someone get back to him about his inquiry. He then went to Attorney O'Donnell's office and met with Alexander, the cousin of James, their estate manager, who had been engaged by his father to defend John. Alexander said that he had been assured verbally that John had been put aboard a merchant ship at New Geneva, bound for the colony of Van Dieman's Land. He had been waiting for written confirmation before getting back to Mrs. Moore and said that Denis Browne had been evading his attempts to meet him and seemed to be staying away from Castlebar. Christmas was almost upon them, and George thought that it was best to assure his mother that all had gone to plan, in order to have some semblance of a family Christmas. He told her that the administration office in Castlebar had confirmed to him that John had boarded a ship bound for the Far East colonies. This news got them through the Feast days of Christmas and lifted the cloud that had been hanging over his mother.

George received an invitation from Lord Altamont to a New Year's Ball at Westport House, obviously orchestrated by Louisa. He decided to go despite his mother's disapproval when she reminded him that this man was the brother of Denis Browne. George was rather intrigued by Louisa, and he figured that Denis would be there and he fully intended to confront him about John's whereabouts – he didn't tell his mother of this so as not to inflame her.

The Ball was an extravagant affair attended by about one hundred guests. Louisa rushed up to him saying how delighted she was that he had come. She was dressed in London finery, somewhat more risqué than what was usual for Mayo ladies. He was introduced to Lord Altamont and most of the aristocratic gentry of the area, some of whom had visited Moore Hall and met his father, but most were people that he had only heard of by name and had never met. There were several other young ladies there who could be described as eligible, and they were suitably impressed by this dashing young man with London manners and local credentials. Louisa always hovered near him and made sure he did not spend too much time with any of these potential suitors.

It was late in the evening when the opportunity to corner Denis Browne presented itself.

"Mr. Browne, I went to Castlebar before Christmas hoping to find you at your office there. Failing that, I spoke to one of your administrators about my brother John, but they were unable to give me information. I made up a pleasant story for my mother to carry her through Christmas, but now I need to know the real situation. What has happened since John was moved to Waterford?"

"It's great to see you again, young man. Thank you for escorting Louisa from London to Mayo ahead of the holidays. I hope you are having an enjoyable evening. Now, what information can I help you with?"

"We have heard nothing since John was moved to Waterford. Please bring me up to date on his situation since then."

"As you know, your mother has no desire to welcome me, hence I did not visit Moore Hall in person. I did instruct my administrator to inform her that John did indeed board a vessel at New Geneva, destined for the colonies and should be settled there very soon. I apologize if they did not follow my instructions – I will investigate. Take it from me, John did board the ship after an improvement in his condition."

"Where exactly was his destination?"

"He was bound for His Majesty's colony at Van Diemen's Land. Do you remember our last conversation? The coming year will see the Kingdoms of Britain and Ireland joining together in a Union that will be a major benefit to Ireland. I hope and expect to be elected as one of the MPs for County Mayo, sitting at the London parliament. Your father promised me his support in that quest, and I fervently hope that you will honor that commitment on his behalf."

"We shall talk about it some more when you come back to me with confirmation of John's arrival and settlement in the colony."

They were both spared further embarrassing moments by a call-out for gentlemen to proceed to the dance floor. They duly obliged and went their separate ways. George danced with several ladies before Louisa was able to collar him as they danced together briefly in part of a dance sequence.

"George, are you having a good time?"

"Yes indeed, I am so glad Lord Altamont invited me."

"I made sure of that. It was a bit chaotic when you arrived – I took the liberty of having your overnight bags moved to one of the cottages. It is the third cottage of the row on the right of the house, the one with the green door. My cottage is next to it, the one with the red door. I'm telling you in case you get inebriated later in the evening – I am saving some dances for you later. Bye for now."

As the evening wore on, George had some spirited discussions with other gentlemen present – John Blake, whose family had sold a substantial amount of land to his father, and Richard Lynch who was a distant relative of his grandmother Jane Lynch. They made no mention of the recent rebellion or of his brother John, but in their conversations, they seemed to be assuming that young George was soon to be master of Moore Hall. They were aware of his literary pursuits and his reputation as a person of high intellectual ability and alluded to their desire to have someone in their midst that could write detailed proposals to government in order to improve Ireland's trade situation, and especially Connaught's trade grievances with Britain. George let it all wash over him and used the occasion to gain insight into local politics. They didn't mention Denis Browne by name, but from their tone it was obvious that to prosper in Mayo it was necessary to be in his good graces.

He enjoyed several glasses of punch during these conversations and by the time Louisa came to get her dances he was feeling quite merry. They danced for almost an hour till she complained of sore feet, and she led him back to the punch bowl. The crowd had thinned out considerably by then, and in due course the pair of them made their way to the cottage with the green door. George was not much of a drinker and was slurring his words at this stage. Louisa offered to help him get settled and got his bed ready while he changed into his pajamas and night robe in the adjoining room. He had to lay on the bed to steady himself and began to feel faint. As he dozed, he had the feeling of being stripped down to his underwear and being kissed on his face and neck, as her body straddled him, and the smell of her perfume filled his nostrils. His underwear was removed, and she was working her way down from his chest — all the way down to his privates. It was heavenly as she worked over him with her mouth and her tongue. He awoke for a moment as she mounted him, and he saw her breasts dangling in front of him like delicious forbidden fruit. She stroked his face and whispered in his ear, telling him to relax and enjoy, enjoy, enjoy — as he drifted into slumber. Sometime later he awoke momentarily in the dark, realized he was in bed, naked under the covers, and that he was not alone. Louisa was asleep beside him with her bare arm stretched across his chest. He was too tired and too cozy to worry about it and went back to sleep. When he awoke in the light of morning, he was alone.

As he finished dressing there was a knock on his door, which turned out to be Louisa.

"Hope you are ready for breakfast — we are due at Lord Altamont's table in half an hour. What a great party that was — I had a wonderful evening, thank you, I had no idea you were such a good dancer, Mr. George."

"I am sorry, but I don't remember much of last night — I think I overindulged at the punch bowl."

"You did get a little tipsy at the end, but I was able to get you tucked up in your bed. Did you sleep well?"

"Eh, yes, thank you."

"Good. Then let us proceed to meet Lord Altamont."

No more was said about the previous night's intimacy. Lord Altamont was very gracious with his time — he was obviously very fond of Louisa and seemed to take a liking to George. They talked about London, the Holland House circle and some of the characters that were connected to it. Lord Altamont made a point of telling George that Louisa was a very good organizer and was especially good at calculating budgetary numbers. He boasted that she was already making a study of the financial operations of his Mayo estate with the objective of improving its profitability and cutting expenses.

"She is whipping the accounts of this estate into shape and has already figured out where we are doing badly, and how to correct it. I had no idea that she possessed such a gift – and look at her; such a pretty girl to add to her talents." This last comment was said loud enough for Louisa to hear it.

She blushed and returned the compliment, – "Thank you My Lord, my number one fan."

No mention was made of his brother Denis, and he was nowhere to be seen – Louisa said he had departed Westport early that morning.

George was nursing a bad head that seemed to take a turn for the worst as breakfast progressed. He braved it out and kept up lively conversation with Lord A and other guests, with the help of several glasses of water. He took his leave an hour later and set off home.

CHAPTER SIXTEEN

Catherine was busy on the estate when George returned from Westport, and she didn't ask him anything about his trip when they ate dinner that evening. He spent the next few days helping his mother with estate accounts and with collecting important documents from his father's desk – putting them into one large file. She also asked him to clear out personal belongings from John's room, saying that she didn't have the heart to do it. He spent time at the lake with Peter and Thomas before Peter had to return to the care home. Thomas was due back to school in a week, so their time was beginning to run short. Eventually Catherine did bring up the subject of John again.

"I want to know that he is safe and well in his new place. I want an address there so that I can write letters to him. It seems that the only person that can supply us with that information is Denis Browne, a man I detest. George, before you leave for London can you please try to find out this information for me – I will be happy once I have that."

Ironically, the very next day a messenger came with a letter from the High Sheriff, asking George to meet him at his Castlebar office on the following morning at ten o'clock – he sent the messenger back with an affirmative answer.

He was waiting at the office next morning promptly at ten and was made to wait another twenty minutes before being called in. Denis was pacing the floor when George entered the room.

"Good morning young man. That was quite a party that Altamont put on for us all last week, eh. You were having a good time when I saw you on the dance floor – Louisa tells me you are quite a dancer."

"It was a very pleasant evening indeed. You summoned me here Mr. Browne – I assume you have details for me with reference to John's destination. My mother desperately wants to know that he is well and wants an address at the colony so she can write to him – surely that is possible."

"Please call me Denis. Here, please sit while I get out the file."

Denis shuffled through a stack of papers at a corner table and then came back and sat at his desk facing the now-seated George.

"George, this is the most up to date information that I have, and sadly it is not good news. I secured permission for John to be treated by two doctors for his illness in Waterford and extended his stay at a tavern there for that purpose. His condition improved greatly and in early December he and three other prisoners boarded a merchant supply ship called The North Star at New Geneva. Five days into the voyage John became deathly ill, and despite the efforts of the ship's doctor he died a day later. He was buried at sea with full Christian rites. The ship's captain reported his death in Cape Town when they took on supplies for the remainder of the voyage. I am sorry."

George's head was spinning as he struggled to comprehend this information – asking Denis to repeat it.

"This cannot be. A little over a week ago in Westport you assured me that he was probably at the colony – now you tell me a totally different story. This news will devastate my mother. It was bad enough that John was being exiled, now he is dead, and his body has been thrown into the sea. There must be a mistake here."

"John was convicted prisoner and when a prisoner dies at sea that is the end of it – standard procedure is to strike the name off the list, nothing more happens – convicted prisoners' families have no special rights and are not informed of these happenings. We have made an exception here by giving you details, because of the closeness of the Moore and Browne families. He committed grave offences against the British government, offences that usually merit execution. I made great sacrifices to have his sentence changed from execution to exile. His health failed him; for that I am truly sorry – we allowed him to be treated by doctors in Athlone, in Dublin, and in Waterford. Many prisoners have made that same journey – sadly John was not able to survive it."

"He was bounced from gaol to gaol, trial to trial, for fifteen months while being kept in filthy conditions – that is why his health failed him. He should have been accorded the same treatment that General Humbert and his French officers received – he was a citizen of Spain, yet he was treated like a dog. Damn you Denis Browne, and your bloodthirsty revenge on my brother John."

With that, George stormed out of the office. He realized he had tears streaming down his face as he mounted his horse and rode away. After a few miles he reined in at a clearing. He was shaking all over, as a range of emotions flooded his brain. How was he going to break this news to his mother, and to Thomas? Twenty minutes passed before his restless horse made him realize that he needed to move. He set off again at a slow pace, wracking his brain for the right words to tell his mother, praying for John and for the whole family.

It was mid-afternoon when he passed through the main gates of Moore Hall. He circled around to the stables in hopes of finding Thomas before going to see his mother – the stable boys told him Thomas had said he would not be home till late afternoon, so he dismounted and after another long effort to compose himself he walked to the house.

Catherine was sitting in front of the fire in the parlor, obviously waiting for his return. She turned to greet him as he entered the room and immediately sensed that something was wrong.

"George, my son, you look deathly pale. Come and warm yourself by the fire. You have bad news; I can feel it."

"Mother, John did not survive the voyage to the Far East colony – he died at sea."

There was a long silence. Catherine turned away and stared into the flames of the wood fire, tears streaming down her cheeks. George sat beside her and cried with her, his arm around her shoulder, steadying her as her body convulsed. They sat there together for several minutes.

"Was it Denis Browne that told you about this? That devil. What else did he tell you?"

"He said they let John stay at a tavern in Waterford while being treated by local doctors for stomach ailments. Once his condition improved, he was put on board a ship with other prisoners for the journey to the colony. He became very ill after five days at sea, while on the first leg of the voyage to Cape Town, and the ship's doctor could not save him."

"Oh my God. Did they, I cannot say it, did they ____?"

"Yes. That is what they do. He said they gave him full Christian rites."

There was another long silence. Catherine was in a state of shock and grief, but she was also consumed with anger – against the British legal system that failed to grant John habeas corpus, and against General Humbert who convinced John to accept the post of President of Connaught, which turned out to be a death sentence. She blamed John himself for being too gullible, for getting lured into the Society of

United Irishmen, and for bringing such pain to his father that it surely caused his untimely death. She blamed herself for consenting to leave their happy life in Spain for the wilds of Mayo, and she blamed the Druids who placed their curse on Muckloon Hill.

"Please forgive me George but I have to say this – John deserves much blame for all the trouble he brought on himself and on our family. God forgive him, he was such an impressionable boy whose head was easily filled with nonsense by Wolfe Tone and others. He didn't deserve to die in his prime and to be dumped into the ocean to be _____ oh God, my John."

Thomas came in a short time later, and her grief returned in earnest as George recounted the sad news to him. The three of them were still in tears when Annie came in to announce dinner. George poured glasses of sherry for the three of them, and they comforted each other with stories from John's youth and his great horsemanship. Very little food was eaten.

The house was back in mourning the next day, once word of John's death spread among the servants. Catherine ordered a carriage once she saw it was a dry day and the three of them went to visit George's grave at Ashbrook, to tell him the news and to pray for father and son.

Thomas and George were due to leave in a matter of days and Catherine insisted that they keep with their plans – Thomas needed to finish his final school term and she didn't want any more disruptions to his schedule. The day before they were to leave, she called George to her private study.

"Son, you are now the rightful heir to Moore Hall and estate. This has come about so suddenly and in a way that none of us expected. I know you have a wonderful life in London and this situation puts you in a terrible dilemma. Please think carefully about what is best for you yourself and don't be rushed – in fact it is good that you are able to be away from here as you ponder your decision. James and I will continue to care for the estate. I will abide by whatever decision you make, and I will support your decision, whatever that is."

"Mother, I confess that I feel much more at home in London than here in Mayo, and I am not at all sure that I am cut out to assume the role of Master of a landed estate at this juncture of my life. So much has happened lately, I feel the weight of the world on my shoulders, and I do agree that I will be better able to collect my thoughts in London. Are you sure you will be alright; I hate to leave you alone again with your grief when Thomas and I leave."

"I am not alone, I have Peter – I will visit with him next week. It will help me a lot when I must explain to him what has happened, in a way that he will understand – and I have George to visit, and my priest. God is good and He will comfort me."

The boys left Mayo a few days later, George dropped Thomas at his school and had a private chat with the principal, telling him of his brother John's death, while leaving out the real details. Then he returned to London and to a form of normality that he was comfortable with. He could not think of a way to explain John's death to his pompous English friends, so he decided to say nothing about it. As far as they were concerned, he had simply returned from spending Christmas with his family in Ireland, and they began inviting him to the usual array of social events. About two weeks after his return, he received a letter from Louisa. She had heard about John's death and wrote to sympathize. She did ask about his plans for returning to Mayo – an obvious reference to the fact that she knew that he was now the heir to Moore Hall, and she assumed that he would be coming home to take up the position of master of the estate. George put her letter to one side and wrote to his mother instead, telling her that Thomas was safely back at school and that he himself was settled back in London. No mention was made about his impending decision on the future of the estate. Then he put all the Mayo issues to one side while he participated in London society and busied himself with research for his next literary works.

Extract from the diaries of Catherine de Kilkelly, Moore Hall, County Mayo

I am now a double widow, first I lost George and now I have lost John. In hindsight, we should have realized that John did not have the fortitude to resist the overtures of the United Irishmen – it was all a big adventure for him. George hoped against hope that the boy would straighten out his life and become a respected member of the Mayo aristocracy – I can see now that would never have happened, even if the French had not come to Mayo and whipped the peasant population into a frenzy, and John too. After their defeat in Longford, Humbert and his French soldiers were treated honorably, and will be sent back to France unharmed. Thousands of Irish have already been slaughtered in revenge for the British loss at Castlebar, and Denis Browne wants every Irish person hunted down who so much as waved to the passing rebel army during the rebellion. That devil is responsible for hanging so many of his countrymen already and his blood thirsty revenge will continue for a long time to come. John was born in Spain and should have received the same treatment as Humbert, but his citizenship claims were ignored.

Young George, at twenty-nine years of age, is now the rightful heir – that is the system – he is the new Master of Moore Hall. Will he decide to leave the great life he has made for himself in London to come here to Mayo, to manage thousands of acres of poor land dotted with mud huts full of poor ignorant peasants, who are but one bad harvest from eviction and destitution? I hope he decides to stay away from this cursed land, that he remains in London as an absentee landlord – at least he will be safe there from the Curse of the Druids.

Blessed God, watch over him and help him make the right decision.

• • •

Catherine, with the help of her manager James O'Donnell continued to run the estate throughout the winter – she kept herself so busy that she didn't have time to dwell on her grief. Mayo was rife with stories of revenge-fueled atrocities carried out by loyalist yeoman and vigilantes against the peasant population. The High Sheriff continued to oversee the hunting down of 'rebels', and his hangmen were so busy that he earned the title among the peasants of 'Denis of the Rope'. Ireland had become peaceful again, from a mix of exhaustion and fear. The rebellion had failed, thousands of Irish had either been slaughtered on the field of battle or died at the end of a rope, and thousands more were sent off into exile.

Catherine's constant letters kept George up to date with estate news and she made a point of never asking him about his plans, about his impending decision. George, despite all the attractions of London and the circle of friends he had there, was haunted by the recent family tragedies. His father and John were constantly in his dreams, where they displayed great love for Moore Hall, Lough Carra and Mayo. By early spring of the new year, a year that had also ushered in the new nineteenth century, he had come to his decision – he would return to Mayo and resurrect the family honor, he would proudly assume the title of 'Master of Moore Hall' – George Moore II. He sent a letter to his mother telling her of his decision and of his plans to be home for Easter.

His London friends were aghast when he told them he was relocating to Ireland. He did not get into details – he simply said he was moving his extensive library to Mayo where he would continue his literary writings while overseeing the family landed estate. Before Easter, he had packed up everything of consequence into numerous crates and engaged the services of a shipping company to ship his precious cargo to Moore Hall. George then boarded a train for Anglesea and caught the ferry boat to Dublin. Thomas stayed at school through the Easter break and through to his final exams in summer, so he did not have to collect him. While waiting on the ferry he wrote a short letter to Louisa, replying to her unanswered correspondence – telling her that he was on his way home to Mayo to take the reins of the family estate.

He was welcomed home by his mother, and all the servants lined the driveway as a mark of respect. Catherine brought Peter home for a few days and the three of them attended Easter Sunday Mass where Father Conolly made a point of welcoming home the new Master of Moore Hall and led the congregation in applause. That night after dinner Catherine made her first notable comments about his return.

"Son, this is going to be a very different life situation for you compared to London. I hope you can settle into this quiet corner of the world, and that you don't feel that you had to do it in order to rescue me. What did your London friends say when you told them you were leaving to return to Mayo?"

"Mother, you are very capable, and I didn't think for a moment that I was coming here to save you. I decided that our family is the most important component of our lives and that I needed to be here to do my part for our family in this trying time. I am going to need lots of help with the estate and I am profoundly thankful for your good counsel as we move forward. Yes, my London friends were surprised at my decision, and I dare to say that some were quite envious. They will have moved on to their next new friends by now, that is the way of the big city."

"You have now become the most eligible bachelor in Mayo and there will be girls fawning over you, from Galway to Westport to Sligo and beyond. Expect visits from the neighboring estates who will be sizing you up for more than just local co-operation. James O'Donnell is planning on taking you on a riding tour of the estate tomorrow. We have many tenants who are late with rental payments and some painful decisions will have to be made soon."

James arrived just after breakfast, a big man with a large beard. They had spoken briefly at his father's funeral; now James welcomed him as the new George Moore II, Master of the estate, and he heaped Irish blessings upon him. When they were out on their rounds James sympathized with him on the death of John – "he was a fine young man and a fine horseman, God rest him. It's just terrible the cost that Mayo has endured since the French came to Killala. I think we are finally over it now and I think there is much prosperity ahead for Moore Hall."

That first day out on the estate was a rude awakening for George. He was quickly exposed to the poverty of his tenants – large families crowded into tiny mud huts that billowed peat turf smoke from a rudimentary chimney, and via the open door. Families had to use most of their small holdings to grow cash crops of grain that were harvested and sold to cover the rent. That left them a very small patch of ground on which to grow enough potatoes to feed everybody. There was usually one cow and one pig per tenant family, and some had a few chickens and maybe a dog or a cat. James explained that the farm animals shared the hut with the family at night. The cow's milk was used to make butter to mix with potatoes for family meals, the rest being drank by adults and children alike. The pig was fattened on waste potato skins to be sold for slaughter, to help with rent shortfalls, not to be eaten by the family.

James was very matter of fact about this situation. "The grain and the livestock all get exported to England. Ireland is the breadbasket that is feeding the cities and the factory workers of England, and the Empire as well."

"I see," said George, while his entire body shuddered at the smells, and the sight of the people dressed in what could only be described as rags. The title of Master of Moore Hall was already losing its appeal for him, and this was only the first day.

Over the following weeks George tried hard to learn the workings of the estate, but he could not develop any enthusiasm for his new position. His spirits were lifted when the crates carrying his library from London arrived safely. He had the unpacked books displayed on shelves in the second-story room that his father had loved so much, the one with the balcony overlooking the lake. The highlight of any day for George was when he was able to lock himself away in that room and peruse his beloved books. For the most part he let his mother and James take care of the day-to-day running of the estate, and politely avoided any further visits to see his tenants in their miserable existence.

By late spring the weather had noticeably improved, which lifted everybody's spirits. He was in his library when a note arrived from his neighbor Mr. Blake – requesting a meeting with him on the following day to talk about ways to improve the influence of Mayo landlords at the government level – he would be coming by with two other gentlemen.

They arrived at two o'clock – Mr. Blake, Mr. Martin and Mr. Russell. Catherine had the servants prepare some refreshments and bite-sized food offerings for the group, then left the stage to George as she had no desire to meet with them. After condolences were offered on his father's death, and introductions were made, Mr. Blake got straight to the point.

"Gentlemen, we all know by now that in the coming weeks the Irish Parliament will be dissolved, and Ireland will become part of the Kingdom of Great Britain and Ireland – and thereafter all the laws pertaining to Ireland will be made in the London Parliament. Those of us who have lived here a long time know that we must elect an MP to represent Mayo who will be a strong and forceful voice. Denis Browne, despite his many shortcomings is the best person to elect in my opinion, and I know that view is shared by many of my fellow landlords. That being said, our main purpose in coming here today is to ask you Mr. Moore, to write a petition on behalf of Irish Agriculture for presentation to the House of Commons. You, Sir, are the only one of us with proven literary ability. We beseech you to compose a document making the case for an exclusive market in Britain that is reserved for Irish agriculture products – a document that can be included in the Corn Bill that is taking shape at present. We would be most grateful if you would consent to do that Mr. Moore?"

"Thank you for placing such trust in a newcomer like me. I will gladly put my hand to such an endeavor – provided you supply me with background information on this subject, and any calculated figures that can be used to support our position. What is the time window in which we must present this?"

"Thank you, Mr. Moore, from all of us for taking on this task. We have brought you what information we possess on the past and current status of this trade and will help you in any way we can. We think that our petition will be best received if it can be presented in the next six months; however, that window of opportunity could lengthen or shorten depending on how politics between the main parties develop."

The rest of their meeting was conducted as an informal get together among neighbors. It was mostly about upcoming social events and general estate management subjects like late rents, weather effects on harvests and the difficulty in finding good servants. The fact that he was an eligible bachelor was mentioned more than once to George and included some references to possible matches – something he managed to deflect. When he talked privately with Mr. Russell, the man was very contrite for his past insensitive utterances to George's father, and he apologized repeatedly. They were very much a group in common cause, and George knew how to meld such a group into a strong voice in support of their objectives. His own standing and the standing of Moore Hall among the Mayo gentry rose to new heights that day.

• • •

Westport House was looking splendid in late spring as the gardens were coming to life. Lord Altamont and his family hosted his usual spring gathering reserved for close family only – his brother Denis Browne was there with wife and brood of children, also his four sisters with several of their children, and his unmarried niece, Louisa Browne, was present. While his five children were busy with their cousins, and his wife was engaged in conversation with other ladies, Denis sought out his niece Louisa, and asked her to walk with him to the lake for a private chat.

As they strolled away from the house, she thanked him for taking her away from the crowd.

"Those ladies all have multiple children and that is all they want to talk about. As a younger woman and being unmarried, I have nothing to add to their discussion and no desire to listen in. Thank you for getting me away from that trap. So, what's on your mind, Denis?"

"Louisa, I'm sure you are well aware of that Mr. Pitt is going to convince the last holdouts to agree to dissolve the Irish Parliament and then pass the Act of Union later this year, which will result in the United Kingdom of Britain and Ireland, all under one Parliament in London."

"Yes, I know about that. I have been working closely with Lord A for several months now, getting his estate and accounts into shape. While I don't waste my time on politics, I have heard him bemoan the fact that his title will disappear once the union is completed – he has gotten used to it and has a strong liking for it. Will he get a new title when this happens?"

"Of course, and it will be even more elegant and important than his current one. However, I will lose my MP position unless I get elected Mayo MP for the London parliament."

"Everything I hear tells me that you have an excellent chance of being elected."

"Louisa, I don't operate on 'excellent chance' theory. I want to seal up that position, so the race is no contest."

"You have been very busy, too busy according to many people – rounding up suspects connected to the recent rebellion. A lot of people have lost their heads, some of whom could have been potential voters. Lucky for you the peasants don't have a vote, or you would surely lose the election and maybe even more than that."

"Don't joke about it my Dear, I have only been doing my job as High Sheriff. Many of the rebels went into hiding in the wilds of Achill and in the mountains of Connemara – it has taken extra time to root them out and bring them to justice."

"Denis, it's time now to break your link to the hangman's rope, give some time for wounds and bad feelings to heal before the election."

"I understand and I am doing just that. One of the people whose support I need is your friend, George Moore. I know that you are a woman of the world; you can be frank and honest with me. What is your interest level in George?"

"That's a blunt question, even for you, Denis. Let's make a deal right now before this discussion goes any further – I am prepared to be brutally honest with my responses to your questions, so long as you pledge to do the same with my questions. Is that agreed?"

"Yes."

"My interest level is very strong – I fully intend to win his heart and to marry him. To use your own words, I want to seal up that race and to do it soon. Now it's my turn for a question – why did you prosecute John Moore to the degree that you did – he was tossed around between gaols and trials for fifteen months, held all the time in filthy conditions? How did he die, where exactly did he die, when exactly did he die, and where is his body? I need to know the truth if I am to marry his brother."

"That is a complicated set of questions which I will try to answer. John accepted the title of President of Connaught, a treasonable offence against Britain and His Majesty the King. The diehard loyalists and General Lake wanted his head, in revenge for the losses they suffered at the battle of Castlebar, especially when Humbert and his surrendering French army were offered good terms by Cornwallis after their Longford defeat. I kept John in gaol for his own safety and moved him between gaols for the same reason – all the while waiting for heads to cool while I figured a way to save his life. Eventually I got agreement on a plea bargain where he would be transported into exile to the far east colonies, in exchange for his life. Sadly, his health failed him, and he died on the voyage."

"He did not take up arms against His Majesty's army at Castlebar – he was for all intents and purposes a guest of Humbert; a captive of sorts may be a better description. He was a citizen of Spain – why was he not treated the same way as Humbert and the French, and returned to Spain just as they were returned to France?"

"In hindsight I think you are right. At the time I did

not think of that option, and everyone was calling him an Irish rebel, and for him to be dealt with via Drumhead Court Martial, like happened to the rest of the rebels."

"My understanding is that he was too ill to be put on a ship – putting a sick man on a long ship voyage was a death sentence."

"Hold on a minute now – I allowed him to stay at a Waterford tavern to be treated by local doctors, while the other prisoners went to New Geneva to be shipped out. He spent several weeks there until he had recovered enough to sail."

"How do you know he was well enough – whose word are you taking for that?"

"I sent my own agent to Waterford to check on him, and he told me that John had recovered and could travel."

"Is that agent a doctor?"

"No, but I'm sure he discussed this with the doctors before he sent him on to the ship."

"Denis – did your agent go there with a mission, a mission to get John out of Ireland, out of your hair – don't lie to me now – it seems odd that John was too ill to sail but as soon as your agent arrived, he became well enough to be sent away on a ship. George and his mother are devastated by John's death. It is bad enough to have him die at thirty-two but worse when they have no body to grieve over."

"Sad coincidence, but I have no reason to doubt my agent. Are you going to repeat all this to George – he already cursed me the last time we met, and I know his mother hates me. Please don't make it worse. Please try to get George to a position where he will not talk badly of me, even if he does not wish to vote for me. You may be wasting your best years trying to woo George when you could be finding a suitor elsewhere."

"You should know how cunning and determined I am. I will find a way to George's heart and to his bed."

"Louisa! My God, what are you saying?"

"Get over it, Denis. You are a man of the world, look at all the kids you have – you have been a busy man in the bedroom. I met George's brother Thomas, a nice boy who will probably study law in Dublin, but I have never met his other brother Peter. What is the matter with him?"

"Unfortunately, he is a half-wit who is not capable of fending for himself. He lives at a care home in Galway and periodically they take him to Moore Hall, like at Christmas and Easter. So, Louisa, what stage is your plan at now, the plan to woo George Moore? His mother may not hate you, but as a cousin of mine she will not have any welcome for you."

"I admit that I have not seen him since the New Year's party here at Westport, but we have exchanged letters. I have been busy helping Lord A and George has been very busy moving from London and settling into his new role as Master of Moore Hall. More attention is needed to get the ball rolling – I will be working on it soon."

"You probably know this already, my dear, but I can assure you that George is a very wealthy man – his father made a large fortune in Spain, and there was plenty of money left over after he bought huge tracts of land to assemble his estate, and the building of Moore Hall. Here's an idea for you. My home in Claremorris was vandalized by the rebels in 1798, as you know. I eventually got reasonable compensation from the government and have recently moved back into the house after extensive repairs and renovations. Why don't you come and stay with us for a week or two. It will give you a break from all those accounting numbers and you will pass Moore Hall on your way. Why don't you drop in for a visit to see George – maybe 'get the ball rolling' as you said, and there is then time for him to repay the compliment by visiting you at Claremorris."

"I think you may be on to something there Denis. When do you suggest I visit you?"

"Very soon my dear – in the next few weeks – whatever works for you. I want George on my side, you want George as your husband. It sounds like we are united in our quest."

CHAPTER SEVENTEEN

Catherine Moore was counting down the days when Thomas would be sitting his final exams, and he would then be home for an extended period. The business of the estate was moving along well despite George's obvious lack of interest. All of this put a lot of work on her slender shoulders, her thin aging frame. Her only trips away from the estate were to visit Peter in Galway and to church. George went along with her to church, listless but at least present. Many of the scars that the countryside had suffered during the rebellion had been repaired, and new growth vegetation covered many of the destroyed buildings. She was still hurting inside, there was no cure for the loss of George and John, and her heart ached every day. At least she could visit George's grave – she had something – but in John's case she had no closure and that hurt even more.

• • •

Louisa Browne took up Denis's invitation and set off for Claremorris on a sunny Saturday morning in May. She had agonized over whether to send George a letter announcing her visit – eventually deciding to make a surprise call. The visit could turn very sour depending on what kind of reception she got from Mrs. Moore, but Louisa was not daunted – she was a statuesque woman who stood tall and was well capable of defending her corner. Her carriage turned onto the driveway of Moore Hall at exactly noon and moments later she was ascending the front steps. The front door was open, taking advantage of the good weather and as she entered, she saw one of the servants, who came over when beckoned.

"Please tell Mr. George Moore that he has a surprise visitor."

"Yes Ma'am," she answered and hurried off. Within moments George came bouncing down the stairs."

"Louisa, what a pleasant surprise," taking her extended hand in his – "I trust everything is alright."

"George, yes, yes – I am on my way to Claremorris and when I realized that I was about to pass by your door, I decided immediately that I would drop in to say hello. I hope my visit is not a disturbance to your day – I will not stay long. How are you and how are you settling into the estate, I hope your mother and brother are doing well."

He led her into the parlor and ordered refreshments while she admired the room and the view.

"Welcome to my humble abode. My apologies for my lack

of communication – I have been acclimatizing to life on the estate – going to 'landlord school' one might say. I am very well, thank you for asking. Mother is very well also – alas she is not here, having gone to visit Peter in Galway. You look splendid yourself, I must confess. What have you been up to?"

"I have been put to work by Lord Altamont, helping him undertake a full review of his estate and properties in Mayo. It has been challenging work but has also been very fulfilling and it is going along fine. I needed a break from my toil and Denis kindly invited me to visit with him and his family at Claremorris – to see the restoration work he has recently completed, in the aftermath of the damage the rebels inflicted on his home. Your home is looking magnificent – from the moment I entered the driveway I have been in awe of the views, especially those of the lake and the house itself."

"Thank you indeed. I was in my library when you arrived, so engrossed in a book that I did not even hear your carriage pull up – I apologize for that."

Louisa was relieved to hear that George's mother was absent and she was determined to make the most of that absence on this visit. During refreshments she hinted strongly to be taken for a tour of the house and gardens. He obliged and they walked the entire house, finishing up in his magnificent library, on the verandah overlooking the lake. She plied him with compliments and saw his obvious pride in his library. Next, they went on a short tour along the lake and gardens – taking her carriage, being that it was hitched, and her driver was refreshed and ready. At a viewing spot at the lake, they dismounted and walked along the shore pathway till they came to a bench which commanded sweeping views of the water and of the islands. They sat down together on the bench.

"There is a ruined castle over on that island, built by a Welshman when he ruled over these lands hundreds of years ago."

"This place is even more beautiful than I had imagined. You are a very lucky man George Moore, to be master of such a beautiful estate. I know you have been through a lot of grief and turmoil of late – has time eased the pain in your heart?"

"It is getting better every day and the peacefulness of this lake has been a big part of it. My mother has gone through much more torment than I have, and she is also healing, but it is a slow process. She has gone to visit my brother Peter today, who resides in a care home near Galway. My other brother Thomas, whom you have met, is taking his final exams at present and will soon be home – mother is so looking forward to his return. Do you miss London? I must confess that I still wake up and think I am back there – I do miss it sometimes."

"I was tired of London, I remember telling you that, and I really do not have any desire to go back there. I fully intend to settle in Ireland and probably in Mayo. Do you ever think of me during your exploits on the estate, or during your time in your library, and in your dreams?"

"Yes, you are often in my thoughts and just the other day I was remembering what a nice time I had at the New Year party at Westport House – do you remember it yourself?"

"Very much so and with much pleasure," – she beamed at George, which made him blush.

"So, how long are you going to stay with Denis?"

"A week or two, until I get bored or outlive my welcome."

"He is a hard man, with a big reputation in these parts – what is he like to be around on a more personal level."

"He is a perfectly charming host. I know you and he have had pronounced disagreements and his actions have angered you, but I also know for a fact that he has no ill feeling toward you, and admires you – he told me that himself, to my face. Please come and visit me in Claremorris. Denis asked me to issue you an open invitation to visit, to stay for dinner, or overnight if you wish. It is time to put the past behind us and enjoy the present and the future in beautiful Mayo – how about someday next week?"

"I am putting the finishing touches to a document that is to be presented to parliament in London – it is a plea on behalf of Irish grain farmers, especially Connaught farmers, to be a given preference under the Corn Act for the supply of grain to the British market. I was asked by a group of Connaught landlords to compose appropriate language for this plea – they seem to think of me as some kind of literary genius, bless their hearts. Anyway, I am to present my draught document this coming week to the committee, at a meeting in Tuam. I could visit you at Claremorris on my way home from the meeting."

"I would like that very much. Of course, the landlords want you to draw up a complicated document like this – because you are indeed a man of great literary ability. Lady Holland and the members of the Holland Circle admired you greatly, and rightly so. I am very proud of you. Send a messenger ahead announcing your arrival if you can – otherwise just come; I will tell Denis and I will make sure he is on his best behavior."

They returned to the house and shortly afterwards Louisa departed for Claremorris, leaving her perfume scent around Moore Hall and in George's nostrils.

George went back to his library to work on the grain document and was still there when his mother returned a few hours later. She picked up the perfume scent the moment she set foot in the house and then found George in his library – he looked up to greet her as she entered.

"Hello Mother, did you have a nice journey and visit with Peter – how is he doing?"

"The countryside was most pleasant, and I found Peter in very good spirits. He likes this good weather, and we were able to spend most of our time together outside. You had a visitor here – I smelled lady's perfume as soon as I walked in."

"Ah, yes – Louisa dropped in for a brief visit as she was passing our gate. I am almost finished this document on grain which I promised to present to the committee next week – it is turning out good, I hope the committee likes it."

"Are you telling me that Louisa Browne was in this house, niece of Denis Browne? Oh my God; why is that person coming round here? I will now have to sprinkle Holy Water in all the rooms."

"Mother, she is a very nice young lady, I bumped into her in London several times when I lived there. She had nothing to do with all the unpleasantness caused by her uncle and should not be grouped together with him."

"Son, it was far worse than unpleasantness. She is a Browne and is tarnished by association. I will see you at dinner."

George rolled his eyes as his mother stormed out of the room. He knew that Ireland was about to undergo a profound change with the passage of the Act of Union. The country would be on an equal footing with Britain – it was time to move forward and relegate the past to the status of history. He could do that, but he feared that his mother could not, which meant that his budding friendship with Louisa was in for a rough passage.

At dinner that evening he struggled to get Catherine off the subject of Denis Browne and all his wrongs. Nobody disagreed that the man had been overzealous in his prosecution of the rebels of 1798, but that didn't make all his extended family guilty of the same offence. Eventually he got her onto the subject of Thomas's final examinations and his upcoming return home.

"Is he still thinking of pursuing Law Studies in Dublin?"

"Yes, in Dublin, Thank God. I couldn't bear it if he was to consider a career in the army, and he doesn't need to be around here getting in your way as you run the estate."

"I must go to Tuam in a few days to present my documented arguments on the case for Irish grain to the committee of landlords, prior to its consideration by the British parliament at Westminster."

"Ah yes, I had forgotten that you were doing that – how clever of you. Do you think it has a good prospect of being passed and of being a help to our Irish farmers?"

"I think it has an excellent chance of passage. Remember, by next year there will be one united parliament and Ireland will be on an equal footing with England."

"Maybe, but I think it even more likely that Ireland will be the poor relation, with so few MPs that our voice will be seldom heard. England doesn't share power; England is the power and controls everything."

George's presentation to his fellow landlords in Tuam went very well and it was decided to move forward with the document in its entirety, and have it be the center piece of the Irish petition on the Corn Bill. The next day he made his way to Claremorris and to Claremount House. It was not in the league of Moore Hall, but it was a fine comfortable house. He had hardly dismounted when he heard a shriek and Louisa came joyously out to welcome him. She escorted him into the house while telling the servants to stable his horse and take his bag to the guest room reserved for him. She was taking control and assuming that he was staying overnight – he let it pass. Louisa introduced him to Denis's wife, Anne, and several of their many children – indeed she was expecting another child, and very soon. Louisa teased her that they would populate the entire county if they did not ease up – bringing a blush to the face of this quiet lady. Denis was not due home till later in the day and Louisa had the afternoon planned for George and herself. After some refreshments and polite conversation, the carriage was brought round to take the couple away to the river, to enjoy the pleasant afternoon weather. She dismissed the driver, saying they would drive themselves.

"George, unless you want to drive, I am happy to do so – let me drive so I can show off my skills."

When they got to the river she pulled up to a small cottage. They unloaded a few baskets and made themselves comfortable on the porch overlooking a deep-water bend in the river that looked like a prime fishing spot. They took a short stroll along the dry riverbank as the gurgling water flowed just feet away.

"Denis tells me there are some fine trout to be caught here – do you fish, George?"

"I have fished Lough Carra many times, but I cannot say that I am an accomplished fisherman."

When they returned to the cottage Louisa spread out some blankets and cushions to make what she called a day bed on the porch and invited him to sit with her. Before long they got even cozier when she pressed herself closer to him.

"George, do you remember the night at Westport House after the New Year's Ball? You were a little tipsy and I helped you to your cottage. I was helping you to get ready for bed when you turned the tables on me and you helped me to get ready for bed – for your bed, and it was beautiful – do you remember?"

"I remember parts of it – I thought it maybe was a dream."

"It wasn't a dream – it was real, and I want it to happen again. I want to be your mistress."

Louisa was wearing the same perfume that she wore the day she visited Moore Hall and it seemed to cast a spell on George. She removed most of her clothing so that her plentiful breasts were exposed, and that was plenty enough to arouse him. With a little encouragement and help from her, he undressed, and he then released those ripe breasts into the afternoon sunshine. She kissed him deeply and he responded by rolling her onto her back – surgically working his way over her breasts while she urged him on with great sighs of satisfaction. This time he was going to be in charge, and he removed her risqué London underwear. "I am sure you didn't buy these in Mayo."

"Dearest – local Mayo girls don't know how to excite a man – keep it going, I love it."

He did just that and made love to her for a surprisingly long time. When he rolled off her, they lay side by side, naked, exploring the curves of each other's bodies, watching the waterfowl playing in the deep pool of the meandering river.

After dressing, they talked while enjoying the picnic she had brought along. Louisa was very matter of fact about how she saw the situation and how she wanted it to unfold.

"Your mother is a wonderful lady and I so want to get on her good side. We know she has an intense dislike for Denis and frankly I don't blame her, considering all the grief she has been through – grief that was caused in part by his handling of the aftermath of the rebellion. But life goes on and forgiveness is a core belief of us Catholics – she probably does not realize that I am Catholic. I can be a fine wife for you, George Moore, and bear you some wonderful children – and surely your mother wants the lineage of the Moore family to continue and to grow, and you are now the head of the family, the seed to start that growth. I know she adores you and your two brothers, but you are the heir, remember, you control the power. Let you and I figure out a way to get Miss Catherine to realize that I am a good person, and the fact that I am a blood relative of Denis is outside of my control – if that detail is put to one side, I am the perfect match for you. I am willing to stay in the background, loving you while you convince her to soften her position. We can do this my darling, from my experiences I know I can run an estate like Moore Hall and that will give you the freedom to continue with your writings, and she can enjoy her grandchildren – life can be nice for her again, we can be a family."

"That all sounds nice when you say it Louisa, but it is not going to be easy to win my mother over. Even though she was born in Ireland she was brought up in Spain and has the explosive mix of Irish and Spanish tempers. Losing both my father and John in such a short time was a terrible blow to us all, especially to my mother. The healing process is slow, and it has not even been a year yet. I need time myself to come to terms with all that is going on in my life before I figure how to win Mother over. As you said, we must keep our relationship very private, and you will have to stay in the shadows for quite some time."

"At present I have as much work as I can handle reorganizing Lord A, and he pays me for my work. We can meet here in Claremount frequently, and at my cottage at Westport House during the regular social events that occur there – we can be the Romeo and Juliette of Mayo."

"We had best be heading back, my dear, it's been hours. We must both promise to tell nobody of the extent of our relationship – agreed?"

"Agreed on one condition – kiss me before we return to the house."

He obliged and they freshened up, gathered the blankets and the remains of their picnic and set off back to the house – with George driving the carriage. Denis was home and went out of his way to welcome George to Claremount. He even produced a bottle of sparkling wine to celebrate the occasion of their first visitors to their recently restored home.

"George, I am delighted that you decided to choose Mayo over London, and we officially welcome you as Master of Moore Hall. To your very good health, and on a secondary note, to all our good health. I trust you two enjoyed yourselves down by the river – it is one of my favorite places to be, whether fishing or just watching the birds and seeing the trout rising for the fly."

"Yes indeed, we had a wonderful time there, isn't that so Louisa."

She nodded, "Absolutely. It was one of the best afternoons of my life."

Shortly afterwards the ladies went upstairs to powder their noses ahead of dinner. Denis led George into his library, talking as he went – "I know this is a meagre collection of books compared to what I hear you have at Moore Hall, but for me it is adequate, and it gives me similar pleasure to what your library gives you. It's the place where I find solitude and where I can think. George, I owe you an apology which I want to offer you here and now. I deeply regret not realizing that John was born a citizen of Spain, and my not using that fact to ask Cornwallis to accord him the same treatment bestowed on General Humbert and his French officers. I don't know if it would have made a difference, but for that oversight I am truly sorry."

George was surprised by this humble apology and was a bit choked with emotion as he accepted it. Not another word was mentioned about John's death and the recent death of his father, George Moore. Denis congratulated him on the petition he had written for the Corn Bill and its likely financial benefit for Connaught farmers. He went on to say how much he admired Moore Hall itself – in his opinion the estate was a model for other landlords to follow, and its contribution to the prosperity of Mayo was significant. The man was a charming host and George was inwardly feeling remorse at his having cursed Denis at their previous meeting in Castlebar.

They were back in the dining room in time to welcome the ladies back downstairs, and all partook of sherry before dinner. Denis knew every landlord in the county and beyond, while George was a newcomer in his own home area, having spent his life to date in London, France and Spain. People had told George that to be successful in Mayo it was necessary to be on good terms with Denis Browne and he knew they were right. He knew that no matter how his relationship with Louisa turned out, he and Moore Hall had to find a way to get along with Denis, and that meant that his mother Catherine would have to confront her ghosts at some stage. After dinner the foursome played whist for a few hours, until Louisa nudged George under the table and said she was tired. They were in adjoining rooms and managed to get a short smooch before going to their separate beds.

George returned home at lunchtime the next day while his mother was out of the house. He went directly to his library – when he met her at dinner later he managed to avoid any mention of where he had stayed the night before.

That summer was a pleasant one, crops came in abundant, and the estate ran along smoothly under Catherine and James, while George kept busy in his library with his literary pursuits.

He accompanied his mother on some visits to see his brother Peter and those trips gave him some opportunities to try to make the case for Louisa – telling her that she had been educated by nuns and was a staunch Catholic, in contrast to all the rest of the Browne clan. He even managed to get Catherine to agree to greet her briefly when she dropped in on her way to Claremorris – it was a short encounter, but it was a start. He also managed to rendezvous with Louisa discreetly several times.

Thomas passed his finals and spent a month at home in Mayo, which made his mother very happy – diverting her attention and it gave George some cover for his courting escapades. The countdown to the abolishment of the Irish parliament had begun, and so had pressure from Denis Browne on George to aid him in his bid to become MP for Mayo at the London parliament. George agreed to pen a letter of support for the Act of Union, and another supporting Denis in his quest for the parliamentary seat. That autumn Thomas moved to Dublin to read law. Catherine was particularly melancholy and agitated in November, as the anniversaries of George Snr and John approached. She had Masses celebrated for their intentions, and George visited his father's grave at Straide Abbey with her. It was a difficult time for them both. George sensed that his mother was aware of the seriousness of his relationship with Louisa, even though she said nothing – she was too silent about it, a fact not in keeping with her personality. The end of year holiday period was approaching, and Louisa was eager to go to social events with George, as well as showing signs of impatience with George's slow progress winning over his mother.

Tensions at home were high during Christmas, despite the presence of both Thomas and Peter at Moore Hall for the festive season. In the aftermath of George's return from a social event his mother commented on the perfume that she smelled on him, reminding him that it was the same scent which she had noticed after Louisa had made her first visit to Moore Hall.

• • •

On January 1st, 1801, the Act of Union came into effect, ushering in a new era for Ireland. In return for the abolition of the Irish Parliament, Ireland was allocated 100 seats at the Westminster Parliament in London and were to have 28 members in the House of Lords. Denis Browne was assured of becoming one of the two Mayo MPs and his brother's title changed from Lord Altamont to Marquess of Sligo. Both men were pleased with the outcome and Louisa had to get used to dropping her Lord A reference. The Act of Union had important implications for the Irish aristocracy, but it had little immediate effect on the lives of millions of Irish peasants who continued to toil in poverty, in a life-or-death struggle to survive. Politicians promised that the Union would make life better for everyone in Ireland – only time would tell if that came to pass, but it was obvious from the beginning that it would bring no real improvement to the daily life of the poor.

George Moore II was an Irishman in name, but by his own admission he was impregnated with the feelings and sentiments of an Englishman, as a result of his time living in London. He became convinced that the Union of the two Parliaments was an important step towards the civilization of Ireland. In his opinion the diffusion of British customs and manners amongst the inhabitants would be good – he abhorred the old primitive habits of the peasants, believing that they fostered idleness and pernicious behavior. He knew that his views were unacceptable to his mother, and he did not broadcast them in her presence. His secret relationship with Louisa meant that in essence he was now living a double life, and it was a situation that could not continue. In February, when the estate accounts had to be examined in detail to ascertain the financial standing of the family, things came to a head between mother and son.

"George, there are some shortfalls in the estate income that need your attention."

"Can I deal with it after I return from Westport next week?"

"Son, I understand and have come to accept that you prefer to spend your time in your library rather than on estate business, but the estate cannot play second fiddle to your social visits to Westport."

"What do you mean by that, Mother?"

"I am your mother and I know you so well, George. I sense what is going on here behind my back. Louisa Browne has got you in her spell – have you forgotten what Denis Browne did to our family?"

"She could not choose her relatives, and she has nothing in common with Denis – she has a totally different outlook on life than he does. For one thing she is Catholic, and she works every day – she has re-organized Westport House estate for the better. There is very little social activity around here that is of interest to a man of my age and position – she has been kind enough to invite me to events there. These events have been my only social outlet – without them I would be living a life comparable to that of a hermit. Surely you do not wish me to live my best years like a hermit."

"She is feathering her own nest. There are many other suitable ladies who do not have the baggage that Miss Browne has. Why can you not make efforts to meet those ladies?"

"I have met several of them and they are dour and ugly, like pillars of salt. Louisa is vibrant and entertaining; she has lived in London and knew many of the people that I knew there – she is head and shoulders over any of the local ladies that I have spoken with."

"Son, you are Master of Moore Hall, and I can only advise you on how you want to run the estate. If it is your decision to have close relations with the Browne's I cannot stop you, but it is unacceptable to me – I cannot be in the same room with Denis Browne, and as far as I am concerned all his relatives are tarnished by what he has done to our family, to Mayo and to Ireland."

"Mother, you are putting me in an impossible position. I value your good counsel and I want you to remain with me in Moore Hall, but I have a life to live also, I want to marry and raise a family here. Louisa is by far the most interesting lady that I have met, and I readily confess that I have great affection for her. Please reconsider your opposition towards her – separate her from the rest of the Browne clan."

"I will pray to the Lord for guidance, and I will pray for you, George. There are only four of us left now. I am old, and because of Peter's condition the future of the family belongs to you and Thomas. Let us both give serious thought to the future and try to find the best solution for our family."

• • •

An extract from the diaries of Catherine de Kilkelly, Moore Hall, Mayo

Ireland has been sold down the river by this Act of Union. Irish MPs will forever be in the minority. They, and all the Irish will continue to be exploited.

I fear that George is lost to me. His sympathies are leaning to the side of accepting that British dominance over Ireland is a good thing; he has little day-to-day interest in the estate, and he has fallen under the spell of Miss Browne. I do not believe that they are just friends. She has her eyes firmly fixed on being Mrs. George Moore and if that is George's wish there is no place for me here. I have given my life to help make Moore Hall what it is, despite my early misgivings about it, but I am now old and tired. The estate needs the energy of a young person to make it prosper, but alas, George does not possess the attributes or the desire to do that. Maybe the next chapter of Moore Hall has another cruel twist of fate – is the Druid's curse about to dictate that a Browne will take charge of the place?

Thank God we buried George at Ashbrook, away from all this.

Thomas is well on the road to passing the Irish Bar and will be able to make his own way in life. Peter is another story – whatever solution I find for myself must include provision for Peter.

Praying for enlightenment.

• • •

George went to Westport as planned, but with a heavy heart. Louisa sensed his depression and worked to lift his spirits. She had excursions planned to St. Patrick's Holy Mountain and to one of the islands in Clew Bay. They went ahead with the trips and kept discussion to simple lively topics. By the third day he was ready to talk about his predicament – she waited for him to bring up the subject.

"Mother has figured out that I have been seeing too much of you for our relationship to be a simple friendship. She is very upset about it and as you know, she lumps every Browne in with Denis. I owned up to some degree and reminded her that you are Catholic and very different from the rest – I pushed all your good traits without telling her too much. We both agreed to take some time to think about the future before speaking about it again, but I fear there is such a wide gap between our positions that we cannot bridge it. She cannot let go of the ghosts of the past – and is struggling to accept that I have my life ahead of me and I need to be able to spend it with whomever I wish. I hate to see her upset like this, but I don't know what I can do to find a compromise and it has me depressed."

"Do you think it would help if I was to meet with your mother and try to talk it out?"

"Maybe but I doubt she will be prepared to meet with you."

"It seems like that may be our only choice. Have you thought about asking Thomas to intercede for you?"

"Yes, but I am reluctant to get him involved in this and he needs to focus on passing the Irish Bar examinations. I am still mulling over whether to speak with him."

"Do you want me to walk away – I don't want to see you unhappy like this?"

"No, please stay. We must find a way to placate mother and accommodate everybody's position."

"Let's give our various options some serious thought while your mother is doing the same – you and her are together many hours of every day so maybe a breakthrough will occur."

• • •

During the previous autumn the deceased estate of George Moore the First, was settled. In that settlement young George became the legal owner of Moore Hall and surrounding acreage, plus the lands at Ballintubber, Partry, and Ashbrook. He also had control of the Alicante property in Spain that was retained by the family when they left Spain – it had been leased out to local merchants since then. The legal documents settling his father's estate included a jointure for Catherine as his surviving wife, a sum of 11,000 pounds which Catherine was entitled to claim at any time. The estate also promised to pay the cost for Peter to live at a care home for the rest of his life. Catherine had not claimed her money from the estate, and now, as she mulled over what to do, she reacquainted herself with these two important provisions of George's will. On a day-to-day basis everything continued as before, with neither young George nor his mother broaching any subjects other than regular Moore Hall operational business. The meeting to deal with the operational expenses that had been postponed still needed to happen, and when it did there was no way of avoiding the subject of Louisa.

George initiated the conversation. "Mother, I think if you

and Louisa sat down and talked over afternoon tea, you could figure out a way out of our impasse. Will you consent to a meeting with her?"

"If that is what you want me to do, I will do it for your sake. Please do not involve Thomas in this, in case you are thinking that way."

"Agreed – I had no intention of doing so. Are you ok with meeting Louisa next Sunday afternoon?"

"That is fine – I have no social engagements in my life."

And so, the two ladies at the center of George's affections met at Moore Hall. George was present briefly to facilitate introductions, and then retreated to his library, having been told that they would ring a bell once they concluded their discussions.

Louisa opened the conversation – "Mrs. Moore, I admire you greatly for the courage it took for you and your husband to return to Ireland and build Moore Hall. I would love to know more about your own background in Spain and in Ireland before you emigrated to Spain."

"That serves no purpose in this meeting."

"Then let me tell you about my upbringing; I was –"

"That story serves no purpose either – I know all I need to know about the Browne's. Why are you trying to take my son away from me? You know full well all the pain and suffering that has been inflicted on our family by the Browne's, especially your uncle whose name I will not even say."

"I am in love with George, and he is in love with me. We want to share our lives together and we want you to be part of it."

"Find someone else – I have lost too much already. I am not sharing George with you. Free him from your spell and let him get on with his life."

"Mrs. Moore, we are in a new century now, where Ireland is in Union with Britain. The days of rebellion are over, and here in Mayo we must bury the hatchet and move forward in forgiveness and hope."

"I have buried my George and lost my son John because of your uncle. Now you want to take young George away from me – this cannot happen, I will not agree to it."

"Please give us a chance. I can lift the burden of running the estate from your shoulders. You can enjoy some rest and look forward to your grandchildren."

"They would be half Browne and half Moore – how could I enjoy them after all the suffering that has been meted out to us by the Browne's. There is no place for you here. I will not have you here so long as I am here."

With that, Catherine rang the bell that had been placed on the table. George appeared at the door as his mother was ready to exit. He was expecting good news; all he got was her goodbye, saying she had a headache and was going to lie down. After his mother left, he turned to Louisa who was in tears at this stage.

"What happened, how did it go?"

She was unable to answer him – she stood up and headed for the front door with George trailing her. They were halfway to her carriage before Louisa was able to speak.

"Your mother had no interest in hearing my story or telling me hers. She wants you all to herself here and wants me out of the picture. I came here today ready to compromise in order to get into her good graces, but she didn't open the door as much as a crack – there was nothing I said that made any difference. Oh George, the meeting was a disaster, and I am heartbroken. Please let me go home now."

CHAPTER EIGHTEEN

George was angry over the failure of his mother to find a compromise with Louisa. Considering that he himself was a philosopher and a deep thinker, he failed to be rational in his analysis of the encounter. He put most of the blame on his mother and failed to examine the facts. Catherine had been at Moore Hall since it was built and had gone through all the heartaches of turning it into a family home – she had been a wonderful mother to him and his siblings. The 1798 rebellion had been a disaster for the family and by the time it ended she had lost her husband and her eldest son. Young George himself had been in London all during that time and was insulated to some degree from the raw pain of those events. He possessed a delicate mental constitution and the grief of the family deaths and the pressure of the decision to return to Mayo had taken a toll on him – he was not mentally ready to face a major confrontation with his mother.

Louisa Browne was a blow-in, who was living off her

relatives in Mayo, relatives who had caused much pain to the Moore family; she was an opportunist who had everything to gain from a marriage to George – a wealthy man from an influential family who owned a Big House and a great estate. His love for the girl blinded him to the cold realities of the situation, and he was not prepared to cut her loose. He could not see his mother's point of view and that backed him into a corner. If Catherine could not tolerate Louisa being in the family the only avenue left was for him to choose between his mother and his lover. He dodged this decision for as long as he could. The situation at home rolled along as before, with Catherine keeping the wheels of the estate turning with James's help, while George immersed himself in his literary works – both avoiding discussion of difficult topics while waiting for the other to give ground. Thomas got accepted into the Irish Bar, and after a short visit home, which was challenging for everybody, he took up a position in Dublin as an attorney. Catherine had spoken to Thomas about the impasse over Miss Browne and he made it plain to George that he sided with his mother. That set the stage for a showdown in September.

This time it was Catherine who opened the discussion.

"This situation cannot continue, George. You must choose between your family and this woman. You are the master of Moore Hall and as such you have the final say. If you want that woman to be here, then I must leave."

"Mother, I love Louisa and want to marry her. That's what young people do. She is a very good organizer and can be a tremendous asset to Moore Hall, and I hope she will be the mother of the next generation of Moore children – your grandchildren. I want you to stay and be a part of this."

"George, I love you and I have given much thought to my predicament and have prayed for Divine guidance. The pain of your father's death is still very real, as is the pain of your brother John's death. I cannot live with myself if I disrespect their memory. If it is your decision that she stays, then I will make plans to leave. No doubt you remember that your father's estate made provisions for me and for Peter. I will take my jointure and the estate will continue to take care of Peter, at least until I get settled elsewhere."

"Where will you go?"

"At this moment I do not know – probably to Dublin to begin with, so that I can be near Thomas."

"Mother, this is crazy, and is giving me so much stress that my head is ready to explode. Do you think you might reconsider and return after a break?"

"Anything is possible, but I really don't see a place for me here if that woman is here – I have no desire to intrude on you and your new life."

They were both in tears at this stage – standing awkwardly and facing each other. Catherine excused herself and went to her room.

• • •

Extract from the diaries of Catherine de Kilkelly, Moore Hall, Mayo

I had hoped and prayed that it would not come to this. I must exile myself from my home and my family in order to defend my principles and the honor of my deceased husband and murdered son. George is a good boy who has now been taken away from me – no, he is an adult now, and has made his decision – upon whose consequences we will all have to live with. There is no point in delaying. I will write to Thomas immediately and ask him to reserve rooms for me at the Dublin hotel that my George used to stay at and spoke well of. Peter will be very upset, so I will have to tread very carefully when I visit him. I will have to say a final goodbye to George at Straide Abbey, and to speak to John's spirit. This is turning out to become the saddest event of my life.

• • •

Young George was caught in a trap of his own making. He had nobody in Moore Hall that he could talk to or get advice from – the only person that was privy to the situation on his side was Louisa, and she was in Westport. He was not a man that drank strong liquor but that day he reached for a glass of brandy and sipped it as he paced around the dining room table, desperately trying to wrack his brain for a solution. The thought of going to Westport came into his head but he dismissed it quickly – he knew Louisa's position already. He was still pacing when the servant came in almost unnoticed to set the table for dinner for two, him and his mother as usual. When dinner was about to be served the servant told him that his mother had declined dinner when called. George sat alone at the big table and ate very little as he continued in deep thought. Sleep that night was very difficult – his parents and John were in his dreams and none of them were happy with him. At breakfast he inquired if his mother was still in bed – he was told that she had left early to meet James O'Donnell and was expected to be out on the estate all day. When she appeared that evening at dinner, they had a short conversation.

He asked, "How did it go today with James?"

"Fine. I told him I was going away for a while very soon, no more detail than that. We were in Ashbrook, and I was able to visit George's grave and say goodbye. Tomorrow I will go to visit Peter; I will tell him much the same, no point in upsetting him. You must make sure to visit him on a monthly basis. Can you go into town and get my jointure money tomorrow and reserve a seat for me on the train for Friday – my destination is Dublin. Please have the money split into several draught orders."

"Are you sure this is what you want to do, Mother?"

"Under the circumstances I have no other choice."

They both took care of their personal business and Catherine had her trunk packed by Thursday. On Friday morning the carriage was ready at the front steps, with her trunk on board. James O'Donnell himself undertook to drive her into Claremorris to catch the train, and there was an uneasy atmosphere among the servants as time came for her to leave. George said his goodbyes privately in the parlor where mother and son embraced silently – and then she was gone. He busied himself in his library, but his mind was not on his books today – it was on the short note that his mother had left there for him.

George,
Life is but a series of chapters, just like your books. Our chapter was wonderful while it lasted. Do not dwell on it but move on to the new chapter of your life, give it your very best and make it as good as you possibly can.

I will contact you when I am settled.

Your loving Mother

The carriage made its way slowly down the driveway and just as James was getting ready to pull out onto the road Miss Catherine asked him to stop for a moment. She turned and stared at the house and its surroundings for many minutes.

James waited anxiously, "Mrs. Moore, are you alright, Ma'am?"

"Yes James. I just wanted to take in the view before I set off. I am ready now, carry on."

He noticed tears on her cheeks but said nothing as they headed towards Claremorris. About fifteen minutes later she asked him how they were doing for time."

"We're fine, Ma'am. I will have you there in plenty of time for the train."

"Good. How are your family doing, James – your eldest boy must be sixteen by now."

"All doing well, Ma'am. You are correct, he just turned sixteen and is working for the Blake's at Tower Hill."

"I hope he turns out as good as his father and I'm sure the other kids will do well also – you have seven in total, right?"

"That's right, Ma'am. God blessed us with seven healthy children."

"I wish them all the best as they grow up."

James was worried about the tone of her voice. "If you don't mind me asking, Ma'am, how long will you be away?"

He could hear her take a deep breath and he waited patiently for her to answer.

"That depends – it depends on business that I must attend to in Dublin, with Thomas's help. I'm sure you can take good care of everything, and George has promised me to be more hands on while I am gone."

"Shur, all I have to do is keep everything straight, Ma'am – now that you have got the estate in good shape."

She murmured something else quietly that he did not hear but sensed the emotion in her voice and left it at that. At the train station he got a hand cart and used it to carry her trunk to the station office, waiting outside while she went in. When she emerged, she said the train was due very soon and he could set off back with the carriage.

"I would prefer to wait and make sure you are safely aboard, Ma'am."

"Thank you, James."

When they heard the train approach, he busied himself getting the hand cart ready. Once it stopped and some passengers got off, the conductor called for boarding. They proceeded to the first-class carriage where James helped to load the trunk as instructed by the conductor. He then turned to say goodbye to Mrs. Moore – who again showed glistening cheeks as she bade him farewell and pressed a sovereign into his hand. "Please use this to help your family."

"You are too kind, Ma'am. I will pray for your safe journey and I'm sure it won't be long till we see you back in Mayo."

"God Bless you James."

He stood on the platform until the whistle blew, and waved to her as she passed by in her window seat – waiting there till the train was almost out of sight. A strange feeling came over him as he pressed the sovereign into his pocket. He wondered if he would ever see Mrs. Moore again – then realized he had a tear in his own eye as he walked back to his horse and carriage.

George was in the front library when he saw James returning to the estate with the empty carriage – he stared at the carriage and was overcome by emotion when he saw James looking directly up at him.

An hour later he had his horse saddled, then strapped on an overnight bag and set off for Westport.

• • •

When Catherine Moore arrived at The Royal Hibernian Hotel in Dublin, she found that Thomas had reserved rooms for her, and had left her a note with his address, asking her to send him a message once she was settled in. This she did the next day, and they ate dinner together that evening after they had a tearful reunion in her rooms.

"Mother, I still cannot believe that George went through with this. He has effectively forced you out of your own home."

"Son, it's a man's world we live in, and women have very few rights, mothers included. George is the legal owner of Moore Hall estate, and he can do what he pleases – that is the system, and he had full legal rights to send me away if he wanted to. I hasten to say that he did not do so, and that I chose to leave rather than share the house with that woman."

"It's still horrible and I told him I was on your side, when I was at home. What will you do now?"

"I am thinking of staying in Dublin for a while. Maybe he will have a change of heart, or she will, and things can go back to what they were – but I doubt that will happen; she knows she has a great prize in her grasp and his personality is too weak to resist her. I have led a very sheltered life in Mayo for all these years – I intend now to spend time taking in the sights of Dublin and would like to go to the theatre if there are any presentations I might like. Your father made generous provision for me in his will, and I have full control of my jointure."

"You may not want to stay in the confines of a hotel for very long. I live close to here and I will make inquiries about the availability of suitable furnished accommodation for you nearby – that would give you more privacy and freedom. Assuming there is no change in George's position, what are your long-term plans?"

"Our former home in Alicante is still owned by the family, owned by George in strictly legal terms. I loved Alicante and loved that house – it would be nice to live there again, but I could not do so unless I had full control of the property – currently it is leased to a local merchant farmer. The other important person to think about is Peter, who is still living at the care home in Galway – I must look out for his interests."

"While you are settling in and waiting to see what happens with George, I will research the legal status of the Alicante property and we will discuss our options in due course."

● ● ●

In Westport, George went directly to Louisa's cottage and waited there until she returned from being out on the estate. They embraced and once inside they kissed.

"Mother has departed from Moore Hall – I tried to

convince her to stay and find a compromise, but she refused, and she boarded the train to Dublin earlier today. I am consumed with mixed emotions – sadness to see her go and to know that Thomas has taken her side against me, elation that a weight has been lifted off my shoulders, fear of the future, but at the same time a feeling of excitement for the future."

"You are visibly shaking, my darling. Come sit with me and let me hold you."

"Thank you."

They embraced again for several minutes and then she took his hands in hers and looked into his eyes.

"Are you sure you have made the correct decision for you, George Moore – are you able to live with yourself going forward, without your mother in your daily life?"

"Yes – I think so, as long as you are with me."

"I will be with you, at your side as I am now – so let us plan to move forward together. I foresaw this and I have been working feverishly to complete my assessment duties here at Westport House. Another ten days will allow me to finish, and I suggest that I then relocate to Moore Hall. That gives you time to get private quarters ready for me. That will avoid any appearance of impropriety."

"Yes – that seems like a good plan. What should I tell my manager James O'Donnell, and the servant staff of Moore Hall?"

"As little as possible – they are your servants, and you are not obliged to tell them anything. Let's ease into this – tell James that your mother has gone away for an extended break, to rest. Have him tell the servants to prepare the rooms for your assistant – being me – and leave it at that. Some of them have seen me there before and it will not be a huge surprise. I will deal with them when I arrive."

"You are so good in this situation, my dear. Yes – I will return home tomorrow and proceed with those ideas."

Louisa continued to stroke his head as they talked their way through the plan. She bedded him down that night in her cabin and continued to soothe his worries.

• • •

James O'Donnell was a bit surprised to see Master George Moore ride out to meet him on the estate, something he had not done for quite some time. He was overseeing repair work to a gate when he saw him approach and rode to meet him in the middle of the field, away from the workmen.

"I wasn't expecting you, Sir, is everything alright?"

It was difficult for George to assess what his mother might have told James at her departure, so the details of his plans for the estate going forward were kept short, just the way Louisa had instructed.

"Yes, James, I just wanted to speak to you about a few things in private. Did you get Mother away safely yesterday?"

"Yes, indeed, Sir. I made sure her luggage was safely in

her carriage and waited until the train was out of sight before returning to the estate."

"Good. Did Mother say how long she planned to be away?"

"Mrs. Moore said she needed some rest and was going to spend time with Thomas in Dublin. I assured her that I would take care of everything in her absence."

"Thank you. Yes, she is taking an extended break. I worried about her overdoing things and putting her health at risk. We will be getting some interior decoration work done while Mother is away – I will be speaking to the housekeeper, Mrs. O'Dowd, about that, but I wanted you to be aware of it also. I will be talking to you some more next week about some estate upgrades I have been planning. For now, carry on with your duties."

"Thank you, Sir."

James knew his place and did not ask any other questions.

George then rode back to the house and resumed his routine of secluding himself in his library.

CHAPTER NINETEEN

Catherine sent a letter to George telling him she had arrived safely in Dublin, that she was staying in a hotel near Thomas and to send any correspondence via Thomas's address – it was a short note with no added personal comments or invitation to reply. She realized how exhausted she was from her labors at Moore Hall and rested up for a few days before venturing out to explore Dublin. Thomas came by and told her of some theatre performances that were currently playing – they picked one for the following week that was lighthearted entertainment.

"Mother, I have been doing some research on the legal status of the Alicante property. Spanish law with refence to property is different than British law, and I cannot get any definitive answers. The Moore estate is listed as the owner of the property and that essentially means that George, as the heir, is the owner now – but it is worth a challenge according to my legal friends with some knowledge of the Spanish system. I think George may not want to fight it – he may offer to negotiate a settlement with me that may lead to my getting control of the property. What do you think we should do?"

"Let us wait a bit longer to see if George has a change of heart, now that I have left him on his own."

• • •

George was indeed alone in his large house – he continued to blame his mother for his unfortunate situation, and he allowed his anger to cloud his judgement. He had become morose and short tempered as he struggled with the guilt of forcing his mother into a decision to leave her home. In a spiteful move he ordered Mrs. O'Dowd to have the servant staff clear out his mother's quarters; using the vague excuse that he planned to do some upgrades and decorating while his mother was away. The rooms were being made ready for Louisa Browne – unknown to the staff. Louisa arrived twelve days later with a lot of luggage: causing even more confusion among the servants. She wasted no time in settling in and reminding the house staff that from now on they would be answering to her – causing a stir of whispers and rumors that were uncomfortable. George felt the need to confirm to Mrs. O'Dowd that going forward she would be reporting to Miss Browne Louisa, which did little to clear up the confusion.

Louisa wasted no time in taking George to task about the state of the house – "My dearest, the decorations are old fashioned, and I will want them upgraded to my liking once I get fully settled. First, I want to take stock of the tenantry situation on the estate – have your manager come here to meet with me as soon as possible."

He meekly nodded in approval. Privately, she had no intention of staying very long in guest rooms and was fully expecting to be sharing the masters' quarters in short order. The next day George called James into a meeting where Louisa was introduced.

George began – "James – Miss Louisa Browne will be overseeing the daily estate functions going forward. She has much experience in estate management and has been recently engaged by Lord Altamont in a similar position at Westport House."

"Yes sir. You are welcome, Madam, and I will be happy to assist you in every way that I can."

Louisa spoke up – "I will be spending the next few days examining the estate accounts and after that I will need you to show me the layout of the estate, the good the bad and the ugly. Be ready for changes as we work to improve all aspects of the estate. I am a hard task master James, so be warned that we have much to do."

During the following months Louisa's domineering personality was in full display as she put her stamp on the house and the estate. Gone were any concerns about his mother's return – Catherine's name was only mentioned when George did so. Louisa brought in carpenters, decorators, painters and seamstresses to make the upgrades that she wanted – including the relocation of George's library to one of the larger guest rooms at the rear of the house – on the basis that he needed more space for his extensive book collection. He was displeased about this move, but his objections were overruled, and he was too timid to stand up to her. James was quickly put under pressure by Louisa to resolve rent payment issues with overdue tenants, and several were evicted soon afterwards when they failed to meet payment deadlines. George was impressed by her hard work but protested the evictions.

"Louisa, we have always had a very low rate of evictions – it's something Father was proud of, and Mother then continued. Let us try to keep that record."

"I am here to tell you that this is one of the reasons that the estate finances are weak. We are running a business and there is no place for sentiment. Your mother didn't understand finances, she was too soft on the tenants, and they took advantage of her weakness. Darling, just you concentrate on your books and leave the business end of the estate to me, my dear – I know how to deal with these people, and I know how to right the ship."

"I suppose you are right."

"Of course, I'm right. They will pay or go and be replaced by new tenants who will pay more."

George sank deeper into his literary world of history, rather than confront her. She became the mistress of the house in every aspect, including the master's bedroom. Neither did she waste time in bringing up the subject of marriage, and George was given orders to make plans for a wedding in the very near future – the only respite he could wrangle from her was to get her agreement to wait till the New Year. Louisa was a staunch Catholic and made sure they were both present in their reserved pew at the local church for Mass every Sunday – Father Connolly could not but be impressed also, and he soon accepted that this new lady was here to stay, and he stopped inquiring of Miss Catherine's wellbeing. Neither did Louisa neglect George's brother, Peter – she sometimes went along with George on his frequent visits to the care home in Galway, admonishing him for not telling Peter that his mother had run out on him.

Denis Browne visited Moore Hall after Louisa had completed her upgrades. He made a point of thanking George in front of her for the help and support he had given him during his election as MP for Mayo, and he proudly announced his brother's new title as Marquess of Sligo. He tried to boast to George about his continued efforts in Parliament to push for Catholic Emancipation but was immediately cut short. George made a point of telling him that politics of all shades were of no interest to him going forward – he was only interested in his family, his estate and his literary endeavors.

With all this home drama going on George had paid little attention to his mother's self-imposed exile, and he had not written to her in a while. He was taken aback by notice of Thomas's claim to the Alicante property and was inclined towards contacting him to negotiate a settlement, when he brought up the subject to Louisa.

"The property in Alicante was Mother's pride and joy. I am thinking of making a deal with Thomas that will give Mother access to the house there."

"Here I am trying to improve the finances of your estate and you want to start giving away some of it. The estate must stay whole – I will not allow any part of it to be carved off in this way. Your mother was given a generous jointure in your father's will, and she made her own decision to leave Moore Hall. Thomas's claim is nothing more than an attempt to take advantage of your good nature and must be refuted. I know an attorney with experience of the Spanish legal system, one who can defeat this claim."

George engaged her suggested Dublin attorney to mount their defense, knowing that the issue would drag on for some time – and he did not personally respond to Thomas's claim.

When George and Louisa settled on a date for a February wedding, he wrote to his mother and to Thomas, inviting them to attend. Catherine's reply was swift and short – she would not be attending any such event, though she did remind George of his responsibility to visit Peter. She was by this stage living in furnished rooms located off Dawson Street, close to Thomas and close to the Hibernian Hotel she had vacated, and she still dined frequently at the hotel restaurant. Thomas eventually decided that he would go to the wedding, as a means of mending family relations and to keep dialogue channels open with his brother. The Christmas holiday period passed with no contact between George and his mother. Catherine marked it as a time of sad remembrance of the deaths of her husband, and son John, and spent the entire month in solemn prayer. Thomas joined her a few times for dinner but for the most part he lived his own quiet bachelor existence in Dublin. After Christmas Catherine told him she was tired of Dublin and wanted to relocate to London. In January Thomas began making enquiries about suitable quarters for her.

The official wedding announcement for George and Louisa was published in the Dublin newspapers, where Catherine saw it. She was named in the article as widowed mother of the groom and there was a tribute paragraph to her deceased husband, George Moore of Alicante and Mayo. Most of the announcement was taken up extolling the virtues of Louisa Browne's family connections – her uncle being the Marquess of Sligo and her other uncle being Denis Browne, the MP for Mayo – both of whom received favorable mentions. The newspaper notice billed the upcoming wedding as a grand affair. Thomas travelled to Mayo for the wedding as a mark of respect for the absent parents, and to rekindle his relationship with his brother, especially in the light of the pending lawsuit over the Alicante property. He noticed that James O'Donnell was not around and mentioned it to George.

"Louisa did not see eye to eye with him – she didn't need

him, and he was dismissed – I heard he was working for the Blake's at Tower Hill, where his son works."

• • •

Extract from the diaries of Catherine de Kilkelly, Dublin

My final break with Moore Hall has occurred. George has taken that woman for his wife and therefore my self-imposed exile is now permanent. Thomas wanted to attend the wedding as a mark of solidarity between brothers and I had no objection to that. Afterwards he wished to tell me all about the event and how all the Browne's took pride of place – I asked him to stop as I could not bear to listen.

While in Mayo he visited with Peter at the care home – who is oblivious to all that has gone on and is being well cared for, according to Thomas. George has assured Thomas that Moore Hall estate will continue to shoulder the costs of taking care of Peter; in view of all this family turmoil I think it best to leave him in his familiar world – God Bless him. Thomas visited his father's grave at Straide Abbey which he said is also being well taken care of.

Thomas has lost his claim to the Alicante property – I shall therefore drop any thoughts I had of returning to Spain. The time has come for me to move on to the next chapter of my life and I will relocate to London. Thomas needs his space in Dublin, and I feel he is giving up too much of his time for me and is neglecting his own life. I will be glad to leave this wretched country and its dreadful politics behind. Ireland's detestable landlord system will probably doom every member of the Irish gentry to an eternity in Hell Fire. The system forces the estate landlords to extract monies from their Catholic tenants, to keep themselves in luxury while the poor tenants live in filth and poverty. It is bad enough for Protestant landlords to do this but there are many Catholic landlords doing the same, George included – we are all part of a system that treats our Irish brethren as little more than slaves.

God, please forgive me and our family for this dreadful practice, and I pray that a future member of the Moore family will have the courage to lead us out of this darkness. These ideals of equality among all Irish, regardless of religion or station in life were held by my dearly departed son, John. He was ahead of his time in this regard, but that is what must ultimately happen in Ireland, for the country to find peace.

• • •

George Moore II and his wife Louisa settled into married life at Moore Hall. He continued to be haunted by his decision to ostracize his mother and as time went passed, he began 'to suffer with his nerves' – he retreated almost completely from estate affairs to become somewhat of a literary recluse in his library. Ironically his thoughts were directed towards the meaning and value of human conflict – he spent his time researching and composing books on the British Revolution of 1688 and on the French Revolution. Louisa had taken over management of the house, the land properties and the family finances – ruling all with an iron fist.

Their marriage produced three sons, George Henry was born in 1810, followed soon afterwards by Augustus, and later by another son, John. George had birth notices sent to Thomas, knowing that he would pass them to Catherine – she did not acknowledge any of the births.

With Louisa busy running the estate, the family employed a French governess to begin the education of George Henry (affectionately known as GH) while he was just an infant. He was judged to be an exceptionally intelligent child, and at the age of nine his parents wished to send him to the best available school. Wanting a Catholic education for the boy left them few choices in Ireland, and his father did not want the boy's accent tainted with a brogue. They settled on St. Mary's College, Oscott, near Birmingham in England – the 'Eton' for Roman Catholics, where clergymen composed the entire staff. The nine-year-old was packed off to school and saw his parents just twice a year for the next several years. His only regular contact with home, apart from those infrequent visits, was through letters, and so began a stream of correspondence between mother and son that was to continue for the rest of her life. Their relationship would prove to be a complicated one, full of conflict between two strong personalities, as she tried to dominate him, while he strived to throw off her shackles.

He survived his lonely childhood schooling experience, and in due course thrived in his studies at Oscott to become one of their star pupils. GH was an accomplished classical scholar by the time he was a young teenager, having seemingly inherited his father's literary gifts. By sixteen he was writing verses so well that they were accepted for publication by the London magazines, and he became a central contributor to the school newsletter called the Oscottian. He left Oscott to attend University at Cambridge at the age of seventeen – carrying with him the reputation of being the most gifted pupil in the school's history.

• • •

Catherine had enlisted help from Thomas when she was ready to relocate to London and he spent a few weeks there getting her settled into a small but elegant home in Kensington, where she planned to live out the rest of her life. Thomas had failed to wrest the Alicante property from George through the courts, but the brothers remained on good terms and when the lease to the Spanish property was not renewed George sent a letter to Thomas, offering him a favorable lease if he wished to go to Alicante and try his hand at reviving the merchant business that his father once ruled. He took up the challenge and Thomas spent several years in Alicante in that quest. Meanwhile, Moore Hall thrived under the strict stewardship of Louisa Moore – she had retained the French governess to continue taking care of the two younger boys. Her husband George, now somewhat well known as the recluse historian, completed his book on the British Revolution of 1688, which he published in 1817.

Tragedy struck Moore Hall once more when their youngest son John suffered spinal injuries from being thrown from his horse at the age of twelve, after which he became an invalid. The accident had scared Louisa so much that she banned family members from horse jumping and from most non-essential riding. George wanted to inform his mother about the boy's accident, but Louisa would not allow him to do so.

• • •

Extract from the diaries of Catherine de Kilkelly, Kensington, London

London was a good choice for my widowhood – a sophisticated city that is a world apart from my previous life in Mayo. My only connections to Moore Hall in recent years have been infrequent personal reports from Thomas, who maintains contact with his brother. George has fathered three sons that by all accounts are blessed with great intelligence, no doubt inherited from our side of the family. The eldest boy George Henry was packed off to an English school at the age of nine – a cruel punishment for any child, regardless of what education privileges it might bring later. I know nothing else about these children, but I pray for them every day, adding them to my prayers for George, John and Peter – and for my dear brother Michel who met an early death from disease in the Spanish Americas. I pray also that the 'Curse of the Druids' does not follow this new generation of children at Moore Hall. Thomas lives in Alicante, having taken up a favorable lease of the family property there which George offered to him. He complains that the French wars are stifling his attempts to rebuild his father's merchant business there – I am too old to take up his invitation to visit him and will stay in London where I have everything I need at my fingertips. Ireland continues to be the poor relation in the aftermath of Union with England, just as I predicted – the news makes for depressing reading in The Times.

• • •

When GH Moore entered college at Cambridge, he quickly departed from the diligent scholar persona that he had been admired for at Oscott. He fell in with a fast set who had too much money and he was not the type to move at a slower pace than his companions. Within a year his parents saw that the only skill he was learning was billiards, in which he had become an expert. They recalled him home to Moore Hall, but the damage was already done. GH was headstrong, violent and extravagant – he had inherited his father's intelligence and his mother's character. His father suffered regular bouts of ill health and knew that he himself did not possess the traits needed for bringing up this headstrong boy; promptly handing that responsibility over to his wife – she who was confident that she possessed the ability to control GH going forward.

They had a clash of personalities that was explosive – they loved each other fiercely and fought as fiercely as they loved. His mother wanted to call the tune on everything – from control of the family purse to her ban of horses at Moore Hall after John's riding accident. All of GH's friends and relations loved horses and for him to comply with his mother's demands would effectively cut him off from contact with all these people. Unlike his mother, GH had a lavish nature and had little to no sense of the value of money. Eventually she had to relent on the rules concerning horses at Moore Hall, and riding and hunting soon became his absorbing passion. George Henry rode madly, fearlessly, and became a leading rider in the often described 'barbarous sport' of Irish steeple chasing – at events such as the Galway Races.

A German prince visiting the area wrote an account of what he saw at these races.

'The peasants were unable to resist strong whiskey and hundreds of drunken men accompanied my carriage to the racecourse during which time I counted a dozen fist fights among them on the way. To enjoy this festival one had to leave pity and humanity at home. The riders were young men from good families dressed in leather britches with elegant silk jackets and caps. The fences were walls of stone without mortar, some being five feet high and two feet broad. During the third heat the favorite led until the horse set his foot on a loose stone and fell backward on his rider with such force that both horse and rider lay motionless. The other competitors coming up behind took no notice of the fallen jockey as they jumped the fence. The horse finally got up but not the rider – he lay with his skull and breastbone fractured. A doctor pronounced his condition as hopeless, he bled the young man repeatedly so that he lay mired in his own blood, while people took little notice of the tragedy before their eyes. The rider was hauled away, and the last heat began on time as if nothing had happened. The eventual winner arrived at the post so exhausted that he could barely speak, having galloped some twelve miles over the time frame of two hours and having leaped over that same fence twelve times.'

GH's riding brought him into the company of the West of Ireland squireens (native small landowners), who led him into gambling and even into dueling – a situation that caused a major confrontation with his mother and she did not shy away from giving him a tongue lashing.

"George Henry, you have gone from being the ideal pupil at Oscott to being a daredevil rider and a reckless human being. You are setting a bad example for your brother Augustus when he is home from school, you are wasting your allowances and incurring debts that you are unable to pay. I control the purse strings at Moore Hall, and I will not stand for it."

"Mama, father said he would help me out on those debts, and I am cutting off contact with these people who have led me astray – please forgive me."

"Your father must not be burdened with your problems. He is too busy with his books, and you are not to speak to him about money matters in future – is that clear?"

"Yes Mama."

A reprieve for GH came in the form of the sad death of his youngest brother John, who finally succumbed to the spinal injuries that had invalided him a few years earlier after a fall from a horse. The family united in their grief and GH's behavioral problems were put on hold.

However, it was not long until GH's bad habits re-appeared; his mother then decided that he had to be separated from his undesirable Irish companions and he was sent to London to study law in the summer of 1829. He agreed to this plan and dutifully signed up for law tutorage with a scholar named Mr. Blick, prior to entry to law school classes for the new term. His mother demanded that he write letters to her every few days and he dutifully obliged, telling her he was studying hard and following quality pursuits like going to the theatre. At this time, he became aware that his grandmother was living in London, a woman he had never met, and he had grown up knowing only his mother's side of the family feud – in which she blamed his grandmother for walking out on them.

GH's personality was such that he asked permission to visit her. His request was denied and, sadly, just a few months later his grandmother died – ending the direct link to his grandfather, the Merchant of Alicante.

• • •

Last entry in the diaries of Catherine de Kilkelly, Kensington, London

I blacked out and fell on the floor last week at home. Doing better now except for the bruises that will take time to heal. The doctor says my heart has weakened – I told him I knew that already as my poor heart has been broken for many years. Nurse Mary has mailed a letter to Thomas asking him to return immediately to London, despite my protests. I feel good today but will probably be a mess tomorrow – that is the way I am now. Thomas told me that my grandson, George Henry, lives in London much of the time but has been forbidden by his mother to come visit me. Maybe that is for the best – I think the emotion of seeing him might be too much for me.

My biggest regret is that I was unable to convince my George that we should stay in Spain. I truly believe that our life would have been happier there, and George would have lived longer. My John would be alive today just like his brothers, George, Thomas and Peter. Poor Peter, locked in his own world – he is blissfully unaware of all the tragedy that has befallen us. I know he is safe, but it pains me every day that I had to leave him behind in Ireland, and that I have not been able to hug him for so many years. God, please forgive me for leaving him, bless him and comfort him and do not let young George forget to visit him regularly.

I made my peace with the Lord many years ago and I am ready whenever He decides to take me. I know I will die soon – with grief staining my heart – grief for my George, for darling John, and for Ireland. The future for our family at Moore Hall fills me with worry and fear.

If there is but one wish that You will grant me, O Lord, please nullify the 'Curse of the Druids' and its effects on those who inhabit Muckloon – banish the Druids to Hell Fire.

• • •

Uncle Thomas's efforts to revive the business in Alicante had been going badly – he had returned to London in 1830 when he received news that his mother was ill. She perked up when she saw him, and as she improved Thomas thought it was only right that she should be told of her young grandson, John's death. She took it very badly, as it rekindled the grief she carried with her for her George, and her son, John, and she mumbled incoherently to Thomas about the 'Curse of the Druids'. He remained in London with her, and a few weeks later she suffered a heart attack and died soon afterwards.

Her son George, Master of Moore Hall, was not informed of her death till almost two months later.

Thomas was the sole beneficiary in her will, and with this windfall of money he went back to Alicante to try one last time.

CHAPTER TWENTY

In London GH slipped back into his old habits of racing and hunting – pastimes he could not afford on an allowance of 400 pounds a year. Despite his constant denials, horses and racing took precedent over law studies; his debts soon began to mount up, to the point of requiring intervention. His mother was furious when she became aware of this and told her London attorney to seek clarification. Mr. Hammersley investigated and confirmed the seriousness of the situation. The twenty-year old GH would not co-operate by telling the full extent of his debts – his creditors included several horse dealers, a tailor and his banker. On Louisa's instruction the attorney gave him just enough money to cover his trip home and he sent him back to Mayo.

The family had to spend a substantial sum of money to settle his London debts. Back home, his parents tried to get him interested in the estate operations, a way to keep a watch over him – a plan that failed despite many heated confrontations between mother and son. He was not contrite, and simply went back to his old habits which meant frequent trips to Dublin, London, and to Bath where his aunt lived. Louisa had her sister attempt to get GH involved in polite society in Bath, in the hopes of having him marry one of the many very agreeable local Catholic girls from good families – thinking that marriage was the tonic to cure her son. Her sister was also acting as her spy. Bath is located very near Cheltenham, a place that attracted wealthy horse people and it became the focus of attention for George Henry. It was there that he became romantically involved with an older lady, but far worse was the fact that she was already married. When news of this relationship was relayed to his mother she flew into a rage and accused him of the deepest treachery; demanding that he cease his attendance upon the woman, or risk forfeiture of the affections of his parents.

Being that GH was in England and his mother was in County Mayo, a stream of explosive letters was exchanged between them as they tried to resolve their impasse. About that same time GH heard through associates of the untimely death of his uncle Thomas, who had contracted yellow fever in Alicante and died there – and he complained bitterly to his mother for her failure to tell him this news timely, when she knew it. GH used her disregard for his uncle's death, and the derangement of his uncle Peter, to strengthen his arguments with his mother and to extract some measure of compromise from her. He offered to winter in Italy, to prove to her that he was ceasing his romantic attachment to the married woman in Cheltenham. His mother approved of that plan and instructed her London attorney, Mr. Hammersley, to see him off at Dover and give him five circular notes of twenty pounds each – his allowance monies.

At Calais, GH had other unfinished business to settle, this being with a West of Ireland squireen named Joe MacDonnell, a chief of the Irish sporting underworld. MacDonnell was known as 'the twenty-tumbler man' meaning that he held the record of being able to drink that number of whiskey punch tumblers at one sitting. Sometime earlier GH had bought a horse from him for one hundred pounds cash, plus a promissory note of four hundred pounds.

"Mr. George, your honor, I could be using that 400 now as I have some debts to take care of."

"Joe – I absolutely do not have that kind of money and our deal called only for payment at a time in the future that satisfied both parties."

"Today is satisfactory for me, your honor."

"Not for me, Joe."

"Your mother would be very upset with you if I was to tell her about this debt – best that us men take care of it and not get the women folk involved, is what I say. How about that?"

"If you cannot wait, then go ahead and contact her but be warned – mother is a very tough negotiator."

"Indeed, I know that. Why don't you pay me 300 and we'll call it a deal?"

"What part of this plain talk do you not understand, Joe? I do not have money for you currently, and I have a train to catch. Good day to you Joe."

GH walked away at that stage and continued his trip to Vienna and Italy, where he stayed till early spring. When MacDonnell did try to extort Mrs. Moore later, she was more than able for him, and she made him settle for two hundred pounds.

• • •

Augustus Moore, GH's younger brother, was by this time showing extraordinary precocity in mathematics at his school in Priors Park, England. WR Hamilton, one of the preeminent mathematicians of the time examined the boy's work and pronounced that Augustus could scarcely fail to become eminent if he persevered with his chosen field. He was accepted into Trinity College, Cambridge. Augustus and George Henry had been inseparable from an early age, and the youngster was getting more and more attracted to what he saw as the fast and exciting life being led by his older brother – bringing an entirely new set of worries to their mother.

GH spent time again visiting his niece in Bath after his return from Italy – he backtracked on his promise to stay away from the Cheltenham racing set, while his mother fretted that his love affair would be rekindled. Added to this was her concern that Augustus might stray from his studies under the bad influence of George Henry. In desperation, she convinced the disillusioned GH to go on an extended trip to the glamorous East – to places like Syria and Persia. Under threat that his allowance was about to be cut off, and having a mild interest in playing the explorer, he agreed to go. He teamed up with his friend Charles Kirwan for the first part of that trip, then continued with other companions exploring the East for a full two years – the Russian Caucasus, Persia, Syria and the Dead Sea, then back towards the West – to Constantinople, Athens and the Greek Isles. He dabbled in history and was quite a good sketching artist – as he tried to find some purpose in his life. His travel diary became an important focus point during this time; it included many sketches of places, people and animals from the East, and he even added sketches to his infrequent letters home to his mother.

Lady Josephine, his Cheltenham love object, persuaded her elderly husband to also travel to the East in order to follow GH – eventually they had a final parting in the Greek Isles. GH felt that he was betrayed by this woman, and he reflected on the affair with an entry in his diary – 'The love of a woman that but yesterday seemed passionate and eternal, may today have passed from her false and reckless heart; but a mother's love lives on through storms and sunshine, with unchanged and unchangeable devotion. Yet, for such a vile thing I would have once betrayed my mother's heart.'

While GH was unable to keep in contact with home for long periods during his Eastern sojourn, his parents received a well-earned break from the financial and emotional struggles that the boy brought on them. During that absence they had developed a friendship with the celebrated novelist Maria Edgeworth, who had a house only fifty miles from Moore Hall. She had read George's 'British Revolution' and 'Life of Pombel' and 'Life of Riperda', plus several Irish locally based Moral Tales that he had published. She liked his works and offered to help him with his research for his work-in-progress – 'A Memoir of the French Revolution'. Maria, then in her seventies, was enchanted by Moore's other son, Augustus, who was continuing to show such promise as a mathematician. Louisa began to confide her hopes and fears for GH's future to Miss Edgeworth – who was very impressed with his travels to places like Russia and Egypt. They had many long and serious conversations by wax light in the drawing room or library. George senior suffered more frequent bouts of ill health, but Miss Edgeworth's enthusiasm for his literary pursuits spurred him on.

George Henry was by this stage focused on his main goal, that of exploration of the Dead Sea – a place that westerners knew little about, other than what they read in the Bible. It was known to be a desolate place, thirteen hundred feet below sea level, with dangerous heat. The first person to visit the place in modern times was an Irish traveler named Costigan, just two years prior to GH. Costigan was overcome by heat exhaustion and died before he was able to make any scientific observations. GH and his companion, a man named Beek, knew they had a very tough task ahead of them – they purchased a good boat in Beirut and hauled it on mules to the Dead Sea shores. Over several weeks they made many important observations such as measuring the length and width of the sea. They found the water so buoyant from high salt content that they had to procure more lead weights, to force their depth lines to reach the bottom when taking soundings. Shortly after this they had to cut their exploration short, when tribes around the east and southeast shores rose up in rebellion, and the chiefs who were protecting GH's party could no longer do so. The intrepid adventurers then spent several months visiting Syria, Turkey and the Caucasus area of Russia, before doubling back to Constantinople and later to Greece.

• • •

During this time period the country of Ireland was largely at peace. The repercussions from the defeat of the 1798 Rebellion had lasted for decades, aided in no small part by the Act of Union in 1801 which abolished the Irish parliament – ushering in the era when Ireland was ruled direct from London and her small allotment of MPs were relegated to a powerless minority. Britain's war with France had led to a strengthened market for Irish agricultural exports. The Royal Canal and the Grand Canal were constructed, to connect Dublin with the

River Shannon to better facilitate those exports. The ending of the war in 1815 hurt the agriculture based Irish economy, resulting in an economic depression. This coincided with agrarian strife over the much-hated Tithes that were charged to Catholic tenants to support the government established Protestant Church of Ireland; a church that the tenant masses did not even belong to. The population of the country grew dramatically during this period which also increased the dependance of the poor people on the humble potato to sustain themselves. This was the era of Daniel O'Connell, the Catholic barrister and MP who made the cause for Catholic Emancipation into a national movement. He was credited with getting the Relief Act passed in 1829 and earned the title of 'The Liberator' among the peasant masses. George Moore II, the historian, paid little attention to any of this, and life on his estate continued as before.

GH came home from his Eastern travels earlier than planned, mainly due to news of his father's deteriorating health. With Miss Edgeworth's encouragement, the young man contributed a report to the Journal of the Royal Geographical Society. However, his mood was one of recurring unhappiness and he was greatly agitated by his mother and Miss Edgeworth reading aloud his own letters from the East and by their urgings to seek fame by writing – he stated flatly that he would rather pay 100 guineas than hear them read the letters again. He got so sick of this continual nagging that he destroyed most of his letters from the East – whatever was not hidden away by his mother was lost forever.

Having reached the age of consent, George Henry was no longer subject to the degree of control that his mother previously had. Nothing amused him but horses and the company of racing men. This passion was shared and carried to even greater excess by his mathematical genius brother Augustus, who had by now returned home on a break from Trinity College, Cambridge. Mayo had the same influence on Augustus as it had on GH, discouraging any ambition other than excellence in horsemanship – to the horror of their mother and the indifference of their ill father.

Augustus terminated his studies, and in a very short time the brothers had thrown aside all thoughts of literary or scientific fame, and plunged into the excitement of horse training, racing and hunting. GH was the better race rider but in the hunting field Augustus reigned supreme. The notion that either should consider earning a living never crossed their minds, and Augustus was even more reckless with money than GH and had a particular flare for practical jokes. Moore Hall soon became notable for the training of racehorses and the schooling of hunters. The brothers' fearless approach to steeple chasing blew away the competition – they would not slow their horses ahead of a jump but take the fence at full stride. Their blue bird's-eye colors began to appear on well-known courses throughout England and the brothers were prominent figures at these events. Those were the days of two-mile heats, with the best of three heats to be the winner of the race. In Mayo all the local squireens who had horses to dispose of sought the attention of the brothers but were on high alert when they visited the stables – wanting to avoid Mrs. Moore, who had forbidden them to sell horses to her sons.

George Moore Senior's health continued to deteriorate during the winter of 1838, to the point that he became paralyzed, and bed ridden. On January 6th, 1839, Ireland was subjected to terrifying windstorms that went down in history as 'The Night of the Big Wind' and caused tremendous damage throughout the country. Moore Hall suffered very little damage other than the loss of some irreplaceable trees.

Shortly after that, GH had to deal with another storm. MacDonnell, the twenty-tumbler man began to harass him for the 200 pounds he had 'lost' when he sold his debt note to Mrs. Moore for a cash discount. This feud escalated into a dueling challenge issued by GH which was refused, but then MacDonnell sucked in another character into the fray – a notorious adventurer called O'Gorman Mahon, whom GH characterized as a swindler's bravo and whom GH challenged to fight. A local newspaper then published details of the exchanges between the parties, causing needless publicity and more pain for his parents. Augustus became involved in the feud and by the summer MacDonnell had filed suit against him for criminal libel. The brothers went to Dublin to fight the lawsuit while their mother prayed that the entire episode would end before the English papers picked up on it – she announced to the brothers that she was sick of these quarrels over horses and declared that she would not spend any more money on stables, or anything connected to horses. MacDonnell's case was thrown out by the court and the brothers returned to Mayo in triumph and set about patching up their relationship with their mother.

In September 1840 George Moore II, the historian, and Master of Moore Hall, lost his health battle and died peacefully at home – he was seventy years old. In accordance with his wishes, he was buried in the family plot of Kiltoom, beside the estate. His extensive manuscript of 'A Memoir of the French Revolution' had not been completed and was put away in a drawer, while Louisa Moore would now finally lose her control of the purse strings to the heir and new Master, George Henry. The income from Moore Hall and the properties at Ashbrook, Ballintubber and Partry, was now to be George Henry's to do as he pleased with. Soon after her husband's death Mrs. Moore compiled a list of the many charges on the inheritance – these charges totaled some 40,000 pounds. Added to that, GH had taken out mortgages adding up to several thousand pounds, in anticipation of his inheritance.

GH and Augustus were undeterred by these debts and the brothers were soon devoting themselves heart and soul to racing and riding. Their favorite hunting fields were in Tipperary with Lord Waterford and in Galway with Mr. St George at

Tyrone House. GH was known by the nickname Wolfdog Moore after one of his celebrated horses and in tribute to the reckless courage with which he rode. The brothers and other young Bloods were not content to just ride home after their hunts – one of them would throw up a challenge and set off at pace to find and jump the most difficult fences they could find as they rode home cross country. The brothers excelled at schooling horses that could jump any type of fence – every morning their horses were ridden over every sort of obstacle. They got many knocks and marks from the stone walls – so much so that blemished knees came to be named 'Moore Hall Marks'.

They had a horse called Faugh-a-Ballagh (Gaelic for 'clear the way'), a wretched looking animal no more than fifteen hands high, incurably thin with big knees who trotted and galloped with difficulty. This horse possessed one great gift – he could jump a stone wall six foot high with the greatest of ease, and hunting men seeing the horse for the first time would readily wager against the horse. It was a constant delight of GH and Augustus to make such a bet and have the horse led down to the stone wall – where these men could see him hobble across the field. Once the horse and his rider neared the fence the horse would cock his ears, gather himself, and hop over the wall with ease. Augustus, on this same horse took part in one of the most famous 'pounding matches' against Lord Clanmorris, a great rider on a fine hunter. The local peasants also delighted in watching these dangerous matches and there was a large crowd to watch this contest. After both horses had easily cleared the early fences, the two contestants in turn then selected tougher fences which they both negotiated safely. Two hours later the two competitors remained equal to the 'challenges' of each other. Then Augustus selected a stone wall about six feet high with an uphill approach and ground in front of it that was very rough. Augustus searched the fence looking for a spot, deciding on a place where there was a huge rock more than half the size of the wall. The little horse clanged his feet on the rock as if using it for a stepping-stone and landed safely on the other side – to the amazement of all present. Lord Clanmorris' s much bigger hunter would not even look at the fence and he had to concede the contest to Augustus.

GH had a horror for figures and money accounting, so he was happy to leave the administration of his father's will to his mother. She was exhausted from caring for her husband during his long illness and she decided to take a break from Moore Hall, spending the winter of 1840 and an extended period through the following summer away in London and other places in England. On purpose, she left her two sons short of ready money while they waited for the will to be approved. The running of Moore Hall was left in the hands of two older servants that she trusted – Mary MacDonald and William Mulldowney, the latter having the combined titles of steward and butler. He was allowed to collect rents from the estate properties and GH had to go to him when he needed money – and provide justification for any monies he received – a ritual he despised and never forgot. Augustus and GH were continually back and forth from Moore Hall to race meetings in England and various places in Ireland and were not involved in the day-to-day estate operations. Mulldowney's responsibilities included keeping 'horse copers' and other undesirables away from the entrances to the estate, as well as sending Mrs. Moore regular correspondence and accounts details from the estate books. While in London she spent time trying to find a publisher for her late husbands 'Memoir of the French Revolution'. Despite help and advice from her friend Maria Edgeworth she eventually decided to abandon the plan and save the 500 pounds that had been set aside in the will for publication. Mrs. Moore struggled with what she should do with herself in widowhood, eventually deciding to return to Ireland and put the financial affairs of Moore Hall in order – finally returning home in October. The brothers were away at races and hunting events at that time, but they did make sure they were home to spend Christmas with her.

The last will and the estate of the deceased George Moore II was settled soon afterwards, and George Henry officially became the Master of Moore Hall. He and Augustus had by now moved up from the company of seedy half gentlemen, Catholic squireens and gig-men – having been welcomed into the 'club' of the English and Irish aristocratic society world – mainly because of their horse riding and training proficiencies. As well as having their own training stables at Moore Hall they hired the acclaimed trainer Boyce, based at Newmarket, for their horses in England. Boyce's son often rode for them, and the son and father made a good income from GH's blue bird's-eye colors. Moore's best steeplechaser was a horse called Anonymous, who won most of the big races at the time and brought home some valuable purses. In October 1843 GH himself met with a horrific riding accident during a race, when he was almost crushed under a horse, and after his recovery he vowed to give up competitive race riding – a promise that was a cherished Christmas gift to this mother that year.

Augustus made no such promise and in March 1845 he went to Liverpool to ride Mickey Free in the celebrated Grand National steeplechase race. The course was hardened by overnight frost and there was talk of cancelling or postponing the race but eventually it was decided to go ahead as planned. Augustus, riding Mickey Free, made the early running, and at his usual frenetic pace he charged towards the difficult fence at the bottom of the hill below the brook. Mickey Free cleared the fence but stumbled on the further bank, then fell back on top of Augustus and snapped his rider's back. The badly injured Augustus was taken to hospital. GH was at Moore Hall when he received the telegram announcement of the accident, and immediately rushed to Liverpool to be at his brother's side, meeting the attending doctor as he entered the hospital.

"Mr. Moore, we have reason to believe that his condition has improved but I warn you that it is still very grave, as his spine is severely damaged."

Augustus knew the sound of GH's step and as he approached his room, he sprang up from his bed to greet him, saying "Thank God you have come." He immediately fell back on the bed in exhaustion and pain, as nurses rushed to attend to him. GH sat by his bedside for the next few days as his condition fluctuated. When he was not asleep or in too much pain they talked a lot, remorseful and tearful conversations.

"George – I have been very reckless and have brought unnecessary pain upon our dear Mother. Father worried about us so much that I cannot help but wonder if we are guilty of heaping too much stress on his frail body. If only we could turn back the clock – I should have made the same pledge as you and quit steeple chasing. Please God deliver me from this and let me atone for my past behavior."

"You must not blame yourself. I was the one that persuaded you to abandon your mathematics studies for the crazy world of horses. Forgive me, dear Augustus."

"Enough of this. Let us not dwell on blame. We both love the excitement of competitive riding and racing – it's in our blood and I would not trade one minute of it. You managed to recover from your accident – help me get through this and let us and start fresh."

"You are right, my brother – we have a great future ahead

of us. I am here for you – for as long as it takes to get you well. You must rest now and know that I am here watching over you."

The doctor came to examine the patient and decided that Augustus needed to 'be bled' again – they were concerned about internal bleeding and this procedure was used to relieve pressure on his spine and other organs. Reluctantly, GH left the room and had to wait for hours outside while the medical people worked to relieve the pain and make him more comfortable.

This situation continued for several days. Just when GH thought they had made progress Augustus would have a relapse. The pain medicine made him so sleepy that all GH could do was to watch over him and pray. It got worse near the end and Augustus summoned up the courage to tell his brother that he was slipping away, and through the pain he said, – "George, take me back to Moore Hall and place me facing the stables and the galloping straightaways. We lost John in a riding accident, and you are all that mother has left now. Promise me you will not lead this wild life any longer."

"Augustus, I will do as you ask and you will always be in my heart, always."

Augustus died on March 22nd, 1845, in the arms of George Henry – who closed his dead eyes with his own hands. Augustus was only thirty-two; ironically the same age at which his uncle John, the appointed 'President of Connaught' had died – as a prisoner of the Crown in the aftermath of the 1798 Rebellion.

George Henry was inconsolable and cried like a baby. Then he accompanied his brother's coffin back to Moore Hall where Augustus was laid to rest just as he had asked of his brother – beside his younger brother John who had died only a few short years earlier from the same type of injury after his fall from a horse. There were reported sightings of the ghost of their grandmother, Catherine Kilkelly, along the woods beside the graveyard – but nobody remembered her warnings about the 'Curse of the Druids'.

Augustus's mother bore her grief with a fortitude and a patience that gave some measure of comfort to George Henry. GH kept his promise not to ride competitively again, but he did continue training racehorses and won the St. Leger several months later.

CHAPTER TWENTY-ONE

George Henry had taken little notice of politics during his early years – even the passage of Catholic Emancipation in 1829 which gave Catholics the right to sit in parliament and occupy political posts didn't grab his attention away from horse racing. It is said that horses, religion and politics have been the preoccupations of 'Modern Ireland' and it was now the turn of politics to come into the life of George Moore III. His father had written of his deep desire that his son should become a model landlord, a wish GH could not fulfill because he was too impatient of detail and routine to adopt such a role. He was definitely 'More Irish' in feeling than his father had been, but he was not comfortable as a 'Repealer' of the Act of Union, or as a 'Nationalist' because they often condoned violent rebellion – he was more comfortable as a 'Reformer'. The year of 1845 was a terrible year for GH – not only did he lose his brother who was his best friend, but it was also the year that the terrible effects of the potato crop failure began to be felt around Ireland, with the worst effects being in Connaught and especially Mayo. His brother's death gave GH a distaste for his former amusements, and he started to cut back his racing business in England as the disastrous 'Great Famine' unfolded in Ireland. He felt a sense of duty to his countrymen – he returned home to do what he could to help his tenants and the starving multitudes in Mayo, and immediately got involved in famine relief work.

An opportunity to contest a parliamentary seat in Mayo came in March of 1846 when a country gentleman named Blake resigned from parliament. GH found himself drawn into politics by the natural order of things rather than any personal ambition. He saw that the famine had highlighted the glaring ignorance of the London parliament, and that the Irish members were selfish and ineffective. Even Daniel O'Connell with his great powers of oratory had failed to obtain any significant relief measures for Ireland. GH did not label himself as a Whig or a Tory, but he had the support of all the big landlords of Mayo – Lucan, Dillon, Sligo and Oranmore – who promised to march their tenants under guard to the courthouse to vote for him. He remarked to a friend that 'emancipation had given Irish tenants the right to vote but their vote was far from a free vote while it was controlled by their masters – the landlords'. Ironically his opponent was none other Joe 'Mor' MacDonnell, the twenty-tumbler man, running as the Repeal candidate for the party led by Daniel O'Connell – and MacDonnell had the backing of all the local priests.

The election got very testy – Lord Dillon locked up some of MacDonnell's voters, and in retaliation a mob of his supporters blocked the roads to stop Dillon's tenants from leaving the estate. GH refused to wear the 'Repeal Badge' and for that he was very unpopular amongst a large segment of the electorate. When he made a personal appearance at the Ballinrobe races he was attacked by a violent mob and cornered until he faced his horse at a very high wall and cleared it to escape – even the mob applauded his fine horsemanship. In the end GH lost the election to MacDonnell and accepted his defeat with good humor. Despite the loss he was constantly being asked for money to feed the starving masses – by no lesser persons than the very priests that had backed his opponent. He could do little at that stage as his own monetary circumstances were bad because most of his tenants were in arrears.

In May, George Henry had a wonderful stroke of luck on the racecourse – his horse Coranna won the Chester Cup in England. Between purse and side bets that he had placed, GH made 10,000 pounds after paying the horse's co-owner, Lord Waterford, his share of the overall winnings. His generous side immediately came out; despite the large estate debts he needed to settle per correspondence he had just received from his butler, Mulldowney. He sent 1,000 pounds to his mother's bank account in Westport and asked her to use her judgement to see that every one of his tenants (and even the squatters) should receive immediate relief in return for making simple improvements to their holdings. He told his mother that 'his horses would gallop all the faster with the blessings of the poor'. She did her best to distribute this aid and gave a cow or other equivalent to every one of their tenants. She utilized the aid organizations of the local priests to distribute general charity to the poorest people but was frustrated by the lack of accountability, which meant that much of the aid was wasted. This information was relayed to GH in letters where she complained that the government had totally misread the seriousness of the famine and were not giving any meaningful help to the people. GH was delayed in England and saw for himself that English opinion was utterly misinformed about the situation in Ireland.

When he next returned to Mayo and saw that matters had worsened, he decided to reduce all his rents to help his tenants survive. All tenants paying less than five pounds a year were given total remission. For those paying five to ten pounds he gave a seventy-five percent rent reduction. For those paying ten to twenty pounds he reduced the rent by fifty percent. He served as Chairman of the Relief Committee covering a large part of the county. It was apparent that the government was not reacting to the crisis in a meaningful way, so GH took matters into his own hands. He persuaded two local landlord friends and kinsmen – Sir Robert Blosse and the Third Marquess of Sligo (still Lord Sligo to his friends) to join him in importing food for the starving people. Between the three of them they chartered a ship 'The Martha Washington' to carry one thousand tons of flour from New Orleans to Westport – where the cargo was discharged in June and was distributed to their tenants over the following months. Those acts meant that not one of GH's five thousand tenants died of want during the famine. He and Lord Sligo toured throughout Ireland, conferring with local leaders on ways to save the starving population. Both were present at an important meeting in Dublin attended by twenty lord peers, thirty Irish MPs, by Daniel O'Connell himself and even a few Orangemen from the north – in a united effort to convince the British government to greatly increase direct food aid to the people.

At last, in the autumn of 1846 the Government was induced to move, but their solution was to create public works projects to pump money into the local population which could then be used to buy food. They had long refused to import corn lest it might interfere with private enterprise, and they failed to understand that the starving people had no money to buy corn from the speculators they allowed instead to bring it in – most of the corn got exported back to English merchants, rather than helping the needy Irish. Thus, while volunteers labored in the cause of charity the Government did nothing but obstruct. Sir Charles Trevelyan was the author and agent of most of these foolish ideas – making people work who were too sick and weak to walk miles to the projects in order to get signed on. GH was a fierce critic of Trevelyan and said of him – 'disaster followed every scheme he originated, and he aggravated every such disaster by his futile efforts to retrieve it.'

By 1850, when the worst of the famine had passed, it was

calculated that out of a pre-famine population of eight million, one million people died as a direct result of starvation; at least another million left the country by any means they could (many thousands of whom died of disease on the so-called coffin ships that carried them to America and other countries). Millions more continued to leave the stricken land in the decades that followed – searching for a new beginning elsewhere. There were numerous deaths from famine sickness among the gentry also – three estate landlords in the greater Mayo region perished from fever they caught while helping their sick tenants.

The parliament seat in Mayo became open again due to a general election in 1847 and GH ran this time as an Independent – against three other candidates, one of which was MacDonnell again. His platform was anti-government, and he continuously criticized their bungling of Famine relief – for which he gained much popular support. Lord Sligo was firmly on his side, and he was also supported by a Tory called Gore, who was a strong supporter of landlord's rights. George Henry won the election; the only handicap he faced was that he entered Parliament when much of the spirit of the Irish constitutional movement had evaporated – O'Connell had died and there was much distrust in all forms of government since their disastrous attempts to effectively help the starving population. People now backed a 'Young Ireland' party who preached a resort to arms, and they did foment an attempted rebellion shortly afterwards in 1848 – it was a total failure.

In the aftermath of the rebellion, John Mitchell, a writer of genius who had founded a nationalist newspaper called The Nation was convicted under the Treason Felony Act and sentenced to fourteen years exile in the far east colonies – other notables such as Smith O'Brien and John Dillon were handed similar punishments.

George Henry Moore cut a fine figure of a man – tall in stature with broad shoulders. What hair he lacked on top of his head he made up for with large mutton-chop sideburns. He was already somewhat well-known in England for his horse racing exploits and his entry into the House of Commons attracted a lot of attention. He was not afraid to speak out on the floor of the House about the errors of British policy in Ireland, speeches that earned him friends in the Protectionist and Country Gentlemen's party but made his landlord class cringe. His blunt criticisms attracted sarcastic rebuffs from The Times, who called him 'Wolfdog Moore' from his racing days, and the 'Tender-Hearted Turfman' – accusing him of speculating at English racecourses instead of attending to his duties during the Famine. He was furious over these false accusations and soon issued a challenge to Higgins of The Times for a duel (with pistols) – while evidence was brought forward by Lord Sligo to show GH's sacrifices in time, money, and other ways in which he had advocated for the poor during the Famine. Higgins was humiliated and later he refused the challenge of 'Wolfdog' Moore.

• • •

At this stage George Henry was approaching the age of forty and was still unmarried. Now that he was a member of Parliament his mother revived her hopes that he would take the time to find a suitable match. She and Maria Edgeworth corresponded about this subject as if GH had asked them to find him a wife. Miss Edgeworth could be described as an open-minded Protestant and she was happy to suggest some suitor names to Mrs. Moore but admitted that she was not acquainted with 'high Catholic people', as she called them. She suggested that Louisa engage the help of a Mr. Bodenham who was hail-fellow-well met with fine and foreign society and could introduce GH into places where he might meet 'an accomplished and suitable lady'. George Henry made his own match in the end, with twenty-six-year-old Miss Mary Blake of Ballinafad. She was the daughter of his near neighbors, good landlords who owned properties in Mayo and Galway, and a family who were well regarded in the area. Mary was described as a mild young woman with a pleasant face, not clever but unquestionably a fine Catholic lady. She was also a virgin and that was important to GH – he had a past himself, and he did not want a wife with any hint of a past that might arouse any talk; even though there were whispers of surprise due to their age difference. They became a happy couple and were married in 1851, at which time she was welcomed at Moore Hall by George Henry's mother and all the staff.

Parliamentary duties took GH to London for a substantial amount of time, and he suggested to his mother that she should remain at Moore Hall as company and advisor to his young wife. Both ladies consented to this arrangement and the pair became great companions – both were fans of Sir Walter Scott's 'Waverly Novels' and they spent time reading aloud GH's old letters from his sojourn in the East and discussing his travel diaries – those that his mother had hidden and had escaped destruction. When Parliament was in recess GH decided to make some major improvements around the mansion's grounds as well as redecorating the interior – as a mark of respect to his new wife. That included the construction of an oak-paneled dining room with a carved mantelpiece and a great mahogany sideboard on which to display all his racing trophies. Next, the drawing room was decorated to express his adoration of Greek classical civilization. A new floor of French parquet was put down and the plastered walls were painted in blue grey, upon which pictures of his horses competed for wall space with gilt framed family portraits. Sadly, his mother suffered a severe fall on the stairs at that time, which left her an invalid thereafter and confined her to her rooms except when she was wheeled about the garden in a bath chair on sunny days. Louisa's dominance faded from that point onwards, and as Mary settled more into her role as wife to an MP and owner of a large estate – she became her own person and was determined not to be a domineering mother to her children like her mother-in-law had been.

• • •

The electoral system in Ireland was one in which the number of voters was very small – only the Mayo gentry and the so-called freeholder tenants had the right to vote. With the full assistance of the local police these tenant voters were commonly caged in pens or houses on voting days and forced to vote for whom their landlord told them to. GH deplored this system and privately criticized his own win on one occasion – where he got 695 votes, to the second-place man at 550 and third-place man at 330 – but he had to play by the rules in place and needed to get elected before he could attempt to change the system from the inside.

In Parliament, George Henry's personality and his oratory ability were quickly recognized, and some twenty-five Irish members soon regarded him as their leader. He set in motion the idea of 'Independent Opposition' – which was to have his group vote in a block against the government of the day on various party measures, and by throwing their weight from one side to the other, the Irish members were able to render party government impossible. However, even from the start, sinister forces began to undermine his position – in the form of corrupt action by the government to lessen his influence, and selfish in-fighting among his own party members. He was a persuasive speaker on the hustings and was fast becoming skilled in the workings of Parliamentary procedures and protocols. GH was a proud Catholic and was ever vigilant of 'popish aggression' by the Protestant majority government; when Prime Minister Russell introduced a bill designed to curb the power of Catholic bishops, George Henry, with the help of Irish Archbishop McHale, organized massive meetings in every Irish county to oppose the plan. He and his twenty-five members were pivotal in preventing the bill from going forward.

GH took interest in the fledgling Tenant League movement, that had been founded in 1850 to fight for tenant rights, and he was especially enamored by the vision of uniting the Presbyterians of the northern counties with the Catholic farmers of the South. He was in full sympathy with the cause of the people and stated their case in Parliament as follows –

'About two hundred years ago the English drove the whole Catholic people of Ireland from every other part of the country into the poor province of Connaught – giving the alternative of hell which they did not choose to adopt. Since that time the possessors of the soil have scarcely reclaimed an acre of the wilderness to which the people of Ireland had been driven to. They have scarcely built a farmhouse or constructed a farmyard or made a fence or dug a drain. The old population, driven by the English conquerors into the poorest countryside, by the sweat of their brows, by the toil of their own hands, had reclaimed a wilderness and made it fertile land. And then, year after year, generation after generation, the landlords had grasped and confiscated the property which the tenant had created, thus driving him further into the wilderness, again to reclaim as before. Was not this a great moral wrong? It was however, not a legal wrong – but we now seek to make it so.'

The League demanded that the government admit the indefeasible right of the occupying tenant to whatever improvements he might make to his land, and in the event of being evicted he would be compensated for all such improvements. GH set himself the task of bringing about a conference between the Tenant Leaguers and the Irish parliamentary members group he had created – with the purpose of cementing an alliance between the two. The conference came together and after difficult negotiations they settled their differences; yet it was an uphill battle to move Parliament with such a minority of Irish members; Lord Derby dissolved Parliament in 1852 when faced with what he called hostile demands.

GH returned to Mayo, to find that his support for re-election was fractured. His advocacy of the tenants' interests had alienated many of the landlords who had supported him previously, and most of the Protestant voters opposed him for his part in the struggle against the Ecclesiastical Titles Bill. Parliament had passed the Encumbered Estate Act to offer relief to bankrupt landlords affected by the famine aftermath. The unintended consequences of this Act were that a very substantial amount of the land of Ireland passed into the hands of speculator investors, who demanded large returns on their investment. The result was increased rents and increased evictions when tenants could not pay. GH had kindly taken in many of these evicted tenants, subdividing his lands to accommodate them and thereby multiplying his tenant numbers. This also became a factor in losing landlord support – many of whom felt that his rising tenant numbers was an attempt to improve his political position with the masses, an accusation he vehemently denied.

His friendship with Lord Sligo faltered over these matters and they had a delicate meeting to discuss the situation.

"Sligo – do you think I should go after that Castlebar newspaper for libel – for accusing me of ordering evictions at Ballintubber – I have never evicted anyone?"

"I care nothing about a Mayo paper, and I think the evictions in question took place while that particular property was in chancery, under the Encumbered Estates Act, after you had given up control of the property. However, you must accept responsibility for losing that land, because of your neglect to attend to the rent paying of your tenants."

"You have carried out many evictions at Westport – have you not?"

"Yes, but care was taken to distinguish between the idle or dishonest, and those desiring to be honest. The honest were put back and were given a new and fair rent. You are following the route of the bankrupt landlord Malley, and if you continue, you will end up exterminating your tenant base."

"I disagree with your assessment."

"Disagree if you wish – time will tell who saves the most of his tenants while at the same time saves most of his rents. Without rents you will follow Malley into bankruptcy. I am sorry, but I cannot support you in this election – I am supporting McAlpine, a Tory."

They left it at that rather than cause further damage to their friendship. GH still managed to top the poll and win re-election, with Higgins taking the other Mayo seat, and McAlpine at the bottom. McAlpine lodged a petition against GH's election, on a 'plea of intimation' – with underhand support from government leaders who wanted to exclude GH from the House of Commons. At the ensuing inquiry hearing held in Castlebar his accusers were not able to substantiate their claims and the plea was withdrawn.

For a time, George Henry's Irish Party held the balance of power in the new House of Commons. To garner support from them and dilute GH's growing power, Lord Aberdeen offered him the position of Chief-Secretaryship. He saw through this veil and refused the appointment, saying he could better serve his constituents by staying outside the cabinet – a decision that drew the rath of the powerful Irish Catholic Cardinal Cullen for his refusal to be in the government. Other members later took the government bait, notably Keogh, Sadleir, Monsell and O'Flaherty – who accepted minor government appointments, in so doing they splintered the Irish Party and diminished its effectiveness. Over the following years GH had several running battles with Cardinal Cullen over his denouncement of what he called ecclesiastical domination of the tenant resistance and the Catholic defense movements, putting himself at further odds with the Cardinal ahead of the 1857 election. Moore again held his seat despite the Cardinal's opposition, because of the support he got from many local priests who defied their Cardinal – but GH was then unseated, on the plea that 'spiritual influence' had been employed on his behalf – a decision that was government-supported in order to remove GH from the scene.

Disgusted with this corrupt interference George Henry withdrew from politics with a farewell address to Parliament that included these words -

"I entered public life with personal reluctance, and were I called to abandon it forever I should do so without personal regret. I leave behind me no sinister ambition crossed and no selfish motive disappointed. I repose upon honest work, honestly performed, and as those who drive the plough and sow the seed must need rest a while before they can hope to hold the sickle, when the harvest time arrives I still hope to be permitted to take my part in that good work, for which many have labored with better ability, but none with more truth and singleness of purpose than your obedient servant."

• • •

His marriage to Mary Blake soon produced two sons – George Moore IV was born in 1852, followed quickly by the birth of another son they named Maurice – and three more children were born some years later – Augustus, Nina and Julian. While out of Parliament he spent time at home in Mayo watching his two eldest boys grow out of babyhood. GH had demoted his old head servant Mulldowney to menial duties and had given the head job to Joe Applely. Joe was an ex-jockey and he looked longingly every day at the empty stables – never missing a chance to make persuasive arguments to his master to get back into horse training. They had a mare called The Cook, from George's previous racing days, which they used as a carriage horse – GH had been told the mare was barren. One day Joe found GH in a talkative mood while he was inspecting the closed stables.

"Your Honor, I have been studying the mare and I think she might be showing signs of wanting to breed – why don't we send her over to Mountain Deer and see what happens?"

"Joe, you are wearing me out with your talk of reopening the stables. Tell you what – let's send her over and see if your instincts are correct – it cannot do any harm."

"Thank you, Sir, I'll get her moved immediately.

Joe's instincts were good, and the mare produced a foal, a dark brown colt with white legs which they named Croaghpatrick, in honor of the local Mayo holy mountain. Joe pointed out how the colt's body was long and sleek, and he prophesied a racing future for him. Young George and Maurice spent a lot of time around the colt and Joe used their stable interest to convince GH to move forward.

"Shur, why don't we lay out a small racecourse in the fields below Drimnashinagh – the wee lads will love it and we can give Croaghpatrick a chance to stretch his legs."

"You'll be the death of me, Joe – but what the heck; let's do it."

They liked what they saw of the young colt as he galloped on the home course and GH decided to put him into training. Joe had filled the young boys' heads with stories of their father's famous riding past – tales of the exploits of Wolf Dog, Anonymous and Corunna stoked their hearts with horse lore and they in turn pestered their father about his exploits. GH had no regrets for withdrawing from politics; he had only entered public life because of a sense of duty and was prouder of owning a good horse than of any speeches he had made in Parliament. He still dabbled in horse racing as a punter and had accumulated a substantial debt to members of the ring. He sold the family property in Alicante, Spain to help his debt problems. His brother-in-law, Blake, and his wife's brother-in-law, Murphy, both bought an interest in the young colt, and they all had high expectations for Croaghpatrick's first race in England – in which the horse did poorly. More failures followed and they decided to leave him with a new trainer while GH and Mary spent time enjoying London.

When the trainer reported well of the horse, they entered him at Goodwood where he was listed at 40:1. The owners couldn't resist those odds and doubled down on their bets. The horse beat a field of 45 and the owners pulled in 20,000 pounds – a wonderful help for GH to clear his debts. They followed this win with another at the Chesterfield Cup and pulled in more substantial winnings. This brought about an inquiry by the Jockey Club over the ownership of the horse. Because GH was in default of stakes, he was not allowed to run a horse under his own name. Moore, Blake and Murphy were ordered to attend the Jockey Club hearing. Evidence was produced to show that GH had sold the horse to Murphy prior to the Goodwood race. GH was cleared of any wrongdoing, while popular myth always held that Moore was the owner of the horse – and Croaghpatrick went on to win several more races including the King's Cup three times in a row at the Curragh.

George Henry once again had a successful horse racing business going. Other winning horses at his stables were Master George, named after his eldest son, and Maurice, named after his second son.

CHAPTER TWENTY-TWO

Irish politics were constantly changing and there was a renewed sense of Nationalism brewing in the country. The Irish Republican Brotherhood (IRB) was founded in 1858; a secret oath-bound society dedicated to the overthrow of British rule in Ireland, by force. They were more commonly referred to as the Fenian Movement and they were destined to play a central role in several rebellions over the ensuing 60 years. GH was attracted to their ideals of independence even though their aims were a direct threat to the Irish land system where landlords ruled the lives of their tenants – a system that he himself was entrenched in as a landlord with tenants. He considered himself a loyal subject of the Crown and in 1864 he was the High Sheriff of Mayo, a position of power within the system of local government. At the conclusion of a court session where GH presided, a Fenian leader named O'Donovan Rossa approached him, and after a brief introduction he was invited to discreetly meet George Henry later at Moore Hall for discussions.

At the meeting O'Donovan Rossa began – "Mr. Moore, the 'organization' are impressed by your history of good deeds on behalf of tenants and the cause of Ireland's freedom and wish to extend an invitation to you to join us."

"I have no major objection to taking the oath, but I am concerned about the strong opposition of the Catholic Church to oath-bound societies like yours. That opposition will be an obstacle that will prevent many good men from joining your ranks and therefore diminishing the ranks to the point that will prevent it from becoming a force to be reckoned with."

"Sir, I disagree with your position on this, but I also understand the complexity of your situation. I do not wish to administer the oath to you under these circumstances and instead I suggest that you call on James Stephens the next time you are in Dublin – he is 'Head Center' and has the power to negotiate an arrangement that fits your high-profile position in County Mayo."

In that subsequent meeting GH and Stephens came to an agreed arrangement that was never made public, one in which GH remained in very close contact with the IRB leaders, without it ever being stated whether he had taken the membership oath or not.

Louisa Moore, George Henry's mother, died in 1861, after several years of being an invalid due to a fall at home. Her death was very hard on him – they had always been very close despite her domineering personality, and he saw firsthand the grief she endured from the loss of her husband George, her youngest son John and her second son Augustus – both boys having died after falls from horses. She had encouraged and pushed GH towards high achievement goals – because of her insistence that he write to her constantly when he was a child at school, he had become a great letter writer. He was still retired from Parliament when she died, and after her burial George Henry wrestled with ways to help his two eldest boys with their education at Oscott, the same Catholic school he himself had attended in Birmingham, England. Maurice, the younger son was a reasonable student, though far below the exulted levels his father had reached when he was that age. George, his eldest son, had lost some eighteen months of schooling due to a child bronchitis illness, and was a deplorably deficient student, according to Dr. Northcote, the school Principal. The boy was observant and lively but had no interest in his school lessons, preferring to be around horses at the stables. By mutual consent between his parents and the Oscott principal, after multiple attempts by teachers to pound the basics of math and grammar into his head, young George was finally withdrawn from the school when he was fifteen. His only ambition was to ride the winner of the Grand National Race, but he possessed none of the skills in horsemanship that his father and his uncle had.

During GH's absence from Parliament the confrontational situation between England and France became so dire that England became seriously alarmed at the prospect of a French invasion, and armed volunteer movements to protect the motherland sprang up all over England. In Ireland there was a strict law preventing the carrying of arms, complicating any similar movements there. GH, being a loyal subject, proposed a different type of volunteer force to circumvent this restriction. He proposed a registration of names willing to bear arms in defense of the country should the invasion threaten Ireland also, and he drew up a manifesto for such a volunteer force accompanied by a detailed scheme of action. His ideas drew surprising interest from the nationalists, and then it became apparent to GH that a generation of young men were already beginning to conspire against the government. He was not an advocate of insurrection and withdrew his ideas from consideration, as an internal quarrel was developing about how best to serve Ireland with the volunteer plan. One faction continued to plot and became the basis for a Fenian rebellion in 1867 that was snuffed out by the Dublin Castle authorities before it got any traction.

GH was one of the best letter writers of his time and was enjoying his 'retirement' doing just that, while keeping his eye on political happenings. He kept on the sidelines when in 1864 the Irish National Association was formed by John Dillon, John Martin and the O'Donohue. It was suspected that the association was under the patronage of his nemesis, Cardinal Cullen and for that reason GH and Archbishop McHale both withheld their support. He kept up regular correspondence with his friend Gavin Duffy, who had given up on the Irish cause ten years earlier, sold his share of the 'Nation' newspaper and emigrated to Australia. GH told him in a letter that he was happy that Dillon and Gray won Parliament seats in the 1865 election, while being glad he himself had not been suckered into running by Cullen. The failure of the Fenian rebellion in 1867 was no surprise to GH; he thought that as a fighting force Fenianism failed utterly, and the leaders at the time were not men of great ability – but the fact that it happened at all changed the mindset of the country. There was now no tolerance for schemers and dishonest politicians, and a sturdy independence had taken its place.

When it appeared that a general election was looking imminent in 1868, GH saw that the time had come when he could be of use to the country again, and without hesitation he decided that he would run. He sold his horses, closed the stables and got ready to fight Ireland's battle in Parliament once more. The representation of Mayo had for ten years been in the hands of an alliance of Tory and Whig landlords and that would be very difficult to break. One Mayo MP was Lord John Browne, brother of his erstwhile friend Lord Sligo, and the other was Sir Roger Palmer. Both resigned ahead of the election and the alliance nominated Lord Bingham (son of Lord Lucan), running as a Tory, with Valentine Blake running as the Whig representative. GH was strongly advised by his friends and his party associates not to attempt to run against such a strong coalition – notwithstanding the fact that his finances were not in good condition. He had confidence in himself that he felt could carry him through and he told his friends that he had made up his mind to run – that he could beat the odds, again. GH had no ill feelings towards his own gentry class and hoped to get some backing from them, but he believed that until the tenants had control of their own votes the county could not prosper. For six weeks he travelled the length and breadth of Mayo making speeches at every town and village, and his rousing nationalist words were well received – per this extract –

"I shall have the question settled whether one lord shall drive a hundred human souls to the hustings, another fifty, another a score – whether this or that squire shall call five or ten or twenty men as good as himself, his voters, and send them up with a brand on their back to vote for an omadhaun (fool) at his bidding. The people should not be constrained by the landlords – let them choose their own leaders, such as the priests. Let those who find fault with the clergy of Ireland for becoming tribunes of the people consider how those people would fare if the clergy did not become their tribunes. If the landlords make common cause with the people, the people will make common cause with them – the priests will make common cause with them also, and the common cause of all will be that of their country. Oppression has become so overbearing here in Mayo that the voters are being ordered to vote, at the same time, for a Tory who is in favor of coercion, and for a Whig who professes to be in favor of conciliation. The voters are the trustees for the great bulk of the people who have no votes and if the landlords insist on forcing their will upon the people it will certainly lead to riot and bloodshed. Mr. Blake and Lord Bingham cannot wash their hands enough, in a fruitless endeavor to cleanse themselves of the people's blood."

During the election cycle GH and Lord Sligo still exchanged several letters which displayed their respect for each other while also showing the gradual disintegration of their relationship. Blake withdrew from the contest before polling day – George Henry and Lord Bingham were elected. The landlord power had been broken in Mayo, but GH's political success was tempered by his personal loss. The men from whom he had snatched the power had considered that power to be their inalienable right and had possessed it for generations – they were his own personal friends. GH bore no ill-feeling toward them, but they bitterly resented his win and that made the quarrel personal.

George Henry Moore was once again MP for Mayo. He decided on further retrenchment by shutting up Moore Hall and took a modest house in South Kensington, London, to be closer to his Parliamentary duties. He and Mary felt that it was better for the children also. Maurice was keen to join the British army and young George had reluctantly agreed to go into the army also – but needed much cramming in order to pass the entrance examination. GH was asked by friends why he was prepared to send his sons into the army, being that he was an Irish rebel. He replied, stating that he was also an

Irish gentleman and as such, what other profession other than the army could he place an idle and backward son – meaning George.

In Parliament GH quickly got involved in the pressing issues that affected Ireland. There were many Fenian prisoners in English prisons since the 1867 rebellion and he led efforts to win better conditions for them. Prison conditions were so bad that four men had gone mad, and four had committed suicide. In June 1869 GH submitted the whole case of the Fenian prisoners to Parliament and asked for amnesty. The government didn't want to hold any public inquiries and his submittal was rejected by 171 votes to 31. GH railed against the decision in speeches throughout Ireland; one of which he gave in Castlebar where he criticized the government with the following lines that made huge headlines in the English Press –

"Her scepter has been the sword, her diadem the black cap, and her throne the gallows during the seven hundred years of her fatal rule."

George Henry used his superior letter writing ability to write a long letter to the Times after their published article criticizing him – a letter which was published by the newspaper, and which caught the eye of none other than Mr. Gladstone. That letter is credited with increasing his uneasiness about Government policy towards Ireland – and spurred him to initiate important changes that were to manifest themselves over the course of the next few years. Monster amnesty meetings in support of the political prisoners were held in Ireland, and GH was a featured speaker at one in Dublin attended by over two hundred and fifty thousand people. He pointed out that in one of the most desperate civil wars ever, the Northern States of America had given a free pardon to all rebels, whereas England was inflicting the most horrible tortures on prisoners who had never fired a shot or committed a single outrage or crime – whose alleged conspiracy was confined to secret oath swearing-in ceremonies and public writings that had not cost a single life.

Mr. Gladstone agreed to grant George Henry's proposal for a public inquiry into the treatment of political prisoners and promised that as soon as the Irish agrarian outrages ceased, he would release all the prisoners who were not connected with crimes of violence – most were liberated soon after this statement. GH pushed for the disestablishment of the Anglican Church of Ireland, believing that it would remove a standing cause of quarrel and dislike between Catholic and Protestant. He also pressed Gladstone for a Land Bill that would satisfy the tenants without robbing the landlords. Such a Bill would in his mind re-establish harmony between the different classes in Ireland – and encourage all creeds and classes to unite for a truly national objective. In January 1870 Gladstone introduced the first Land Bill, amid great hopes and expectations among the Irish people. GH thought it was insufficient, but he supported it because he thought it was as much as could be achieved at that time, considering public sentiment inside and outside Parliament. The Times and other mouthpieces of government expressed astonishment that Ireland was not completely satisfied with the generosity of the proposed legislation, initiating another stream of back-and-forth correspondence between GH and the papers – per this example from George Henry –

"The experiment of Imperial legislation set foot in 1800 has signally and notoriously failed; failed by general admission of all thinking men in Ireland, and, indeed, of the select few in England who think for themselves. It is not that this or that grievance has remained too long unredressed, but that the British Parliament has for seventy years shown no capacity and no disposition to redress the grievances or advance the prosperity of Ireland. A conviction has been gradually growing, upwards from the starving to the needy, from the needy to the struggling classes, from the struggling classes to all above them who are still left in Ireland – that the Government under which we all live is a very bad Government for our country. Imperial legislation stands self-condemned; nothing will satisfy the people of Ireland but self-government."

A meeting of the Irish members in early March 1870 was attended by many Ulster members and a resolution was proposed by George Henry Moore, and seconded by William Johnstone, the 'Orange' member for Belfast; and shortly after that, a motion about party emblems was made in the House of Commons by William Johnstone, seconded by GH Moore.

George Henry remarked – "The Orangemen of the North are beginning to see that their favorite fruit is likely to flourish best amid the green leaves in which Nature had placed it. I think I can already perceive in the Irish orange tree what I have often seen in other lands – the fragrant blossoms of another crop filling the air with the perfume of promise."

Mr. Gladstone was coming around to the idea of a federal arrangement for Ireland – he had stated that he intended "to compete for popular approval in Ireland with the honorable member for Mayo."

Once GH felt that the ground had been sufficiently prepared to make a move in Parliament, he gave notice that on May 3rd he intended to 'call attention to the state of Ireland under the Government which the Union had established and move a resolution thereon.' He had overcome the three great forces impeding the progress of Ireland towards freedom and prosperity – namely, political corruption, ecclesiastical tyranny, and landlord domination – and was confident that the field was clear for a fight against foreign misgovernment.

● ● ●

After the failure of the 1867 Fenian rebellion, secret societies driven by the ongoing agrarian strife, became popular in many parts of Ireland. They often sprang up spontaneously due to the actions of some tyrannical landlord, and their local leaders were usually the village ruffians. In Mayo many landlords had made a complete clearance of their tenants and turned their estates into grazing land – finding themselves in the happy position of having no small tenants who might combine against them over some grievances. George Henry had never evicted a tenant, and had generously, if unwisely, taken in some tenants that had been evicted by his neighbors, and so the density of his tenant numbers increased. This dense population was ripe ground for these Ribbon societies, who directed their actions at first against his neighboring landlords that had evicted many of them.

In due course, personal greed and dishonesty spread among these local ruffians, and without any regard for the work that GH was doing in Parliament on their behalf; they demanded a considerable reduction of rents on his estate. The first demand of this sort arose in 1868 before the election. GH decided to refer the matter to an arbitration committee composed of local people of good standing in the community. The arbitrators examined the land holdings – listened to the statements of the tenants and fixed what they considered a fair rent in each case. These fixed rents were paid that year, but the next year the situation was repeated, and in 1870 matters ballooned into a crisis. In February, George Henry received a copy of a notice in the mail at his London home – in red ink –

To the tenants of Mr. Moore's property – whom it may concern –

> 'Notice is hereby given that any person who pays rents to landlords, agents, or bailiffs, above the ordinance valuation, will be at his peril – mark the consequences.'
>
> By Order Rory

GH was furious, and wrote a letter to Father Lavelle, the parish priest in nearby Cong, County Mayo, who was one of his biggest supporters, attaching a copy of the notice and asking him to intercede.

"I have just received the enclosed. If it is supposed that because I advocate the rights of the tenants, I am to surrender my own rights as a landlord; if it is suspected that I am so enamored of a seat in Parliament that I am ready to abandon my own self-respect rather than imperil its possession – those who count upon taking advantage of my political position will find that they have mistaken their man. I am determined to vindicate my own rights without fear or flinching, and if it is necessary to evict every tenant who refuses to pay his rent in full – I will take that course.

I place the matter in your hands as the first and most honorable resort. If I am driven to the 'ultima ratio' of an injured man, I shall be found as unbending as I have ever been in the path of right. I hope to receive a letter from you in reply as soon as may be. My course must be taken at once, and once it is taken it will be hard to turn me from it."

Ironically, at that very time GH was busy in Parliament speaking in support of tenant relief. Gladstone's Landlord and Tenant Act was in second reading, and during debate GH announced that he would vote for the bill because it included the Three F's – Fair Rent, Fixity of Tenure and Free Sale – even though he stated that the bill did not go far enough in protecting tenants against unfair increases in rent. He spoke again on the floor during the week of March 26th, this time against Gladstone's new Coercion Bill, that was an attempt to suppress a resurgence in Fenianism – taunting the British authorities in Ireland for not stamping out random acts of agrarian violence, in a veiled reference to Ribbonmen.

Father Lavelle was not able to make progress in his intercession attempts, so, when Parliament went into recess for Easter, George Henry set off for Mayo. He crossed on the ferry Thursday night and on Good Friday he found that train service in Ireland was restricted due of the holiday, and he had to take an exhausting coach trip the last thirty-five miles to Moore Hall. On Saturday he consulted with Father Lavelle and his agent Sebastian Nolan, arranging for a Monday trip with the agent to meet face to face with his troublesome Ballintubber tenants. On Easter Sunday he attended Mass at his parish church in Carnacon. He was feeling tired and unwell Monday and left a note for his agent to stay overnight in Moore Hall, while he took to his bed for extra rest, and said they would make their tenant visit Tuesday.

His valet found GH asleep Tuesday morning and decided

to let him rest longer: finding him still asleep on the next call he became worried and called the agent to come with him to see Mr. Moore. The agent was so concerned that he could not be awoken, that he sent for the local doctor, who arrived without delay. The doctor found GH's breathing to be very shallow and the patient was unable to speak – he diagnosed an attack of apoplexy, that he said statesmen often get, and he sent for another doctor to help him. Together, they did everything their medical training had taught them to do, finally pronouncing George Henry dead at two o'clock on Tuesday, April 19th, 1870, at the age of sixty. The cause of death was determined to be a stroke – but Father Lavelle maintained, after he administered the Last Sacrament to him, that he had died of a broken heart.

Mrs. Mary Moore was notified by telegram, and she came immediately from London, accompanied by their oldest son and heir, George. They were comforted in their grief by Father Lavelle and Father Conway. The steward, Joe Appely, led them to the bedroom where GH was laid out, the same bed where young George was born eighteen years before. Mary questioned Appely about any strange visitors or incidents that may have occurred, and whether his master had shown any signs of despair: Joe answered all questions in the negative. She could not believe or accept his sudden death and insisted on removal of the white cloth covering the face of the corpse – revealing a face that was terribly changed in death.

The wake and funeral were attended by over five hundred tenants, filling the avenue with carriages and donkey carts. Three Keeners were present to perform their essential part of the Irish death ritual, and their wailing was said to be audible ten miles away. Eight tenants carried his coffin to the hearse and the precession of mourners made their way to the local church. Other than Mary Blake's family members, there were very few of the local gentry, but their absence was more than made up for by tenants and clergy. Twenty priests led by Archbishop McHale concelebrated Requiem Mass, led by the local parish priest, Father Browne – who's oration focused on how faithful George Henry was to his Catholic faith. After that the cortege made its way to the family mausoleum at Kiltoom, where George Henry's parents and two brothers lay. Once the final prayers were completed, and the coffin was sealed into the mausoleum by the firm tapping of the mason's hammer – Father Lavelle mounted the tomb to address the assembled crowd, in their native Irish language.

He began – "God Save Ireland! Woe, woe is Ireland today! George Henry Moore is gone. The pale of death has fallen on her most gifted and devoted son. O my country, now mayest thou weep – weep scalding tears from your million eyes until their very fountains are dried up – those weeds of ages of thine he had resolved, should be changed into nuptial robes of brightness and joy ____."

He did not make any reference to the conspirators, whose actions had prompted George Henry's sudden and fateful journey back to Mayo. Once again, Ireland had lost a champion who was fighting to improve the lot of the poor masses, and ironically, it was people acting selfishly, while claiming to be acting in the best interests of the poor, that brought about the stressful conditions which doomed their champion.

Newspapers in Dublin, Liverpool, Manchester and London carried obituaries on the death of George Henry Moore – one of which called him the last of the Irish Nationalists.

A large meeting was held in Dublin to mourn his passing and it culminated in an oration by Isaac Butt, himself a Protestant, and the leader of the Irish cause championed for so long by George Henry.

Isaac Butt stated that George Henry Moore had been the most eloquent voice of Irish nationality.

CHAPTER TWENTY-THREE

George Augustus Moore was born on February 24th, 1852, at Moore Hall, in the same bed in which his father later died, on that fateful Easter day of 1870. In infancy he was a slow developer, so slow to begin speaking that his parents feared he was mute. He almost drowned as a child when he fell into a well – and was only saved by a servant hearing and recognizing his grunts during a search for the missing boy. He did not show any early desire to learn and was happiest running about the stables with the stable boys, at a time when his father George Henry was making a comeback in the horse racing business at the usual circuits.

It so happened that GH had a horse called Croaghpatrick, being groomed for the Steward's Cup at Goodwood at the same time as he and his wife thought that young George should be sent to Oscott, the Catholic school near Birmingham that GII himself had attended. His parents took the nine-year-old with them to England when they visited Cliff, the horse's trainer, a few weeks before the race. They left the boy at Cliff's house as the race date approached – where he hung about with the other kids on the farm. The horse won big at Goodwood and again two weeks later at another race meeting, with the result that a month went by before young George was picked up by his father and deposited at the school. He was the youngest of all the boys at the school, and there was not even a matron on the staff to take care of his childish needs. From day one young George suffered physically and spiritually at Oscott – he was not cut out to be a schoolboy. The piercing cold draughts at the old stone buildings soon took a toll on his delicate chest, and he developed severe bronchitis after a year – so severe that he had to be taken home to Moore Hall where he spent eighteen months recovering from near death. After recovery he was allowed to stay home for several more months to build up his strength – happy times for him around the horses. He learned every curve of Lough Carra and made a collection of wild bird eggs.

During his absence from school his father engaged tutors for the boy with minimal success, other than an improvement in his French that his governess taught him. On his return to Oscott he was put into the lowest classes where he learned nothing. During the next summer holidays his father proscribed books for the boy to read – such as Scott, Macauley and Burke; books that young George was unable to get interested in. Riding one day in a carriage with his parents, he listened as they talked about a new book they were reading.

"I'm inclined to think that Lady Audley was involved in the murder of her husband," his mother was saying to his father, "what do you think, my dear?"

"I have not read as much of the book as you, but I'm of the same opinion."

The boy was intrigued by the book title – 'Lady Audley's Secret', and at the first opportunity he 'borrowed' the book from his parent's room and devoured this passionate adult novel, cover to cover – without their knowledge. He then read other books by the same author, which eventually led him to the pocket edition of poems by Shelley – a book he kept constantly on his person until it was confiscated from him at school. However, he made no progress at Oscott, despite all the efforts of the teachers and scolding by his father. George continued to resist elementary teaching – simple arithmetic, spelling and basic grammar. After two more years of frustrating attempts by the Oscott staff, it was amicably agreed between George Henry Moore and the Oscott principal, Mr. Northcote, that young George be removed from the school – at the age of fifteen. His brother Maurice was making his grades and he stayed at the school, where he was later joined by the third brother, Augustus.

Moore Hall was a fully-fledged horse training enterprise at this time and young George was attracted to the sport – he suggested to his parents that he should adopt steeplechase riding as a profession, leading to a discussion at home, led by his mother.

"George Henry, I am terrified by the idea of him riding races, after all the race tragedy we have seen in the family."

"I totally agree, my dear. He does not possess very good horsemanship abilities, according to people whose opinion I respect. Let us try some home tutoring with Father James."

This plan was put into effect and the good priest reported to Mrs. Moore at the conclusion of the first month, in the presence of young George.

"Mrs. Moore, I do believe that this young man will one day soon give up hunting and fishing, in order to concentrate on the classics."

"Father, you must surely be joking," she chided him, and laughed out loud.

The boy reacted immediately.

"Mother – you think I'm just stupid, don't you."

It was an awkward moment for mother and priest, but the expressions on their faces didn't give young George much encouragement.

"Of course not, my dearest – I was taken by surprise by his statement. We have a great library here. You can have the run of it – pick poetry, or history, or the classics Father James referred to – choose whatever you like, so long as you read every day."

Most of his reading over the following year was not from the library but from racing papers like the Sporting News, as the lad trailed his father to race meetings and spent much of his time with Joe Applely and the grooms at the stables. When it came to estate matters, like dealing with the tenants, young George had no interest in accompanying his father. From early childhood he felt no kinship with the tenants, just fear at first, followed by bewilderment and repulsion, and later by a reluctant acceptance of the landlord role in Irish society.

His father's racing enterprise ran into a period of bad luck around the time that a general election looked imminent, and George Henry decided to have another try at politics – he sold his horses and closed the stables to secure the time and money to win back his Mayo seat in Parliament. By advocating land tenure reform, he was able to get the priests over to his side, and he toured the county making speeches condemning the outgoing government and the outgoing Mayo MPs – taking young George along with him on the hustings several times. Despite opposition from most of his fellow landlords he won a seat, and the boy was with him when the poll was declared. Young George had little interest in politics and was far more affected by the closure of the stables. After the election his parents decided to shutter Moore Hall and move to London to be near Parliament, and to facilitate the education of the other children who were at English schools. Joe Applely was left in charge of Moore Hall and the staff were let go, other than a few. Horses continued to be the mainstay of young George's life and he kept up a constant correspondence with Joe, while spending most of his time in his two favorite London betting clubs – the Alliance and the Exchange. He began to revel in the big city life.

His parents were still burdened about how to educate young George and pry him away from the betting shops. They made him continue reading and he attended a literary course on Charles Dickens.

He overheard a parental discussion one day – "Mary, I fear those two older boys are stupid, and the army is probably the only place for them to go."

"Perhaps Augustus and Julian will be better."

Their father took George and Maurice to the National Gallery several times, where young George received his first introduction to art – a subject that George Henry had been attracted to when he was young, and his sketches during his sojourn in the East were well regarded.

A distant cousin of the family lived in London, a painter named Jim Browne who had been patronized by George Henry – a large painting of his, 'The Burial of an Indian Chief' hung above the staircase at Moore Hall. He was a handsome man, very well dressed who came regularly to the Moore residence in London, where his conversation and lifestyle excited young George. He talked about art and women, and made George think that the life of a painter was very jolly indeed. Both older boys were enrolled in evening classes at the School of Art in the South Kensington Museum. George was able to wander about the museum, and chat to young girls who were often in there copying the paintings – his sexual interest in them was well received by girls despite his gangling looks. When his parents found revealing photos of the two daughters of a Hammersmith tradesman in his room, it was a wake-up call for George Henry. He immediately enrolled the boy in Jurles's School, run by an army tutor famous for his success educating stupid boys, to the point of getting them to pass the entrance exams for the army. George had no interest in being a battlefield casualty but attended classes to please his father, while befriending two boys there who shared his passion for betting on horses. Furthermore, they convinced George that they could introduce him to the beautiful girls of the fast and fashionable London scene.

One day George returned home with an easel, and all the rest of a painting kit he bought from an artist material shop – and proceeded to paint a copy of a colored print he had acquired. Calling his brother Maurice into the room, he asked, "What do you think about that?"

"It's a daub as far as I'm concerned."

"You know nothing about painting – get out of here."

George had the painting bug, and he convinced his parents to hire a local quality artist called Lutyens to give him some painting lessons.

A week later the family's routine was upended, when an agrarian disturbance on his father's Irish estate came to a head and caused the normally unflappable George Henry great annoyance. Parliament had just recessed for Easter, and instead of spending the holidays with the family, he announced that he had to make an urgent trip to Ireland during the week of Easter.

"I would like to go to Ireland with you, Father," young George offered.

"Son, this is nasty business that I must take care of on my own. Thank you for the offer but it is best that I go alone."

His parents talked in hushed voices for quite some time upstairs and shortly afterwards his father appeared with a packed travel bag. Mother came down to see him off and just before he departed, he sought out young George in the back room to say goodbye.

"You are the man of the house for this Easter. Escort your mother to Easter Mass and show good example to the younger kids by your behavior while I am away."

"Yes Papa. Please say hello to Joe Apply for me."

"I will indeed."

He put his hands on George's shoulders and then pressed a sovereign into his hand before he went to the front door and was gone. His siblings arrived home later that day, and it was left to George to calm them when they were told that their father was not going to be home for Easter – a job he managed so well that he gave himself a clap on the back. Mrs. Moore insisted on the family going to church each day from Holy Thursday through Easter Sunday, in observance of Holy Week. George fulfilled his duty, even though he had long since lost interest in religion and was tending towards atheism. They were at home on Tuesday when the fateful telegram arrived. Mrs. Moore dropped the paper after reading it and had to be helped to a chair. George then read the message from their Mayo agent with his siblings –

> Dear Mrs. Moore – George Henry Moore was taken ill on Monday night. The doctor's diagnosis is that he has suffered a stroke. He is being cared for at Moore Hall by two doctors and is resting as I send this. Please come to Mayo immediately upon receipt of this telegram.
>
> Your humble servant
> Sebastian Nolan.

They were all numbed by the news – finally Mrs. Moore managed to compose herself. She scribbled a message and had Maurice wave down a carriage to carry it to Jim Browne, their cousin who lived not far away. Another message was sent with Julian to her close friend and neighbor down the street. She told George to pack a bag to travel to Ireland with her. Within hours she had plans in place to have the three younger children cared for by her maid, overseen by her neighbor, and Jim Browne duly arrived to help. George and his mother then caught a carriage to Kings Cross and boarded the train to Anglesea, where they caught the overnight steamboat to Dublin and then the train west to Claremorris in Mayo, some twelve miles from Moore Hall. As their carriage approached the house George could see a flurry of activity around the front steps. A man opened the carriage door for them, identifying himself as Sebastian Nolan, and, as Joe Apply took care of the carriage driver, mother and son were ushered inside the house. Two priests awaited them – Rev. Lavelle and Rev. Conway.

Rev. Lavelle began, "Mrs. Moore, I am wholeheartedly sorry to welcome you to Mayo under these circumstances. Our brother in Christ, George Henry Moore, departed this life yesterday afternoon and is now seated at the right hand of God Almighty. I am truly sorry to be the bearer of such terrible news."

Mrs. Moore was by this stage better prepared than George for the tragic situation and bore it with dignified tears, while the boy just fell apart. She had to comfort him, and those circumstances helped her to be strong.

Rev. Conway enjoined, – "Ma'am, they are almost ready to place Mr. Moore in the coffin. If you wish to see him, please follow me."

She nodded and took George's hand, – "We must say a prayer for Papa," and followed the priest to the bedroom where George Henry was laid out on the bed, the bed that young George was born in, and where his father had just died. They knelt in prayer at the bedside, looking at the corpse whose face was covered with a white cloth. Mrs. Moore was reaching toward the cloth when Rev. Conway spoke from the other side of the bed.

"You may be best not to uncover him. He is changed."

"I don't care. I want to see my husband's face one last time," and she removed the cloth, revealing a face that was very much changed in death – a face that shocked Young George a great deal.

As heir to the estate, he was the chief mourner at the funeral. The coffin was carried to and from the hearse on the shoulders of Moore Hall tenants, while the Keeners wailed in high pitched cries and waved their arms towards the sky. Very few of the local gentry attended, while the poor came from all over Mayo to honor the man they regarded as their champion. After Requiem Mass at Carnacon church, concelebrated by twenty priests led by Archbishop McHale, George Henry was buried in the family vault at Kiltoom, set between the two arms of Lake Carra. Young George was not prepared for the wild and fiery speech that Rev. Lavelle delivered from atop the stone vault – even though he didn't understand Irish, he knew the speech was inflaming the crowd. Then, all eyes seemed to turn towards the young heir as if they were waiting for him to say something. He was eighteen years old, shaking in his shoes from a mixture of grief and fear – he could not have spoken even if he wished to do so. His mother took his hand and they turned away from the grave and went home to Moore Hall.

Despite all his ups and downs, George Henry Moore had left the affairs of the family in pretty good shape. George Augustus Moore was the heir, as George IV, but being a minor, he could not take full control until he reached the age of consent. Mrs. Moore's grief continued to pour out for days, that stretched into a week. Conversations were held at the house that clarified the situation going forward: his mother's brother Joe Blake who owned a local estate, was chosen to be the agent for the Moore estate – he would be collecting the rents and allocating monies for at least the next three years, till George reached twenty-one. Lord Sligo, George Henry's closest friend till their recent estrangement, had been listed in the will as guardian of the heir, young George.

The will left Mrs. Moore a secure 500 pounds a year as a first charge on the properties; the younger children had small inheritances, and provision for their education. Everything else would pass to young George, with an entail being listed in his brother Maurice's favor. The estate consisted of some twelve thousand acres, which provided an income of 4,000 pounds per year from the rents of the tenants. Out of that had to come his mother's annuity, and the maintenance of Moore Hall, leaving George with an expected income of about 2,000 pounds a year. His mother was perturbed that such an inheritance was coming to a boy who had been expelled from Oscott for being unteachable, and who was making very little progress in his studies to pass the entrance exam for the army, but she was powerless to change the system. His three brothers would be obliged to fend for themselves when they were grown up. In consultation with his mother and her brother Joe, it was decided that the expenses at Moore Hall were to be cut to a minimum, to allow Mrs. Moore to remain living in London while her children's education was completed.

After their stay went into the third week, George was bored and felt the need to speak up.

"Mother, we cannot spend our lives here, going to Kiltoom every day to visit Father's grave. We must return to London immediately, where the younger children need to be taken care of."

"You are right, George. My grief has caused me to neglect them – we shall leave tomorrow."

On the train journey to Dublin from Mayo, George told his mother he would not continue at Jurle's academy – he would abandon the plan to join the army and would study painting instead. Being underage, he could not yet pursue any personal plan, and under pressure from Lord Sligo, his guardian, and his uncle Joe Blake, who was overseeing the collection of rents for the estate, he agreed to stay in London till he was twenty-one. Basically, he was to be a young man about town for a few years, with a good allowance. Going forward in that role, he spent much of his time imagining himself becoming famous in some way, while he frittered away most of his time and his allowance money. After he got to know the two Bridger sisters, he travelled down to Sussex to spend time with their family. He had by this time moved on from the sporting weekly's to reading Kant's 'Critique of Pure Reason' and tried to engage Mrs. Bridger in a theological discussion. Mrs. Bridger was a very pretty woman and George had wild fantasies about her. He thought of himself as being a manly charmer of women, while women looked on him as a boy who was not yet sure how to behave as a man. Returning to London, he continued with his art by taking lessons at the studio of a French artist named Barthe, who advertised that James Whistler was to be the visiting master. Whistler invited the students to visit his studio one Sunday, shortly after he had completed a painting named 'The Artist's Mother'. George tried to engage Whistler that day by praising Pre-Raphaelites and was put in his place by the artist with a cutting anecdote – thereby setting the stage for a long and testy history between Whistler and Moore. One day George was hanging around Jim Browne's studio when he saw a six-foot by four-foot painting of a naked Nymph that he really liked.

"Jim, this is the best painting of yours that I have seen, so why do you have it turned to the wall?"

"My sisters visit me often and it is too explicit for their taste."

"How can I learn to paint like that?"

"France is the only school of art where you can learn to paint like that – if you want to learn real painting you must go and study in France, in Paris."

This idea resonated with George, and he began to formulate a plan in his head to go to Paris. He could not do so until he turned twenty-one, so he continued to waste his time at theatres and music halls – spending his money on scent, toiletries, tickets and women – many of them being women of ill repute. A friend persuaded him to invest in a theatrical production, and they brought a troupe from Paris to perform at St. James's Theatre – with George's main interest being the hope of a stage-door romance. The show was a flop and creditors demanded money from George – he managed to get out of being answerable to creditors because he was underage. Mrs. Moore got wind of these antics and she asked Lord Sligo to speak to Jim Browne, whose influence was encouraging George's bad behavior. Lord Sligo suggested to George that he needed to have some project to embark on, something to focus his mind on – and he put forth ideas along the lines of what the boy's father had done when he went to the East and explored the Dead Sea.

George was approaching his twenty-first birthday and he already had a set plan in mind. On March 13th, 1873, when his mother and his guardian lost their authority over him, he set off for Paris, accompanied by his valet, William Mulldowney of Mayo (son of old Mulldowney who had worked for his father and grandmother) – a good servant but with rather primitive manners. George brought along several trunks full of clothes, books, pictures and his French phrase book – because he had not bothered to improve his French in preparation for his new life. He lodged first at an old-fashioned family hotel called the Quai Voltaire, where he had reserved an apartment consisting of three rooms. His first school was Beaux Arts under Cabanel but he quit after a few weeks because he disliked getting up early in the morning. He then spent ten days walking around the Paris boulevards looking at the salon pictures. His valet became worried – "Master George, maybe you should return to London where your mother can advise you."

"No, William, I must figure this out on my own."

With advice from his bankers, George moved to a less expensive hotel and became a pupil at Jullian's Academy, among a class of twenty, and in a friendly atmosphere that encouraged him to greatly improve his French speaking, all done by ear – while his painting skill improved little. His valet Mulldowney had a wife in Mayo, but that didn't stop him from enjoying life in Paris. Mulldowney wrote to Joe Applely to update him of their Paris exploits – "Dear Joe – Mr. George is as happy as a prince here and works hard at his painting from 8 in the morning till 5 in the evening. I am broiled to death both day and night with the hate(heat) – but brandy for two francs a bottle, all kinds of fruit for a song, and women for the asking does make up for a lot. Went to the Grand Prix race of course and put money on the English Derby winner – he looked great at the parade but was well beaten at the post."

By the following spring George was so homesick that he returned to London, and released his valet, who had allowed Paris to get to his head. In London, George took a studio where he got pretty girls to model for him and went back to his old habits of carousing with women of ill repute. His only contact with his Moore Hall estate was his frequent requests to Joe Blake for money advances, so he could pay off debts. Joe advised him to take more interest in his estate, but George didn't want to – to the point of not even wanting to see the yearly accounts.

"Send me fifty pounds – I want the money even if you have to borrow it or sell something at Moore Hall."

Joe told Mrs. Moore that George should come home and collect his own rents, but George recoiled from the thought of living life as an Irish landlord beside a lonely lake. He wanted to return to Paris and told Joe that he had reformed his spending habits and would need no more than twenty-five pounds a month going forward. As soon as he was back in Paris, he resumed friendships and the lifestyle he had led during his previous stint there, including his high spending. Because of his disinterest in learning during his early school years in Oscott, he was dreadful at spelling and grammar – even his mother cringed when reading his letters. His family visited with him in Paris in 1875 where they saw George continue his efforts to become a painter, and he bragged about the long hours he was putting in.

Only a year later, at the age of twenty-four, he began to despair of his progress and gave up on his efforts – at which time he said, "as much as I loved the idea of being a painter, I was not fitted to become one." To get his mind off his disappointment he sought out the Irish colony in Paris, and met with the exiled old Fenian leader John O'Leary, who had known his father very well and greeted him warmly on that account. The company of the Irish exiles was not stimulating enough for George, and he started to pursue French high society, what he called 'the circle of Alphonse Rothschild', and the Duchess de la Tremoille. He began to talk about finding a rich heiress to marry, and delighted his mother with news that he was in pursuit of the heiress Miss Mary de Ross Rose, a bright and intelligent girl with Irish connections.

"My dearest Mama – I am dining with Miss Rose on Thursday. I went to church with her last Sunday and my sources tell me the girl has a lot of money. I have, as we used to say in racing, 'run up with the leaders' but if I go to the front, I will compromise myself. I really do not know how to proceed."

Nothing came of his pursuit of Miss Rose. He told his uncle Joe Blake that he abandoned his endeavor when he discovered that Miss Rose's income was only eight hundred pounds a year, not the two thousand he had been led to believe earlier.

George's mother had given up the house in London to save money, and was living again at Moore Hall, mostly alone, as her three younger children were still at school in England, and Maurice was stationed in India with the Connaught Rangers since graduating from Sandhurst. She was hopeful that George would return to live at Moore Hall and bring a rich bride home to share his life there.

In the latter part of 1876 George began to think more seriously about becoming a writer and had made a commendable effort to drag himself up from his almost illiterate state, in order to be able to write with proficiency. He had befriended an elderly literary Frenchman named Bernard

Lopez, who helped him on his first literary effort, a comedy called 'Worldliness'. Lopez's mother was English, and he spoke English fluently – they then began to collaborate on a play in English for the London stage – a religious tragedy about Martin Luther under the same title, a play that would take him several years to finish. Meanwhile, George continued to work on his poetry and to build up his contacts in Paris, becoming friends with an English poet named Villiers and a French writer named Mallarme. Through them he began to frequent a café in Montmartre called Nouvelle Athenes, and it was there that George became acquainted with such notable figures as Monet, Degas, Manet, Pissarro, Renoir and Zola – a 'university' which launched him into the artistic and literary life of Paris.

He also got to meet many young ladies from French society, one of which was later to become Madame Duclaux, and became a life-long friend. She described what George Moore was like in those early days –

'His dress was that of a Frenchman and he wore a beard. He was not handsome and looked vaguely comic in appearance. His neck was long, shoulders too sloping for a man of his height and strength. His chin was too small for his forehead and nose but was mostly hidden behind his fair beard. The color of his hair was amusing – fine pale-yellow hair without the least tint of red, that fell on his absolutely white forehead. His grey blue eyes were a little too prominent, with the vague, spiritless expression common to the very observant

– and sometimes they would light up and become strangely adventurous.'

He succeeded in getting a small volume of poems published in London that made him a little money while being criticized in the newspapers for their immorality – one reviewer suggested that 'the author be whipped at the cart's tail while having the book burned by the common hangman'.

George was blissfully uninterested in the life and politics of Ireland, as he slowly began to make a literary name for himself in London and Paris, with the publication of several novels, plays and books of poetry during the following years. His happy life in Paris was interrupted by a letter from Joe Blake in 1880 demanding that he come home and look after the affairs of his estate in Mayo. Agricultural prices had fallen and the poor tenants on the estate were unable to pay timely rents. Even worse was the recent rise of an organization called the Land League, founded by Mayo man Michael Davitt only fifteen miles from the gates of Moore Hall – whose policy was to offer landlords what the League thought was a lower and fair rent, money that was paid into a holding account until the landlord was willing to accept their offer. Joe told George that he was not going to risk his life serving eviction notices while trying to collect overdue rents.

George was frightened for the safety of his estate and for his loss of the income that he depended upon, and wrote back – "If you don't collect the rent what is to be done? I have never looked into my business but at all events I have never committed any follies. I have never spent more than 500 a year, and I was told when I came into the property that I had ever so much. Enfin, I suppose you will do your best. I will try to meet you in Dublin if you like and have some understanding – about Christmas."

Soon after that, Joe Blake was in London and George was compelled to cross over from France to meet him there to discuss the affairs. They met at Morley's Hotel, where Joe opened the conversation –

"There is no easy way to say this. You are a grown man, master of one of the largest estates in Ireland. Times have changed and with this Land League organization there has been an increase in agrarian aggression. I have had enough problems with my own estate at Tower Hill without adding the Moore Hall problems to my load. Besides, you have accumulated over two thousand pounds of debt to me personally for all the advances that I have kindly sent to you. The situation cannot continue this way – you must leave the fancy life of Paris behind and secure the finances of Moore Hall before it is too late. It is your estate – you must take personal control of it, collect your own rents, and figure out a way to get my debt satisfied."

"Joe, I am extremely grateful for all that you have done for me and for Moore Hall over the years, and I fully acknowledge the debt that you are owed. After so much time away from Mayo I am out of touch with the situation on the ground, and I may be at a great disadvantage trying to collect rent, not to mention danger. You told me already that Mother has relocated to Dublin from Moore Hall, because of fear for her safety – what about my safety?"

"I cannot guarantee anything, but you are a Mayo gentleman, and you are master of Moore Hall – you must show your tenants that you will defend your estate and use the power of the law that you have on your side to do that. There is no alternative."

"Can you not find me a suitable person to take over being my agent – in your place?"

"I have tried but nobody wants to take on the job."

"I have so much to do here in London – with publishers and writers that I am collaborating with – I don't see how I can possibly spend time in Mayo chasing those, those ghastly tenants in their stinking cabins."

"If you can make enough money from your books then forget about Moore Hall. If not, then you must resume your place as Master – it's your choice. I have a train to catch – I see no point in continuing these discussions until you decide whether you want the estate or not."

They left it at that, and George went on to meet with the publisher Tinsley and told him of all the novels he had in mind to write. When he sat down later to assess his financial status, he realized that he could not afford to lose Moore Hall. He went back to Paris where he terminated his apartment lease and gave orders to sell his effects to cover debts there – leaving quietly because he knew the auction would not bring in enough to cover all his Paris debt.

CHAPTER TWENTY-FOUR

Reluctantly, George Moore returned to live at Moore Hall in the spring of 1880 where he was joined by his sister Nina. He found the solitude of the place to be conducive to his writing and he mined much of his material from his childhood remembrances and interactions with past characters. His brother Maurice had returned from fighting in the colonies and was in barracks with the Connaught Rangers in Mullingar. The next brother, Augustus, was working as a society journalist with the London newspapers of Fleet Street. Julian, the youngest, was studying for a career in book bindings and book collections while living with his mother in Dublin.

This was not a good time to be a landlord in a Big House on an estate in Ireland, surrounded by hostile, hungry and penniless tenants. It was the third year in a row of crop failures, and the tenants had little of value left to sell in order to pay rent and repay loans to local shopkeepers. There was a knock-on effect up the line of the precarious West of Ireland system of life, one that was totally dependent on the agriculture base. Agrarian violence had increased greatly, including assassinations – rent due notices could not be served without a substantial police presence. A nearby landlord in County Galway was murdered in September, and just up the road in Ballinrobe, there was major incident. Lord Erne's agent, one Captain Charles Boycott was ostracized by order of the Land League, because of his actions against tenants – his servants left and nobody in the entire area would supply him with any goods or services. A party of Orangemen came from Northern Ireland to bring in Boycott's crops, and despite a constant police and army escort they were harassed the entire time they were in the area. Boycott's name became synonymous with a new form of political intimidation endorsed by the Land League – Boycott capitulated eventually and took his family back to England. There was little that a landlord like George could do other than offer his tenants a big reduction in rents, and hope to collect that amount rather than nothing at all – and forget about the arrears that were owed. He and Joe Blake had a disagreement about the accuracy of the estate accounts, and rather than start a family feud George signed off on the books while continuing to hold a grudge against Joe.

A Protestant from County Wicklow, named Charles Stewart Parnell, was the new chairman of the Irish Parliamentary Party, and he continued the legacy of George Henry Moore's parliamentary career by using the Irish vote at Westminster to force concessions on land issues. Parnell referred to landlords as the 'enemy' and openly agitated for confiscation of their property estates, estates and operations that were rather similar in set up to Moore Hall.

George Moore held liberal views on these agrarian political issues and would happily depart in peace if he could get decent compensation. His letter addressing his fellow-landlords that was published in the Freeman's Journal was proof of this –

'Landlords and tenants may now become friends as before. The golden opportunity has arrived. The Lords have rejected Gladstone's Relief Bill, and the tenant farmers are in despair. Let the landlords coalesce with their archenemy, the Land League, and offer to the people of Ireland a better, not a stronger Land Bill. Let old differences of opinion be put aside – let the landlords give way a good deal on their side, and the League a little on theirs. Let them draw up together an efficient Land Bill, one that popular opinion will enforce as strongly as any law coming from England is enforced by the bayonet. By its acceptance let it forever divide the good landlords from the bad and establish the basis for a great principle for which we are all striving – Home Rule.'

He and his sister went on a visit to their cousins, the Ruttledge's, in Roscommon, and George took a shine to their young son, Tom, whom he persuaded to become his land agent. Together they devised a plan for the forgiveness of rent arrears and a reduction in the current rent – as a means of collecting some money to keep the estate going. The local papers were very critical of the returning George Moore, describing him as 'the degenerate son of a worthy father, who was a devoted and fearless champion of Ireland's Bishops and Priests – and a great Catholic.' George was relieved to appoint Tom as agent and free himself from the landlord duties he despised, so that he could concentrate on his writing projects. He had kept in touch with his London literary friends, like the poet Arthur O'Shaughnessy who was helping him to get some of his new works published. When a publishing issue arose in London, he was happy to go there and leave the affairs of Moore Hall in the hands of Tom Ruttledge. Tom knew the local people much better than George and was able to negotiate a deal with a timber agent who would pay 500 pounds to thin out the woods around the Big House.

This money allowed George to live for quite some time in London while he sought to improve his standing as a writer there – he reignited old friendships with Richard Mansell, Lord Tennyson and Oscar Wilde – who had been a boyhood friend when the Wilde boys often spent time at nearby Cong, County Mayo, with their father. Someone advised him to change his wardrobe – to drop his Parisian top-hat and high-heeled boots, which he did, and the change allowed him to blend better into London society. After this change he made immediate progress there and said later that he had at last found his real business in life – that of being a storyteller. By the age of thirty-five George was a successful novelist – author of such titles as 'A Modern Lover', 'A Mummer's Wife' and 'A Drama in Muslin'.

It was now in the late 1890's and the various Moore siblings were getting on with their lives. Maurice and Augustus and Nina were all married, while George himself continued to be a bachelor, as was young Julian. In these marriage partners there was a definite family movement towards Protestantism: this pleased George, who still held his great-grandfather in contempt for embracing Catholicism in Spain and derisively called him the 'Catholic Celt'.

In 1891 George published a novel called 'Esther Waters' which was a resounding success – it sold very well and moved George to the top ranks among living authors of the time. It was even read by Prime Minister Gladstone who sent George an approving postcard.

• • •

Mrs. Moore, George's mother, died in May 1895 at Moore Hall, and that event brought all the family together at the estate. His relationship with her had always been good for she never quarreled with him – her Catholic piety was pure, and she never scolded him for turning away from the Catholic faith. He was reluctant to return from London too soon when his brother told him of her failing health, not because of any lack of love for his mother – he just didn't want to see her die, and he delayed his arrival till after she was dead.

She had always feared premature burial, and so they waited several days before she was laid to rest at Kiltoom. George used that time to reacquaint himself with Lough Carra – the enchanted silence, the shapes of every island and the reflections on the water. After he returned to London his mind continued to be consumed by the subject of death, the pomp of the funeral and the wailing of the Keeners that accompanied death in Ireland. In death he wanted to avoid the 'horrible' vault at Kiltoom, and wrote to his brother Maurice – "Remember, I have but one wish – to be cremated and my ashes scattered on Hampstead. On second thoughts I like the idea of a great funeral pyre on Castle Island in Lough Carra.'

While in Ireland George had taken the time to break the entail that listed his brother Maurice in their father's will – the entail would leave the estate to Maurice if George died without having any children of his own.

"Why did you want to do this George?" Maurice asked him.

"It is the usual thing to do, our uncle Llewelyn Blake did it many years ago – it is of no consequence."

"Anyone has a right to do what they like with money made by themselves, but money made by our forefathers should remain in the family – that is my opinion."

George did not respond to that comment.

Being the eldest, the heir and owner of the estate – and now making a decent income from his writing, George felt that he needed to act more like a father figure to his siblings. He offered to pay for the education of Maurice's eldest son, Rory, and he also wanted to financially help his sister and his youngest brother Julian – but George always had to attach strings, such as demanding that the children get a Protestant education, and this caused friction in the family. The fact that George didn't want to live at his Moore Hall didn't sit well with the others. His land agent Tom was keeping an eye on the place and George had specifically told his siblings that they could stay there any time they wished, with Maurice having first choice. Only London was good enough for George, and he hoped to become a celebrity there – he was always chasing new love interests and thrived on rumors of his love affairs, whether they were real or in his imagination. Meanwhile he continued a frenetic pace of writing and collaborations with others.

George was leaning towards more involvement in the budding Dublin literary revival and assisted in founding the seminal Irish Literary Theatre in 1899. In May of that year, he crossed to Ireland to direct a play called 'The Countess Cathleen'. During rehearsals, there was criticism of the theology of the play and George had to ask Yeats and Lady Gregory to keep a close watch on his collaborator friend, Edward Martyn, a devout Catholic, lest he resign from his directorship of the theatre because of heresy accusations. He got through the production and spent more time in Ireland on other collaborations, presenting plays at the Gaiety Theatre and the Antient Concert Rooms. George's actions were important early steps that led later to the founding of the Abbey Theatre in Dublin in 1904 by Yeats, Lady Gregory and others.

Despite spending substantial time in Dublin during this period, George, oddment that he was, continued to keep away from Moore Hall.

The outbreak of the Boer War in South Africa in September that year greatly distressed him – he feared for his brother Maurice, whose Connaught Rangers regiment were being sent to the war, and he was disgusted with Britain for its cruel actions on the battlefield. Maurice's wife Evelyn and her children were frequent visitors to Moore Hall and the grounds around the lake while her husband was stationed in Africa, but they had to endure interference from George. He knew that Maurice spoke fluent Irish and had developed a great interest in the revival of the Irish language – that he had engaged a native speaker as tutor to his kids in the language. While the soldier was away, George injected himself into the situation by paying the children's tutoring, and he then bombarded Evelyn with letters about their progress – even to the point of suggesting disinheritance if they did not become fluent very quickly.

As the war in Africa turned nasty George formally withdrew from London in protest, and took a house in Dublin, at Ely Place near St. Stephens Green, announcing that he intended to assist in the revival of the Irish language, while admitting that he didn't speak it himself. A friend remarked on this, saying to him, "Moore Hall would be the ideal place from which to grow your language plans, being that it stands in an area where Irish is spoken by most of the people – why not live there instead?"

George replied, "Moore Hall will not be lost to the language revival and my nephews are learning their Irish from there. I am neither a recluse nor a bookworm – I need to live in a place with more social intercourse, where friends can drop in for conversation after dinner."

To his brother Maurice he wrote, "The Irish tutor is now at Moore Hall, and I am sure the children are speaking Irish every day. Their mother deserves credit for the fact that while they will soon speak fluent Irish, they don't speak English with a brogue. I love to hear Irish spoken but I hate to hear English spoken with a thick brogue."

Meanwhile, George quickly moved on from language revival patriotism to his next new cause – he now began waging a campaign against clerical influences in Irish life, using his new novel 'The Lake' as his attacking tool. Britain prevailed in the Boer War and Maurice returned home with the rank of Colonel, after distinguished service – to find George seeking formal admission into the Irish Protestant community of the Church of Ireland. This led to a serious confrontation between the brothers.

"George, this is an act of disloyalty, like going over to the enemy."

"Au Contraire, Mon Frere – the Moore's were originally Protestant, and it is my understanding that our great-grandfather joined the Catholic Church in order to save his Spanish business from confiscation. I also point out that the tone displayed in our grandfather, George the historian's writings, were very English liberal and swayed towards Protestantism."

"George, very few facts are known about our great-grandfather's religion, George of Alicante, but we do know that he included a private chapel in Moore Hall when he built the place, and it contained mostly Catholic vestments and chalices from Spain. You cannot deny that he went to Mass or that he was a champion of Catholic causes."

"Our patriotism doesn't amount to much in my opinion. Father was a sympathizer, I agree, and our own Grand-Uncle John got caught up in the Rebellion of 1798, but Grandfather George, the historian, regarded himself as an Englishman. You must admit that the best Irish nationalists were Protestants – such as Wolfe Tone."

"I agree with you on Tone's credentials, but you have just admitted our family connections to him, by mentioning John Moore's involvement in that same rebellion of 1798, and I remind you that Grand-Uncle John was President of the Republic of Connaught."

The brother's disagreement didn't prevent Maurice from making use of Moore Hall, or George from paying for the education of his nephew. Their mother's family, the Blake's, were devout Catholics and they both accepted that fact – Uncle Blake had even taken Catholic monks into his home, and when he died, he left all his money and two homes to those same Catholic monks, and to the missions they supported.

Maurice remained in the army for another four years while his regiment was stationed at Mullingar, some forty-five miles from the estate. He and his family spent much of this time at

Moore Hall, and in conjunction with George via correspondence, he proposed to make some much-needed repairs at the Big House. They both loved the old house, and they usually were able to agree on anything that involved its upkeep. As usual, George had to get involved too much in the details, such as wallpapers and paint color – he hated the large plate glass windows and pined for the old-fashioned small panes but held off. Sadly, neither of them knew enough about what was in storage in the cellar and didn't know that the original eighteenth-century little panes were sitting there, having been replaced by his grandfather. Sales of Irish estates to the government, for splitting up into parcels and subsequent sale to local Irish tenants were still going ahead under the auspices of the Wyndham Act, and negotiations were begun for Moore Hall to be included. George, Maurice and their agent Tom Ruttledge all proved to be hesitant in moving the negotiations forward quickly enough, and the opportunity was lost as a change of government came about. The Nationalist party put pressure on the new Liberal government to alter Wyndham legislation in a manner that would be more hostile to the interests of the landlords. The Gaelic League was fast becoming more of a force to reckoned with – they pushed for love of the Irish language, and tenants' rights, but their real objective was said to be full separation from England.

George complained to his brother about the money he had spent improving the house. "Despite my vision I spent 800 pounds on the house, and nobody will ever live there after your temporary term – do you seriously imagine that your children will live in it?"

• • •

The closing days for the great estates of Ireland had indeed arrived. There were fewer violent outrages but Moore Hall neighbors like the Lamberts and Browne's had all gone – even the old home of their agent Tom Ruttledge was empty. The Irish peasants knew that they were soon to be rid of the landlords, and cheaply at that. Colonel Maurice didn't see this situation coming and was busy convincing George of the vanity of keeping up Moore Hall as a gentleman's house, and he was full of blind enthusiasm to revive rural industries like weaving and brewing. Maurice possessed a true patriotism for Ireland, and having retired from the army he was able to devote his full attention to supporting various national movements. To that end there was a constant stream of notables visiting Moore Hall to confer with him – he didn't suspect their motives, but he was being used by many selfish men for their own advantage. The siblings were all well into their middle age by this stage and seemed to be enjoying good health. Then, Augustus, the third brother, who was a career journalist in London's Fleet Street, died suddenly at fifty-four following a medical operation. George took issue with the obituary description that 'he came from an Old Roman Catholic family' – and he decided not to attend the funeral, leaving it to Maurice and Julian to represent the family.

Just after this, in 1911, a new 'Land Purchase Bill' came into operation in Ireland and the negotiations required George's attendance at Moore Hall. His two nephews, Rory and Toby were home from school and their uncle inquired about their education – becoming distressed when he was informed that they were both at Catholic schools, and this became a focal point for a serious clash with his brother Maurice.

"I am disgusted that I allowed money to be taken from estate accounts to be paid to Priests for Rory's education. If I am to continue this assistance and make Rory my heir, the boy must be brought up as a Protestant."

"Your proposal is preposterous, and I will not stand for it. You will not dictate the education I desire for my children – they will attend the schools I want them to attend. Withdraw your funding if you wish but don't tell me how to educate my sons."

"I will have to think long and hard on this. In the meantime, you and Tom Ruttledge must engage in a conference with me on the issue of selling our estate lands through this commission."

George then suddenly became reluctant to sell any part of the estate lands – his stubborn nature coming through. In the end George decided that he would be prepared to sell the outlying lands of the estate – at Ballintubber, at Partry and Ashbrook – via the new Bill, if an agreeable price could be realized, while Moore Hall itself and the five hundred acres around it would be retained.

Maurice then took the initiative on the education issue with George – "I have decided that my family will leave Moore Hall, we will leave Ireland. We will relocate to Belgium where I will finish the education of my children."

"So be it, Maurice."

• • •

Moore Hall was locked up again, the family furniture was covered with dust sheets, the pictures and bookshelves sat like sentries guarding the rooms – and the two brothers left Mayo. Running expenses at the estate were cut to the absolute minimum and Reilly, the new steward, was the only person left to oversee the estate and the house. George refused to lease out the house or the closely attached acreage – he decided that the demesne proper, the lawns and gardens were to be preserved just as they sat. These several hundred acres made up the original core of the estate put together by George Moore the First, the Merchant of Alicante, and George Moore IV was not willing to part with them. Maurice had moved his family to Belgium and George moved to London, to a house in Ebury Street alone, where he continued his writing career – and Mayo was pushed to the back of their minds.

In Ireland the transfer of vast land holdings from landlord to tenant was far from complete when a new Home Rule Bill was introduced in Parliament in 1912. This was done to satisfy the Irish Parliamentary Party who held the balance of power at Westminster, and whose vote kept the Liberal Government in power. George flew into a panic and decided that it was only a matter of time before landlords would be legally compelled to sell their property at reduced prices – and putting aside his recent altercation with his brother, he wrote to him and to his agent Tom.

"The Home Rule Bill is certain to pass the House of Commons and the House of Lords seem ready to pass it also. I urge you to press forward with an application for the sale of all tenanted properties through the land courts. There must be no time lost in settling with the Congested Districts Board – or we may lose everything." In reality, there was no 'we' – George was the sole owner.

The Congested Districts Board offered 40,000 pounds in cash and Government stock for the entire estate and demanded that the locals get grazing rights for the demesne around Moore Hall itself. George refused this demand and brought his case in front of the Irish Secretary, Mr. Birrell. He won that battle, and the Board relinquished the grazing request, allowed him to keep the house and 500-acre demesne, and they even upped the purchase price by 3,000 pounds. After repaying all the mortgages, George cleared 30,000 pounds profit from the sale and he happily went back to his writing, knowing that he had retained his 'dreaming house' and the core demesne. Many of the main ties that bound him to Ireland were now severed, but Ireland continued to play an important role in his imagination – he had several more Irish stories in mind that he hoped to write. He even found time to embark on a trip to the East where he visited Egypt and Palestine – adding an extended stay in Paris on his way home to London.

George saw that the Ulster Protestants were preparing to disrupt Home Rule, and he resorted to writing letters to the newspapers supporting Ulster's claim for special treatment – citing his own family experiences as proof that 'Catholic and Protestant do not mix'.

Maurice was Nationalist leaning, and he disparaged his brother in public statements – 'George contradicts himself and he stands for nothing. When the Gaelic League rejected his attempts to pose as the leader of an Irish literary movement, he took revenge by abusing Irish Catholics. Now he poses as an Irish Protestant as he tries to compel attention.'

Relations between the brothers deteriorated further. Eventually they agreed on a six-month truce during which time they were not to discuss politics and religion. As a goodwill gesture George travelled to Belgium to help Maurice with the manuscript of a biography he was writing about their father, George Henry Moore. A publisher suggested that George contribute the preface for Maurice's book – it was agreed but soon afterwards the very description of their father's death became another source of disagreement and deepened the rift between them. They had both changed so much and disagreed so much that separation and silence was the only mode of life that seemed appropriate.

After his return from Belgium to live in London, Colonel

Maurice Moore heard of a plan for the establishment of The Irish Volunteers, a permanent force to defend Ireland and her liberties. He offered his services and was promptly appointed Inspector-General by the organizing committee – a body that, unbeknownst to Maurice, included Padraic Pearse and other radicals who were all Irish Republican Brotherhood members. Maurice felt that he was finally doing something tangible to help Ireland on the road to her freedom, and he attracted instructors from his old ranks to the Volunteers – retired sergeants from the Connaught Rangers and other ex-soldiers from the Dublin Fusiliers. Redmond's Irish parliamentarians were hostile to the Volunteers at first, but changed their stance as the threat to the Home Rule Bill posed by the Ulster Protestants grew – and Redmond himself was on friendly terms with Colonel Moore. The Volunteer ranks swelled quickly with recruits and by June of 1914 they significantly outnumbered the opposing Protestant Ulster force. Redmond succeeded in getting the Home Rule Bill put into the Statute Book just as the European War broke out. However, the operation of the Bill was suspended until the end of the war.

Large numbers of Volunteers from Ulster were being recruited to the British Army for service in France and Redmond called for his Irish Volunteers to do likewise. Colonel Moore was not opposed to Irishmen going to fight in France, but he thought the Volunteers should only be used to enforce demands for national liberty, and worried that a call to join the British Army would provoke dissension in the organizing committee that could lead to a split. Twenty out of the original twenty-seven promoters of the Volunteer movement denounced Redmond's call to enlist. The movement split into the National Volunteers, supporting Redmond and enlistment, while the remaining Irish Volunteers supported the Irish Nationalist agenda. Reluctantly, Colonel Moore supported the Redmondites and continued for several months as Inspector-General of the National Volunteers. He never made recruiting speeches and when requested to do so by a senior commander of the British Army, responded – "My business is to arm the Irish people, not to supply the British Army with recruits."

As the First World War intensified Colonel Moore's own two sons enlisted to fight in France in January 1916. He resigned his position of Inspector-General of the National Volunteers after a disagreement with Redmond, rejoining the British Army and was stationed at a fort in Southern Ireland. The following April brought the news of the Easter Week Rising in Dublin, led by Pearse and other IRB Rebels – which was put down with great brutality by the British forces, causing the near-total destruction of central Dublin. The execution of fourteen leaders of the Rising infuriated Colonel Moore and he resigned his commission in protest – not knowing how he could best serve the everchanging cause of Irish Nationalism.

• • •

George was living in London at the outbreak of the 1914 European War and was so consumed with his literary endeavors that he took little notice of it. The political developments in Ireland and the Easter Week Rising of 1916 were events of no real interest to him, although he regarded it as a stab in England's back, in her hour of need during the Great War. He visited Dublin late in the summer of 1916 for a book publication event and was taken on a tour of the devastation of central Dublin, before traveling to Westport to meet with his land agent, Tom Ruttledge. The brewing insurrection sentiment and land trouble in Ireland began to prey on his mind and he had frequent dreams of Moore Hall going up in flames. The two brothers were on such bad terms that once in Dublin they passed each other on the stairs without speaking a word. Both of Maurice's sons were at the front lines in France, where the younger one Ulick (nicknamed Toby) was wounded and sent to London for recuperation. He visited his uncle at his home there, where George was less than a gracious host.

"Your father and I are not on speaking terms and never shall be again."

"Uncle, even the Germans and our side talked and played football during the Christmas truce. Rory and I desperately want you and Father to mend whatever it is that is keeping you apart – especially in this time of war."

"Young man, I am not going to scold you for speaking out of term. The matter between your father and I is very personal, very deep and I will not discuss it. The fact is that I despise

Roman Catholics, and one cannot change oneself. Whether you be Protestant or Catholic, you are certainly a brave young fellow who has done the right thing. So, you are going back to the front again, now that you are healed – Bravo."

"Thank you, Uncle."

George didn't tell anybody that he had already decided to disinherit his brother Maurice, and Maurice's two sons. In the summer he visited Ireland and felt alienated in the company of his friends such as George A. E. Russell, because of their Sinn Fein and pacifist sympathies. The war was close to ending and George now began to show his admiration for the Allies. Ironically, all four grandsons of the Irish patriot George Henry Moore were fighting England's battle on the front lines of Flanders – Maurice's two sons, Augustus's son and Nina's son. Not long before the war ended, Maurice's youngest son Ulick (Toby) was killed in battle on the front lines at St. Emilie, and even that tragedy didn't open any dialogue between George and Maurice. After the Armistice, the surviving brother, Rory, called in to visit his uncle in London, and was invited to dinner and to stay overnight. George had kept regular contact with the lad's mother, Evelyn, his sister-in-law, because she was a Protestant, and he wrote to her after the boy's visit telling her what a fine young man her son was. At the beginning of the war Rory had joined the American Expeditionary Force and was stationed in the US state of Wyoming, before enlisting for frontline duty – now that he was demobilized, he returned to Wyoming to take up cattle ranching.

Colonel Maurice Moore and his wife had settled in Dublin after the war, from where he watched the new Irish political situation and the threatening military confrontation unfold. Sinn Fein won almost all of Ireland's Parliamentary seats in the autumn 1918 general election: they refused to sit at Westminster and set up their own Irish Parliament in Dublin, named 'Dail Eireann'. Mr. Eamon De Valera, a survivor of the 1916 Rising was elected President of this rebel government – ushering in a strange era of two governments in Ireland at the same time. Sinn Fein set up their own court system and the nationalist population of Ireland began to ignore the British government institutions that had long been put in place by the British – preferring the Sinn Fein courts and their own Irish police force. There were many raids, stand-offs, arrests and imprisonments of the Irish leaders – as the British forces tried unsuccessfully to suppress the Irish Dail, while also negotiating with Sinn Fein for a compromise both sides could accept.

A solution eluded the parties and informal hostilities broke out in January 1919 between the Irish Republican Army and British forces. A nationwide and bloody guerrilla war followed – with assassinations, ambushes, reprisals and counter-reprisals, until a cease fire was agreed in the summer of 1921, followed by negotiations in London that led to a Treaty later that year. Colonel Moore had been a member of Sinn Fein since 1917, and he kept a low profile during this War of Independence, despite his Nationalist sympathies. He was arrested by British forces at his house a few times and courteously detained for several hours each time. Later he was appointed by the Dail shadow government to be their Irish envoy to the Union of South Africa – he travelled to Cape Town and was well received there by Prime Minister Smuts because the Boers remembered him as being sympathetic to their cause during his service in the Boer War. His main objective for the trip was to persuade Smuts to support Irish independence, and the following year Smuts met De Valera in Dublin – his influence was an important voice in getting both sides to agree to the Truce in July 1921 that ended the Irish War of Independence.

George was horrified by Maurice's embrace of the Irish Republican Dail government and worried constantly for the safety of Moore Hall. Maurice was back in Dublin when the Dail met to debate 'The Treaty' that Michael Collins and Arthur Griffith brought back from their London negotiations. The Treaty terms proposed the partition of Ireland into a twenty-six county Free State and a six-county Northern Ireland entity that was to remain part of Britain: it caused a split among the members of the Dail and a split in the country – into 'Free Staters' and 'Republicans'. The Treaty was eventually passed by a small majority in the Dail, and the Free Staters, being in the majority, drew up a new Constitution. This provided for an Upper House or Seanad (Senate) consisting of sixty members, thirty were nominated by the President of the Executive Council (Mr. Cosgrove), and thirty were elected by the members of the Dail.

Colonel Moore was offered a Seanad seat as a mark of recognition for his services to the emerging nation. He was not the only Nationalist, or member of the gentry nominated, as the selection method was designed to give the political minority a voice in the affairs of the new Free State. Therefore, his Senate colleagues were mostly drawn from the Protestant minority of Southern Ireland – people like W B Yeats, Gogerty and Plunkett. The Republican defeat in the Treaty vote soon festered into a Civil War, which took a terrible toll of Irish patriots killed on both sides, among people who had until recently been fighting side by side for Irish freedom.

The Colonel felt very uneasy in his position as Senator on the Free State side, and he particularly objected to the partition of Ireland, and to the concession of the six Ulster counties. The Free Staters had military supplies and logistic support from the British Army, and they quickly gained the upper hand in the Civil War hostilities. Colonel Moore participated on a public stage at a large meeting held by the Free State army leader, Michael Collins, held in Castlebar, County Mayo – which was an act of poor judgement he later regretted. He personally knew many of the local commanders of the East Mayo Brigade of the IRA and knew that they were predominantly anti-treaty – they were good men who were about to be on the losing side of this Civil War. He tried to use his influence to stop the violence between the two sides in Mayo, and he knew that reprisals were being considered against Senators and their property. Some of his IRA acquaintances, like

Thomas Kane, had refused to fight in the Civil War against their old comrades – they were already imprisoned by the Free Staters in internment camps at the Curragh and could not do anything to defuse the worsening situation.

The losing Republican side accused the Free Staters of supporting wealth and privilege – they decided to drive the remaining gentry out of their demesnes, so that their land could be divided among the Irish peasants. They also decreed that Senators were guilty of collaboration with the enemy and gave permission to their local commanders to burn the houses of legislators. When George Moore learned of this decree, he accused his brother of bringing certain calamity on Moore Hall by getting mixed up in what he called 'the absurd politics of Ireland'. One night he had such a realistic dream of Moore Hall burning that he jumped out of bed and tripped over a carpet, breaking his wrist. His favorite painting at Moore Hall was a portrait of his grandfather, George Moore the historian, that hung over the main staircase. He admired his grandfather because he was a renowned literary author of several books, and because his political leanings were very much in line with his own – namely that he had always regarded himself as more English than Irish. George asked his land agent, Tom Ruttledge, to take down the picture and bring him the canvas – Tom made a special trip to London to deliver it to him a short time later.

CHAPTER TWENTY-FIVE

On February 1st, 1923, Reilly, the steward who took care of Moore Hall, sent an identical telegram to George Moore in London and to Colonel Moore in Dublin.

"Moore Hall house burned down last night, nothing saved."

The gruesome details were revealed later. At midnight, armed strangers came to the estate lodge where Reilly lived and demanded the keys to the house. He asked why and was told that a column of Republican fighters was coming through and were going to be billeted there for the night. They would not allow Reilly to go with them to the house. He feared the worst and pointed out that the house belonged to George Moore the writer, and was not owned by the Senator, Colonel Moore. This protest was ignored, and one of the armed IRA intruders reminded Reilly that Colonel Moore had participated in the Castlebar meeting with their enemy, Michael Collins. They took the keys of the house and warned Reilly to stay in his lodge. At 4am he heard two loud explosions and at 5am he ventured out into the dark rainy night to investigate. He got to the hill overlooking the gardens and saw the entire house engulfed in flames, with clouds of sparks like snowflakes being carried away in the wind. Fearing the fire would spread to the outlying barns, he let out all the livestock and stood in horror as the roof caved in with a mighty crash. When the worst flames subsided, he and his friend Joe Roney put up ladders to the upstairs windows, establishing that there was nothing to be salvaged. The only objects that were saved were vestments and religious objects from the house chapel, which had been carried out onto the lawn by the burning party before they torched the house – having first looted some of the furniture which was carted away.

George was saddened by the destruction of Moore Hall and issued a statement – "I am purely a man of letters, disassociated from Irish and English politics, and have no opinions on either side of the dispute going on in Ireland."

The detailed account of the burning that Reilly sent to George was so well written that he had it published in the Morning Post newspaper, and then sent a check to his steward for twelve guineas.

He submitted a claim to the Free State government for 25,000 pounds and eventually ended up with a third of that amount in compensation. He wrote to a friend – "Since the burning of my house I don't think I shall ever be able to go to Ireland again – I fear I should crumble into dust the moment I set foot on the shore. My dreaming house is gone, with only a portrait saved to hang on the first landing in Ebury Street, in a little lobby whence it looks out and catches my eyes as I come downstairs, a sort of fetch-light or corpse-candle, reminding me that my race is over, betrayed, scattered and in exile."

There were rumors that the burning of Moore Hall had been ordered by De Valera himself, but Colonel Moore would have none of that – he also determined that the locals had no hand in the destruction and stated this publicly.

"This was the one Big House in Mayo which all the people of Mayo had been brought up to love and to respect; a sort of historical monument which all revered on account of the many generations of the Moore family who had stood by the people, served them, and suffered with them."

George had no interest in restoring the house and Maurice quickly realized that its restoration was far beyond his financial means. He conveyed this information to his son Rory in America, in a letter describing the utter destruction of their entire family history, the magnificent library, the paintings and even the manuscripts of his grandfather's literary works. The dispute between the two brothers continued and they were still not on speaking terms – both got on with their lives. George was now a successful writer living in London and busied himself with new projects, having vowed never to set foot again in Ireland. Colonel Maurice went back to his politics and started to plan privately for some kind of restoration of Moore Hall – feeling it his duty to save it somehow. First, he had to own it, and he was finally able to purchase the ruined house and the few hundred untenanted acres around it in 1929, in the name of his son, Rory. He hoped for good fortune for the boy in Wyoming, but the economic depression was taking hold in America, coupled with a drought in the West which decimated Rory's cattle herds.

George continued with his writing projects in London and visited Paris frequently, while keeping away from Ireland. By this time, he was a highly regarded and somewhat famous author, but not at the top of any of the 'best' lists, while his publications and his fan base increased. He entertained and was entertained by all the top celebrities of the time, a raunchy and crotchety old bachelor who wrote freely about his friends, enemies and conquests. Many of the settings for his stories continued to be Ireland, and his beloved Lough Carra made its way into many of his works. Lady Maud Cunard was a lifelong friend, and it was rumored that George and she had been lovers for years while she was married to another, and that he was the biological father to her only child, Nancy – a fact that was never admitted nor fully denied by the parties. Lady Cunard applied all her energies to convince the British government to award George Moore the Order of Merit. George himself said he cared nothing about such things and the OM award never did come to pass.

George was lucky in his health into his late seventies. In 1928 he suffered with a severe stomach illness and spent months in a nursing home, returning home with a catheter that became permanent for the rest of his life. He was a cantankerous individual all his adult life and more so in his final years, as his faithful housekeeper, cook, and his secretary did their best to humor him. He selected Charles Morgan to be his biographer and began a series of meetings with him to shape the work the way George wanted it – "literature in front and a background of women." To that end he asked Lady Cunard to let Morgan see all his letters to her over the years.

"All – why there are far more than a thousand?" she replied.

"Yes, all – because I think that no proper story of my life can be written without them."

"I will require some time to think this this matter over before I can agree to that."

Morgan found George's male friends very approachable, but his interviews with his female friends did not go so well. He reported this to George who wondered why, out loud.

"George, they have their pride to consider, furthermore they are acutely aware of the commercial value of whatever materials and intimate information they possess. If Lady Cunard refuses to let me see all the letters I will not continue with the project."

"Oh, blast," replied George, "I think she will relent."

George made many wills and made several changes to them. He made his final will on October 31st, 1930. He had by this time published fifty-one books and he bequeathed the rights to these works to C. D. Medley, his advisor and agent – 'he understands my literature and I wish him to deal with them according to his best judgement. He shall retain all proceeds in the memory of his old friend.'

Lady Cunard was to get all his furniture and pictures, with a few exceptions – most notably he left the portrait of his grandfather to the National Gallery in Dublin. The net monies in his estate amounted to some sixty-eight thousand pounds and there were various money bequests – to the five children of Tom Ruttledge, to St. Peters Hospital, his secretary, cook and housekeeper, and to several old friends. The residue of his estate, subject to an annuity to his youngest brother Julian, was left to his sister, Nina Kilkelly and to his nephew, Peter Moore, son of his deceased brother, Augustus. His brother, Colonel Maurice Moore and his family were totally excluded from the will.

He continued writing despite his failing health, and in late 1932 he began an autobiography to be called 'A Communication to My Friends'. The following January his condition deteriorated, and he was confined to his bed under the constant care of a nurse and a doctor. A week of misery ensued, dulled by pain killers and sleeping pills until the morning of January 21st, 1933, when George Moore IV died peacefully – he was eighty-one years old.

• • •

Meanwhile in Ireland, the ruling government was getting weaker, and the Republican opposition had morphed into the Fianna Fail party – in 1928 Colonel Moore joined that party. He was nominated for the position of vice-chairman of the Senate but lost that contest to Mr. Kenny, while being re-elected as a Fianna Fail member of the Senate. The Cosgrove government fell and in the election of 1932 De Valera and his Fianna Fail party took over the government. Taoiseach (Prime Minister) De Valera refused to continue paying the hated Land Annuities to Britain and abolished the Oath of Allegiance to the Crown that had previously been taken by all Dail members. The Senate was abolished also, and with it went the salary of 350 pounds a year that Colonel Moore was paid – further dooming the chances of any rebuilding of Moore Hall. He approached the Forestry Board with a proposal for their taking over Moore Hall: when that proposal was rejected, he had no choice but to sell the demesne to a timber business, whom he expected would probably demolish the ruin in due course.

That was the end of the Moore family ownership of Moore Hall.

Ironically, just after the sales papers were signed, the Colonel had a preplanned meeting with Taoiseach De Valera and during the meeting he told him what had transpired.

"This is dreadful," said De Valera, "I can't bear to think of a fine old place like Moore Hall being torn down."

• • •

The day after George Moore died, Colonel Maurice Moore went to Ebury Street to view the body of his dead brother from whom he had been so long estranged. He was joined there by his younger brother Julian, and his sister Nina. George had asked to be cremated and his ashes taken to Lough Carra, and on January 25th the mourners gathered at Golders Green Crematorium for a funeral service.

The family members were there, plus a group of George's friends, including the British Prime Minister, Ramsey MacDonald. They listened intently as the elderly Irish Protestant minister, Canon Douglas, tried while very drunk to recall the words of the burial service – mixing them up badly with the Lord's Prayer. George's best friends struggled to contain their sadness while they were rendered helpless with internal laughter at the antics of the officiating minister. There were many floral tributes on display including a large one from his literary acquaintance, James Joyce.

Maurice faithfully shouldered the duty of returning the ashes to Castle Island, Lough Carra, which ironically, he now owned – he took delivery of 'George' into his own hands after all the bad blood that had transpired between them. He had a brass urn made – a copy of a bronze age original housed in the National Gallery. The ashes were shipped in a case to Dublin and then taken by train to Balla, County Mayo – the very same route that George had taken as a boy with his mother sixty-three years earlier, for the Moore Hall funeral of his father, George Henry Moore. The family and several of his friends took the train west for George's last trip. Word had got around locally that there was to be a 'pagan, non-Christian' burial at Lough Carra the following day. The local parish priest warned his parishioners to stay away – 'pay no more attention to that event than to a man burying his dog'. It was a meagre crowd compared to the throngs of people that had come to pay homage to his father George Henry.

The mourners were rowed over to Castle Island in a few boats. Maurice had selected George A. E. Russell to write the funeral address – a man George had fallen out with over the previous ten years and who did not personally attend the service. The brief oration was read by Richard Best, a friend of George – it was a caustic piece, full of double meaning.

'If his ashes have any sentience they will feel at home here, for the colors of Lough Carra remained in his memory when many of his other affections had passed. It is possible the artist's love of earth, rock, water and sky is an act of worship. It is possible that faithfulness to art is an acceptable service. That worship, that service was his. If any would condemn him for creed of theirs he had assailed, let them be certain first that they labored for their ideals as faithfully as he did for his.'

At the head of the grave a plaque was placed with the following inscription –

>George Moore
>Born Moore Hall 1852, died 1933 London
>He deserted his family and friends
>For his art
>But because he was faithful to his art
>His family and friends
>Reclaimed his ashes for Ireland.

As the cairn of stones were being piled on top of the urn, Colonel Moore produced a wooden crucifix which he planted into the top of the pile.

Reilly, the old steward was there and surveyed the scene while the workmen completed the cairn, and as the afternoon light wore away. On George's behalf he took the time to admire the scene – the level shores of the lake, the bluish tinge of the Partry mountains rising in the west, the great woods standing unchanged around the burnt shell ruin of the old house itself, now gone with the old life. The Colonel came over to him after the proceedings and spoke to him – "What are you thinking about all of this, as you survey the spectacle?"

"Well, Your Honor, I'm thinking that George would be happy with everything, and I might add on my own behalf that you have been exceedingly kind and true to his wishes, probably more than he deserved – if you don't mind me saying so. I'm also wondering whether the Curse of the Druid's will now be lifted, after all the sadness that has befallen those who inhabited Muckloon Hill – I daresay those wicked Druids must have had their curse fulfilled, now that all is in ruins."

"That is indeed food for thought. Thank you for coming – God Bless."

• • •

Colonel Maurice Moore continued to labor in the cause of his country. The new Fianna Fail Republican Government led by Taoiseach De Valera passed a new Constitution of Ireland in 1937, and shortly after that they created a new Seanad (Senate). Colonel Moore was one of De Valera's eleven nominees to the new Seanad and he remained a Senator till the end of his life. He had seen three provinces of Ireland achieve political independence and saw the Gaelic Irish language of Ireland given official recognition everywhere in the country. He remained convinced to his last breath that the province of Ulster would be regained some day to make a united thirty-two county Ireland.

His main regret was that the Moore family had been dispersed, and therefore would not share in the greatness and the future prosperity that he foresaw for Ireland.

Irish Senator, Colonel Maurice Moore died on September 8th, 1939, in Dublin – he was buried at Kiltoom, Moore Hall, alongside his forefathers and in accordance with his wishes.

THE END

EPILOGUE

John Moore, First and only President of the Republic of Connaught, perished in the aftermath of the 1798 Rebellion. For reasons that defy explanation, his death was not investigated at the time of death, nor during subsequent years. As far as is known, his family did not demand or ever receive a detailed account of his final days.

In 1960, a gravedigger at Ballygunner Cemetery in County Waterford stumbled upon a simple headstone with the name John Moore on it. Further investigation revealed that this was the final resting place of John Moore, President of Connaught. In August 1961 his remains were exhumed and carried under escort to Castlebar, County Mayo.

The President of Connaught was reinterred at The Mall, in the center of Castlebar with full military honors. The ceremony was attended by the President and the Taoiseach of Ireland, the Ambassadors of Spain and France – and other dignitaries from Church and State. The Moore family was represented by the late Colonel Moore's son, Rory Moore and his wife Nancy, who travelled from their home in America. A large crowd of local Mayo people attended the event – which was treated as a joyous occasion.

It was said locally that there were ghostly sightings of John and his mother Catherine that August – both at The Mall and at Kiltoom on the shores of Lough Carra – during the long summer evenings when twilight can stretch till almost midnight.

• • •

Thankfully, Moore Hall did not get demolished. The ruined Big House has stood up surprisingly well during the intervening years. In due course, the house and grounds became the property of the Irish State – it is now a public park that is much loved by the thousands who visit every year to enjoy the tranquility of its setting – to be enchanted by a Big House with a famed history, still standing tall on the Hill of Muckloon, overlooking Lough Carra.

Grave of John Moore in center of Castlebar, County Mayo

Moore family motto 'Fortis Cadere Cedere Non Potest' (The Brave May Fall But Cannot Yield) Pray for the soul of John Moore of Ashbrook and Moore Hall. Ireland's First President gave his life for his country in the Rising of 1798. He died in Waterford Dec 6th, 1799. By the will of the people exhumed and re-interred here with all Honors of Church and State – August 13th, 1961

NOTES / RESEARCH ACKNOWLEDGEMENTS / INSPIRATION FOR THIS BOOK

This book is based on real people who participated in important events of Irish history. However, there are many substantial gaps in that history and records of conversations between those people are almost non-existent. To help the flow and readability of the book, the author has created several fictitious characters to interact with these real people. He has recreated substantial segments of the leading character's life experiences, plus multiple conversations between the various characters – for that same reason. Any inaccuracies or misconceptions, real or perceived, should be excused as being in the realm of fiction. In all instances the guiding principle was to stay true to history and to treat all the historical characters with dignity and respect. The four generations of the Moore family that hold center stage in this book contributed immensely to Irish history and deserve our profound gratitude. Even today, Moore Hall and its associated grounds are a haven of tranquility – a national treasure that should be visited by every reader of this book.

The author would like to mention the following books that were instrumental in his research and provided inspiration to get this book to the finish line.

> The Making of Modern Ireland by JC Beckett
> Spain's Men of the Sea by Pablo E. Perez-Mallaina
> The Year of The French by Thomas Flanagan
> The Moores of Moore Hall by Joseph M. Hone
> An Irish Gentleman by Maurice Moore
> The Life of George Moore by Joseph Hone
> Letters from the Irish Highlands of Connemara by the Blake Family
> George Augustus Moore by Adrian Frazier

MEET THE AUTHOR

Michael Gerard lives in South Carolina, USA. He was born and reared in County Mayo, on Ireland's rugged west coast. Like so many Irish before him, he was inclined to roam, and after stints in Galway, Limerick, Cork and Dublin, he moved on to England. His mining equipment career took him all over the UK and he met his wife in Manchester, England. Next stop was South Africa where he worked in the supply of equipment to the vast mining businesses there and travelled extensively throughout the Southern Africa region in that role. They moved to America in the 1980's, set down roots in South Carolina and established their family processing equipment sales company that they still operate today, alongside their American-born sons. Despite being constantly busy with business, Michael Gerard has managed to find the time to follow his passion for writing. The Irish Merchant of Alicante is his third published book. His books are available on Amazon and through a link from his website www.MichaelGerardAuthor.com

Follow him on twitter @MgerardK
Facebook – Michael Gerard-Author

Printed in Great Britain
by Amazon

2ee7636d-c5ad-4ffb-a4af-93c09a7adf65R01